BOAT
CRAZY

BOAT CRAZY

The Collected *WoodenBoat* Stories of Stan Grayson

STAN GRAYSON

WoodenBoat

Brooklin, Maine

Essex, Connecticut

WoodenBoat

WoodenBoat Publications, P.O. Box 78
Brooklin, ME 04476; www.woodenboat.com

An imprint of Globe Pequot, the trade division of
The Rowman & Littlefield Publishing Group, Inc.
4501 Forbes Blvd., Ste. 200
Lanham, MD 20706
www.rowman.com

Distributed by NATIONAL BOOK NETWORK

British Library Cataloguing in Publication Information available

Library of Congress Cataloging-in-Publication Data
Names: Grayson, Stan, 1945- author.
Title: Boat crazy : the collected woodenboat stories of Stan Grayson / Stan
  Grayson.
Description: Essex, Connecticut : Lyons Press, 2024. | Includes
  bibliographical references.
Identifiers: LCCN 2023050191 (print) | LCCN 2023050192 (ebook) | ISBN
  9781493078974 (cloth) | ISBN 9781493078981 (epub)
Subjects: LCSH: Yachting--United States--History.
Classification: LCC GV815 .G68 2024 (print) | LCC GV815 (ebook) | DDC
  797.124/60973--dc23/eng/20231122
LC record available at https://lccn.loc.gov/2023050191
LC ebook record available at https://lccn.loc.gov/2023050192

♾™ The paper used in this publication meets the minimum requirements of American National
Standard for Information Sciences—Permanence of Paper for Printed Library Materials, ANSI/
NISO Z39.48-1992.

For Roger Taylor and Llewellyn "Louie" Howland III,
friends, sailors, book men

CONTENTS

PART FOUR: BOAT CRAZY

FOREWORD

THERE IS A small portion of Marblehead (Massachusetts) Harbor that was known informally as "Catboat Cove" when I was growing up in that area in the late 1970s and 1980s. It was populated by a stalwart group of wooden boat aficionados whose boats included an assortment of classic types centered on a core fleet of catboats. Stan Grayson was one of the catboat sailors; I didn't know him back then, but I certainly knew his name.

When I became editor of *WoodenBoat* magazine in the mid-1990s, Stan was already something of a legend. He was then running his own book imprint, Devereux Books, and had written several authoritative tomes, including ones on antique marine engines and catboats. Briefly, I thought of him as only an expert on these niches within the niche of classic wooden boats, but as our editor–author relationship blossomed over the following years and decades, I came to realize that Stan had a preternatural gift for researching and writing about all matters related to boats.

Stan's breadth of interests still surprises me. Recently, he wrote an article for *WoodenBoat* on the great yacht designer Charles D. Mower, who was active in the 1920s and 1930s. I'd owned a Mower-designed boat in the early 2000s, but information about the designer had eluded me for years. His collection had been largely destroyed in a fire, and I knew very little about his origins. Stan, however, working with detail from a wide range of sources, managed to make a crystal-clear profile of the man, illuminating not only his career but also his personality and origins. It resonated for me like a first-person interview in which I was startled to learn that Mower got his start in Lynn, Massachusetts, not far from Catboat Cove. That profile forms the second story of part II of this book.

Stan's interests range farther afield than the North Shore of Massachusetts. In this book, you will also find chapters on the New York–based catboat designer Gil Smith; the pioneering marine engines of the Detroit-based Joe van Blerck; new detail about the world-girdling voyage of Capt. Joshua Slocum; and the search for the mysterious small boat of Henry David Thoreau—not to mention a broad cross-section of America's yachting past in a profile of the incomparable boat collection of Connecticut's Mystic Seaport Museum.

But don't be mistaken: Stan's interest is not only in the past—at least not as a locked-in-amber artifact. He has also embraced new technologies, especially as they fit into the practicalities of classic boats. His chapter in part IV, titled "Electric Experiences: Small Voyages toward a New World," examines his experience with, and embracing of, state-of-the-art electric-motor technology as it relates to its seamless installation in his Herreshoff-inspired, Chuck Paine-designed Pisces daysailer (a modern boat that's based on a classic). And that serves as an apt metaphor for Stan's career, and for this collection of his writings: Stan brings a strong element of practicality and relevance to every historical piece he writes. He does not place his subjects on a dusty shelf, but rather enthusiastically relates them to what is now, and what is possible. And there's nothing crazy about that.

—Matthew P. Murphy
Penobscot, Maine
June 20, 2023

INTRODUCTION

I N OCTOBER 2019, my wife and I took a vacation trip to Italy's Amalfi Coast. We based ourselves in Sorrento, a colorful little city overlooking the Bay of Naples and boasting *two* harbors. Whatever the coming days might have in store for us, I reasoned that there would always be boats to look at.

Soon enough, we took a day-trip to the nearby Isle of Capri with a local guide who was surprised when I paused our introductory walk at a little sand beach. Hauled up there were several double-ended rowing boats. While the guide watched curiously, I prepared my camera and began to examine these craft, each about twelve feet in length. The boats were strongly built with closely spaced, steam-bent frames and sturdy knees to support the thwarts. Each had a single thole pin to which the oar was secured with a loop of rope. When I knelt down to run my hand along the curve of the bottom, the guide scratched his head and turned to my wife.

"Your husband," he said, "seems to be crazy about boats."

What could she do but agree? A couple of hours later, we watched as craft just like the ones on the beach ferried visitors from tour boats to and from the famous Blue Grotto. The oarsmen, each clad in a white shirt and khaki shorts, rowed facing forward and standing up until they approached the Grotto entrance where they sat down, timed the small surge then running, and pulled into the cave.

Well, it was a fine way to spend a beautiful day.

This book is the product of a longtime curiosity regarding the historical development of yachts and small working craft, and those who designed, built, and sailed them. As a historian in a field that deserves more attention than it usually receives, I was first inspired by the work of four men: William Piccard Stephens, Thomas Fleming Day, Howard Irving Chapelle, and John Gardner.

Stephens's *Traditions & Memories of American Yachting* remains a key resource because Stephens lived throughout the sport's nineteenth-century formative period and well beyond, and knew personally all the principal figures. Day's editorship of *The Rudder*, which he founded in 1890, meant he could pursue historical aspects during a time when many key players were living and could provide firsthand information. Born in 1901, Chapelle recognized the need for scholarship in the preservation of America's working craft before they disappeared. Chapelle's work is reflected in the Smithsonian's National Watercraft Collection and his several books. John Gardner, born in 1905, brought a similar approach to the subject. As the personable Associate Curator of Small Craft at Mystic Seaport Museum, he shared his interest with the public and discussed in his books the history of various boat types together with instructions on how to build them.

A yachting historian these days, of course, can't have the personal connections to nineteenth- and early twentieth-century historical figures and boats enjoyed by the pioneers in the field. But that's true of historians no matter what their area of specialty. On the other hand, the ever-increasing scope of the internet permits the diligent researcher to access material that previously would have required visits to far-flung libraries, archives, and museums. What's more, digital indexes make possible an efficient, wide-ranging information gathering that hands-on research with hard-copy primary sources would struggle to equal. When the knowledgeable researcher combines digital tools with old-fashioned detective work and email exchanges with reference librarians wherever they may be, an unprecedented level of information can be mined.

Access to great artwork involving yachts and working craft is more limited, but studying paintings remains a special treat for me. Many are the artists who were inspired to record their impressions of yachts and working craft and their ever-changing environment of sea, light, and sky. Besides being a worthy subject for art historians, the best marine paintings can also be a rich source of information for the sailor-historian who knows what to look for regarding specific details of rigging, mast placement, hull forms, fittings, and burgees.

Each of the following stories—originally published between 2004 and 2023—represents an effort to combine informed scholarship, story-telling, and experience afloat into narratives that bring the past to life. That these stories were first published in *WoodenBoat* is thanks to Matt Murphy, who has long had his editorial finger on the pulse of the wooden boat world, both past and present. Invariably, the manuscripts I've submitted have been handled with sensitivity, the end result always meeting the original intent while often being improved in subtle but appreciated ways. There's not a boat-crazy bunch of publishing professionals anywhere that I'd rather be associated with than the *WoodenBoat* crew.

The twenty stories collected here don't represent all of my published work in *WoodenBoat*. However, those omitted for reasons of space—mainly book reviews or pieces that focused on a specific boat—can be accessed in back issues of the magazine. While the stories' text is as it appeared in the magazine, each piece in this collection is prefaced by an introduction that offers some background on the subject and my personal interest in it. As appropriate, there is mention of events post-publication. For space reasons, there are fewer pictures than in the magazine. However, there are also some new images and, here and there, a new table.

The stories fell more or less naturally into four areas. Part I, "Catboats," may come as a surprise to some. However, although catboats today represent a small but dynamic niche in the market, for at least four decades, they were fundamental to yachting and working craft. If you learned to sail between the 1860s and the early 1900s, it would often have been in a catboat, and the type became very highly developed as a racing yacht before being eclipsed. The stories in part II: "Yachting" present a sense of the sport's growth and variety. Part III: "Power" explores both the lasting fascination steam can still exert and the impact of internal combustion. Although we have long since taken for granted the convenience of a diesel or gasoline engine, developing such machines was anything but straightforward. Finally, part IV includes a variety of pieces related to boat obsession of one sort or another.

A few of the stories are more or less contemporary in nature but, mainly, the book is an exploration of the past which, for reasons never easy to define, holds a fascination for each of us. The questions arise: how did they *do* that? Where did their ideas come from? What were their successes and failures? Sometimes, the most boat-crazy among us recreate or restore a classic yacht that accurately reflects the design and technology now a century or more in the past. Such boats permit us to step back in time and experience the sport as it was known to those we can only read about. Invariably, what one learns is how well the "old-timers" knew what they were doing, not to mention the beauty of the boats and the craftsmanship involved in their construction and finish. Never underestimate the performance of a yacht designed a century ago or the skills required to sail it.

Ultimately, *Boat Crazy* is a meandering among the designers, builders, mechanical geniuses, and sailors who dwell in history. They're a group as diverse as the great subject itself. Included, to name but a few, are Henry David Thoreau and his homemade skiff; Nathanael Herreshoff who designed *America's* Cup defenders but found personal delight in simple, small sailboats; Raymond Hunt whose genius at the helm and instinctive flair for design made him a legend in his own time; and, of course, my longtime acquaintance, Capt. Joshua Slocum.

In the old days, in the rigorously class-conscious nineteenth century especially, yacht designers were considered to be artists who occupied a social and professional position of unusual distinction. Boatwrights, spar makers, sailmakers, riggers, and mechanics were viewed as "practical men" of a different stature. In my experience, however, I've found that those who've devoted their careers to boats—at least the sorts of boats being discussed here—to be artists in their own way. Such professionals, invariably intelligent, thoughtful, and creative, have added immensely to the pleasure I've found during my years of research and writing.

To those who know that sailing and all it entails can be a metaphor for living, to those thoughtful and insightful folks who appreciate the art involved in boats, and to those who understand that there is wisdom to be gleaned from the past that can enrich us, I hope that *Boat Crazy* will serve as both a lasting affirmation and inspiration.

—Stan Grayson
Marblehead, Massachusetts
July 2023

PART I

CATBOATS

HERRESHOFF CATBOATS

The Roots of a Boatbuilding Dynasty

Right at the start of my sailing days, things took an unusual turn during a Cape Cod vacation. It was the first time I ever saw a Cape Cod catboat. The boat was propped up on stands beside a shingled building and its rounded form and lowered centerboard resting on a block of wood immediately captured my interest. Soon enough, I developed an intense curiosity regarding how local waters and winds influenced boat design and construction back in "the old days." How was it, I asked, that a beamy, shallow draft boat with a single mast right in the bow came into being in the first place? That curiosity would persist down to the present day and for many years, my boat ownership involved catboats.

The more I studied catboats, the more it became clear that although they now represent a small but devoted niche in the sailing scene, they were once a large and important aspect of both American yachting and working craft. Scratch the surface of the early days of sailboat racing from New Jersey to New England (and elsewhere, too), and you'll find a catboat of one sort or another.

I was not aware of the Herreshoff connection to catboats until I made a visit to what was then called the Henry Ford Museum and Greenfield Village. I was really in Dearborn to photograph several antique cars in the museum's collection but, during an exploration of the place, I chanced upon a catboat displayed there. Although I soon afterward bought my first catboat, it would be many years before my research would focus on the important role that catboats played in the Herreshoff family, in the Herreshoff Manufacturing Company, and in the boating lives of those who bought a Herreshoff catboat. This piece tells that story.

My first visit to the Henry Ford Museum in the mid-1970s was memorable for many reasons. The collection of automobiles, steam and gasoline engines, locomotives, bicycles, and other objects ranged from marvelous to mind-boggling. But it was the surprise I got that remains foremost in my mind. During my wandering on what is said to be the world's largest expanse of parquet flooring, I suddenly encountered, of all things, a catboat. There she sat in a well-fitted wooden cradle with a plaque identifying her as *Sprite*, built by the Herreshoffs of Bristol, Rhode Island.

The boat had clearly been restored and, as I learned later, important original details had been lost, an all-too-familiar tale with old boats. However, her basic shape was still intact when *Sprite* arrived at was then called the Edison Institute of Technology in 1930. Whether Henry Ford recognized the boat as important because she represented a uniquely American type of sailing craft, or because she'd been built by the famous Herreshoffs, or both, is a matter of conjecture.

On July 3, 1929, Mr. H. H. Weston, the Ford assistant branch manager in New York who'd discussed *Sprite*'s acquisition with the Herreshoffs, wrote to J. A. Humberstone, the Ford executive responsible for such matters at the Edison Institute in Dearborn. "Captain Herreshoff," wrote Weston, "will donate the Catboat to Mr. Ford's museum for safekeeping."

Here is how *Sprite* was displayed at the Henry Ford Museum when the author first encountered her in the mid-1970s. (The Henry Ford Museum)

Three months later, on October 2, 1930, Humberstone wrote to Nathanael Herreshoff asking, among other things, whether *Sprite*, built in 1859 for Nat's older brother John Brown Herreshoff (1841–1915), was the first Herreshoff boat. Nathanael's detailed response not only recalled *Sprite* but also made clear that catboats had been important to the family, to John's boatbuilding efforts, and to the Herreshoff Manufacturing Company for over fifty years.

The Early Family Boats

Nathanael Greene Herreshoff was eighty-two years old in 1930 when he replied to Mr. Humberstone's letter. "The sailboat *Sprite* was not the first of the Herreshoff boats," Nathanael wrote. He noted that beginning in 1834, his father Charles Frederick Herreshoff Sr. (1809–1888) had owned four boats, all named for his wife, Julia. Nathanael recalled that these boats were kept "in fine order and spick and span in every way. . . . Any boat coming along side must be held clear and not touch 'Julia.'"

Although the *Julia*s were cat-rigged, none were what we'd consider a typical catboat, in part because none had a centerboard. The first, launched in 1834 when Charles was twenty-five years old, had a full-bodied hull—detrimentally full in her aft sections, Nathanael reckoned—with a raked transom. She had a loose-footed gaff sail, and resembled what historian Howard Chapelle called a "Newport Boat," a type he dated to "prior to 1840."

While *Julia* was used for transportation and family outings, the twenty-two-foot *Julia II*, built in 1855, was designed by Charles for day sailing and racing. Deemed lacking, *Julia II* was replaced by the 22'2" *Julia III* in 1856. With a rather full-bodied hull, 3'3" draft and 500 sq. ft. sail, she had a long career before being wrecked at Bristol during a September 1869 storm. She was replaced in 1870 by *Julia IV*, another shallow-draft (2'7") hull with topsides and rig resembling a catboat.

During this period, ballast was carried inside the hull and it was typical for a portion of it to be moveable, either in the form of sandbags or stoutly constructed canvas bags containing iron or lead bars. The bags had handles and the crew member whose job it was to move them from leeward to windward was known as the "ballast shifter."

Although it was for years a necessary part of sailing, being a ballast shifter doesn't sound like a particularly fun job. To ease the task, around 1864, Charles Herreshoff devised what his son Nathanael called "a ballast box on small wheels that ran on cross tracks. [It was] controlled by ropes at each side and had a strong toggle with notches forward and aft to hold the box either amidships or at either side, as desired." The box was secured amidships in light weather but was used as soon as the wind was strong enough to appreciably heel the boat. The potentially dangerous nature of the ballast car—it weighed 550 lbs.—is obvious. However, Nathanael emphasized that "when sailing with strangers aboard, [father] was very careful they did not monkey with it."

Sprite

In 1859, while Charles Frederick Herreshoff was enjoying *Julia III*, his eighteen-year-old son John Brown Herreshoff decided he needed a larger boat than the twelve-foot *Meteor* he'd been sailing all over Narragansett Bay for several years. Having lost his sight at age fourteen, John relied on his younger brother Nathanael to be his eyes when on the water. According to Nathanael's son, L. Francis Herreshoff, John described to his father the shape he envisioned for *Sprite*'s hull. Charles then began shaping a graceful half-model for a 20' catboat, which John reviewed and made suggestions regarding "where he wanted it changed or cut away."

Historian William Piccard Stephens, who knew the Herreshoffs, never forgot witnessing John's ability to "see with his hands" when examining a model or full-size boat. Nathanael was eleven and a half at the time and wrote later that the result was "a very perfectly formed model of a twenty foot boat." In a meaningful way, *Sprite* launched young Nathanael Herreshoff on his career. It was his job to cut "templates to fit the model and from these, drawing out sections where frames . . . were to be, and measuring them and [drawing] profile[s] from the model at one-twelfth its size."

In October 1859, John and Nathanael borrowed another family cat-rigged boat owned by their older brother Charles Frederick Herreshoff Jr. (1839–1917) and sailed to Wickford, Rhode Island, to purchase oak stock for *Sprite*. John made *Sprite*'s cordage himself and, with some assistance from Nathanael, turned the lignum vitae sheeves for the wooden blocks made by his father.

The ongoing attention paid to ballast is made clear by Nathanael's references regarding *Sprite*, which, most importantly, was a centerboarder. In his letter to Humberstone, Herreshoff wrote: "Originally she was ballasted with about ½ ton of scrap iron stowed low down, under cabin and cockpit floors, and 400 pounds of ballast [bags] to shift to windward when tacking, which was the custom in those days. . . . They were in quite constant use. . . . Weighing about 56 lbs. each, the weights were padded and covered with canvas, with canvas strap handles and painted straw color, same as deck and cockpit."

Sprite was launched on June 28, 1860, the day the 692' steamship *Great Eastern*, the world's largest vessel, arrived in New York. In July, *Sprite* together with *Julia III* set off for New York, the crews of both boats hoping to tour the ship. Nat Herreshoff was twelve at the time and his lifelong memories of this adventure reveal a great deal about *Sprite*'s performance and the mid-nineteenth-century skills and attitudes of these expert small boat sailors.

Never in recalling this cruise did Nathanael Herreshoff mention sleeping, cooking, toilet arrangements, or comfort. These matters seem to have been deemed irrelevant by comparison to a boat's sailing ability. *Sprite*, with her low coamings and flat cabin top offered a sheltered place to lie down but little else in terms of comfort. But *Sprite*'s low freeboard and its attendant reduction in windage would enhance performance and remain typical of many Herreshoff designs, catboats or not. The catboats also had well-proportioned, well-located centerboards, usually made of white oak but sometimes cut from steel or tobin bronze.

After overnighting in Newport, *Sprite* and *Julia III* cast off for New York at around six in the morning despite fog and a southerly wind that lasted until mid-afternoon off Watch Hill, Rhode Island. Then came a favorable northwest wind. The two boats reached New York in twenty-eight hours and returned in twenty-six. "Very good time," Herreshoff recalled, "for a 20 foot boat to cover 175 miles."

This is a very thought-provoking performance. Engineless *Sprite*, sailing night and day through tricky waters averaged, for good periods, a bit over six knots. Nathanael noted that "both boats tied in reefs for night sailing" and that, on the return, "[i]t was rather rough outside, but it did not bother us."

That fall Nathanael sailed *Sprite* in what he called "her first real race." This event was held off Fox Point in Providence, Rhode Island, an area not far from where Route 195 now exists. Three other catboats were involved: *Planet*, a twenty-five-footer said to be the fastest boat on the Providence River, and a twenty-two- and twenty-three-footer both owned by a local sailor named Ben Appleton who ran a livery business. Appleton was so interested in *Sprite* that he asked to sail aboard her as the ballast shifter. *Sprite* finished close behind the larger *Planet* and easily won on time allowance.

"This was my first formal race," Nat Herreshoff wrote years later. He recalled that the Providence boatmen showed "much surprise and chagrin at being beaten by a smaller boat from Bristol and sailed by a boy of twelve."

Sprite became known as the fastest boat of her size on Narragansett Bay and Nathanael never forgot what it was like to sail this twenty-footer with her 450 sq. ft. sail and long boom that overhung the transom by several feet. "I remember well how my back and arms would ache in steering her, and often my brother John had to assist me. In sailing to windward, my brother John could sail her as well as anyone, even without sight."

It is not uncommon for knowledgeable catboat enthusiasts today to assume the old-timers had some magic tricks that helped overcome the weather-helm issues common to the type. In fact, some boats were more magical than others. *Sprite*, though fast, could be a handful and Nathanael was never really happy with her sail plan.

"Her boom was very long and it swung very low and [was] a menace to all on board when tacking, besides being dangerous by catching in the water when reefed and making her steer very hard in a breeze." Later, with a taller mast and shorter boom, *Sprite* was improved.

John Brown Herreshoff sold *Sprite* in 1863 to fund a larger cruising sloop and Nathanael grieved at the parting. However, twenty-eight years after *Sprite* was sold, she was acquired by James Brown Herreshoff (1834–1930), eldest of the eight brothers. In August 1891, when the *Boston Globe* did a story on the Herreshoff family and its achievements (James invented, among other things, the coil boiler used in the speedy Herreshoff steam launches), it reported that "even at this comparatively late day [*Sprite*] possesses remarkable speed."

At the time *Sprite* was donated to Ford's museum she'd been resting on the lawn at Nathanael's house for some time, a reminder of his youth. When the Edison Institute wrote Nathanael regarding missing components, he did his best to assist. "I have taken interest in making a drawing of the boat showing rudder, centerboard, spars and rigging," he wrote, "for it was the first of what became my life's work, and details of that boat stand out more distinctly than any of a thousand that came afterwards."

A Start in Business

John Brown Herreshoff used the proceeds from *Sprite*'s sale to build the larger cruising boat he wanted, a 26'9" foot sloop named *Kelpie* launched in April 1863. She was quickly followed by a similar-sized yacht named *Magic*, initially cat-rigged but later with the mast moved aft, jib-and-mainsail-rigged.

Around this time, John Brown Herreshoff became acquainted with a local yachtsman named Dexter S. Stone (1837–1887), four years his senior. The peculiar-looking 21'10" catboat *Secret*, launched in 1864, is listed in Herreshoff records as designed by Stone and built at the yard begun by John. In 1865, the two men entered into partnership. "We want to build a 'big thing' in the yacht line," Stone noted, "and have concluded to spend say $50 on advertising the *Kelpie* and *Magic* to see if we can't sell them and use funds to put into a larger yacht."

Herreshoff and Stone promptly began receiving orders for boats of different sizes and types, most based on John's models. Nathanael recalled that several small catboats were among the output. In 1864, when Nathanael wanted a boat for himself, he carved his first half-model. "I had a desire to have a boat, and I designed and made a model for a 16-foot [overall] catboat. This was not built then but the following year for a Mr. Holden and named *Henrietta*."

By 1865, while a student at MIT, Nathanael was creating more half models for boats to be built by Herreshoff and Stone. Among them was a 23'8" catboat ordered with the express purpose of beating an existing catboat. Such motivations—often involving wagers—were not unusual then. When *Fannie* failed in this mission, her owner asked Nathanael to try again. He shaped a new half-model for *Fannie II* launched in 1867. The yacht achieved the intended goal and went on to a long racing career.

After the Herreshoff and Stone partnership ended in 1867, John carried on business alone for a decade, building commercial fishing boats and pleasure craft ranging from smaller catboats, both with and without a centerboard, to larger sailing yachts. In 1870, John modeled a 14' overall catboat for nineteen-year-old Walter Burgess, one of the wealthy "Burgess boys," as the press referred to them, on Boston's North Shore. Walter hoped his new catboat would be faster than the small sailboats in his home waters around Beverly, Massachusetts.

Pink was delivered on a rail car to Boston where she was eagerly met by Walter and his family. He was so anxious to get his new catboat home that he insisted she be launched and rigged despite a gusty southwest wind. Having reefed the boat's 192 sq. ft. sail, Walter and crew set off for Beverly. Sailing a new boat little larger than a Beetle Cat, Walter made this voyage of a good seventeen nautical miles, much of it in open water, and soon defeated the local fleet.

Comparing Two Nathanael Greene Herreshoff Champion Catboats

	LOA	LWL	Beam	Draft (Board up)	DISPL (Lbs.)	Sail Area (Sq. Ft.)	Sail Foot/Hoist/ Head/Leach
Fannie I (1866)	23'8"	21'0"	11'8"	2'1"	9,000	504	28'/22'/ 12'3"/34'
Fannie II (1867)	23'4"	21'5"	10'	3'0"	11,000	575	29'/24'/ 12'1"/ 37'

Notes: Subtle changes resulted in markedly better performance for *Fannie II*. Herreshoff was careful to note that neither boat had a bowsprit. He also calculated additional data such as freeboard at bow and stern. In *Fannie I*, it was 1'10"/1'3 1/2" while in *Fannie II*, it was 1'8"/ 1'4". Both boats reflect Herreshoff's long-standing goal of modest freeboard and windage.

See Herreshoff Catalogue Raisonné (Herreshoff.info/index.htm) for additional information.

Originally built in 1872 for Edward Burgess, *Bluebell* was still winning races well over a decade later. Owned by Swampscott, Massachusetts, yachtsman W. Lloyd Jeffries in 1886 when this photo was taken before the start of a regatta she won at Nahant, *Bluebell* (17'1.5" x 16'8" x 7'7" x 1'9" board up) raced in the Third Class Catboats based on her waterline length. She shows the comparatively tall mast and not overly long boom preferred by Nathanael Herreshoff. (Claas van der Linde)

In 1872, John designed the 17' *Bluebell* for Walter's brother, twenty-four-year-old Edward Burgess. Edward, commodore of the newly formed Beverly Yacht Club, later gained great renown as the designer of the *America's* Cup defenders *Puritan* (1885) (see *WoodenBoat* No. 283) and *Mayflower* (1886). In 1873, Sidney Burgess, who would later become uncle of and guardian to designer Starling Burgess, bought a 21' catboat designed by Charles Frederick Herreshoff and built by John. Sidney, who was said to be the Burgess family's best helmsman, scored many victories in Beverly Yacht Club events.

Nathanael recalled that the Burgess boys "were very successful . . . so that the growing generation of North Shore men were brought up in Bristol-built catboats."

In fact, Walter moved up from *Pink* to acquire *Fannie I*. He renamed her *Posy* and had some success after getting a new sail. Although Walter soon sold *Posy*, she remained so competitive that, despite being one of the oldest Herreshoff catboats racing at Boston during the 1889 season, she won fifteen firsts and captured the Hull Yacht Club championship for the fourth straight year.

Meanwhile, in 1872, *Fannie II* was purchased by Benjamin Dean, a wealthy attorney, founding member of the Boston Yacht Club, lawyer, and congressman. *Fannie II* was well-remembered by a keen observer of post–Civil War yachting around Boston who wrote an occasional column for the *Boston Globe* under the pseudonym Water Line.

Fannie II was recalled by Water Line as "undoubtedly the fastest boat in that class [and] had a swingin' big mainsail, but she could carry it off pretty well, and her skipper wasn't afraid of [double] reefin' when the boat needed it . . . while some of them would bite off their own heads [meaning battle extreme weather helm] by draggin' whole sail."

Yes, advice about reefing and catboats goes back well over a century.

Herreshoff Manufacturing Company Catboats

On December 31, 1877, Nathanael Herreshoff quit a $1,400-a-year-job at the Corliss Steam Engine Company in Providence to join John at a $1,000 salary and establish the Herreshoff Manufacturing Company. A year before he officially teamed up with John, Nathanael designed the 25' *Gleam* with the understanding that if she defeated the fastest catboat then sailing in Providence, she'd be bought by two enthusiastic brothers.

With Nathanael at the helm, *Gleam* won a two-of-three series. Years later, Nathanael's son, L. Francis, noted that *Gleam*'s method of construction was important. She "was the first boat built upside down with [perhaps for the first time in this country] screw fastenings, a construction method that was used by the Herreshoffs on all later small craft: in fact they later built steamers upside down."

Most Herreshoff catboats that followed *Gleam* were 16'–21' long overall, open-cockpit models. Company records frequently identify them as "racing catboat." While this suggests a certain "sweet spot" was recognized by both customers and the designer, larger models were ordered as well.

In mid-October 1891, Nathanael Herreshoff signed a contract with Dr. Edward Williams of Philadelphia and Beach Haven, New Jersey, for a 29'10" catboat named *Sayonara*. With her overhanging bow—reminiscent of Herreshoff's famous 73' cutter *Gloriana*—and stern, and her high-peaked sail, *Sayonara* made an immediate impression when she became the first Herreshoff boat in Little Egg Harbor. "Owing to her capabilities and speed in windward work," the *New York Herald* reported, she "served as an

Low, sleek, freakish, magnificent were all terms that could apply to *Wanda*. A catboat by virtue of her single sail and not much else, *Wanda* dominated older, more traditional designs. (Library of Congress)

object lesson to the New Jersey yachtsmen between Barnegat and Atlantic City."

A second boat produced to *Sayonara*'s model and launched in 1892 was *Merry Thought* built for John P. Crozer, a wealthy cotton mill owner from Upland, Pennsylvania, who had a summer home at Beach Haven. Not only did Nathanael Herreshoff assure him *Merry Thought* "would be a good boat when his grandchildren had children of their own," but she proved so superior to her competition, whether working catboats or yachts, that interest in competing with her dwindled.

Perhaps the most dramatic example of Nathanael Herreshoff's catboats was *Wanda*, a boat that owed nothing at all to the classic catboat. *Wanda*, 36'6" overall but with long overhangs and a waterline of 21'9", was essentially a racing machine with a stayed mast and a shallow, lead fin keel through which her big centerboard passed. *Wanda* was purchased for $2,100 (about $75,000 today) by New York yachtsman Frederick T. Bedford. On June 26, 1898, the *New York Times* reported that *Wanda* "literally spread-eagled her field in the twenty-five-foot class and even sailed away from the thirty-footers." *Wanda* won every one of the thirteen races she entered that year.

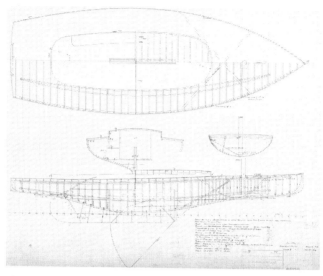

Anatomy of a racing machine: the construction drawing for *Wanda* (dated January 24, 1898) shows her unique hull shape with long overhangs that would increase the boat's waterline as she heeled. A pair of Tobin-bronze straps, each 13 ½' long, reinforced the bow section against the loads imposed by the mast. (MIT Museum)

The Herreshoff Style

It is safe to say that Nathanael Herreshoff never was bound by traditional thoughts on catboat design. He was always innovating or refining. Even in rare cases where more than one boat was built from the same half-model, dimensions varied slightly, as did details. By comparison to the Cape Cod catboats or those developed around Newport, Rhode Island, New York City, and New Jersey, the Herreshoff models were a species unto themselves.

Although the earliest models might reflect the plumb-stem or canoe-like bow we often associate with the classic catboat, designs evolved, particularly after Nathanael entered the picture in a full-time way. Then, gracefully curved stems and overhangs appeared. These hulls were proportionally narrower than most other catboats, with beams well under half the waterline length. The size, shape, and location of the centerboard were all carefully calculated. Transoms were normally raked and rudders were usually underhung, seldom the "barn-door" style often associated with catboats.

Masts were precisely tapered to reduce weight aloft. They were often a bit taller than one might expect (and booms shorter), some with shrouds in addition to the expected forestay. Masts of some smaller models were freestanding. Booms and gaffs tended to be slender and shaped to minimize weight. To resist bending, gaffs were well-supported by bridles and the peak halyard rigging.

All this added up in performance terms. "It were peculiar," Water Line mused in the *Boston Globe*, "that the Herreshoff cats always did beat [so well] in a breeze."

It was not unusual for boats to be designed from the outset to have a removable bowsprit on which a jib could be set to improve balance when reaching. Also, it was not uncommon that two mast positions were indicated, one for a cat rig, the other, further aft, for jib-and-mainsail. A boat that started life as a catboat might well "mature" into a sloop, a matter guided by owner preference though disappointing, no doubt, to the catboat purist.

A Herreshoff boat was comparatively expensive. In 1892, when the average worker earned about $675 annually, the 18'10" Herreshoff catboat *Viola* cost her owner $750, likely more than twice the price of a comparably sized product from another yard. "Our object," Nathanael wrote, "[was to] deal only with those who appreciated and could pay for good, honest work."

But Herreshoff owners also got value for their money. In the May 1900 *The Rudder*, sailor Lewis C. Walter wrote about the 24' Herreshoff-built catboat, originally named *Trojan* that he'd acquired when she was nearly thirty years old. The boat had been built by John Brown Herreshoff's yard in 1870. Walter noted that, "So strongly was she timbered and planked that today she is in good condition. . . . She has never been replanked nor has any frame been renewed."

In Retrospect

The radical *Wanda* marked the end of an era that had begun decades earlier with Charles Frederick Herreshoff's well-loved *Julia*s and the open cockpit racers of the 1870s, 1880s, and 1890s. The seventy-six catboats built between 1867 and 1907 account for at most 3 percent of all production by John and the manufacturing company combined. It was an era that saw the rise and decline of catboats as newer, easier-to-handle types gained popularity. But these catboats were meaningful because of their racing successes, quality, Nathanael's design innovations, and the sailing pleasure they gave their first and subsequent owners.

If one were to attempt to name a "classic Herreshoff catboat," a good candidate might be *Mab*, a 16'6" LWL design with an underhung rudder launched in the spring of 1891.

Few images show a classic Herreshoff catboat better than this one of *Mab* being sailed comfortably by two women in Victorian garb. Launched in 1891, *Mab* had dimensions of 18'6" x 16'6" x 7'4" x 1'4". *Mab's* 4 ½"-diameter tapered mast and slender spars were spec'd to minimize weight, a typical Herreshoff goal. *Mab's* 318 sq.-ft. sail was comparatively modest yet she reportedly defeated others in her class quite easily. (MIT Museum)

Mab was one of five "racing catboats" (*Viola* among them) built to half-model 221 carved in 1890. Each of the five boats differed somewhat in dimension, and Herreshoff also drew an optional bowsprit and sail plan that included a jib. Still, the cat-rigged versions looked like one expects a catboat to look. One imagines they would have been wonderful to sail and it's a shame that none have survived.

Sprite, of course, has survived. In 1979, she was returned by the Ford Museum to the Herreshoff Marine Museum. Former curator John Palmieri recalls that in 2010, based on Nathanael's drawing and photos taken before *Sprite* left Bristol, improvements were made. "We made corrections to the stemhead and mooring bit and rigged *Sprite* as she should be. Dearborn had the boom higher than shown by NGH." Remaining tasks include fabricating two blocks attached to the deck and running lines to the cockpit, replacing the manila cordage with cotton, covering the deck and housetop with canvas, and painting them the straw color Nathanael knew as a boy.

Sprite is the oldest surviving Herreshoff boat and may be the oldest American yacht in existence, a type seen only in very rare paintings from her

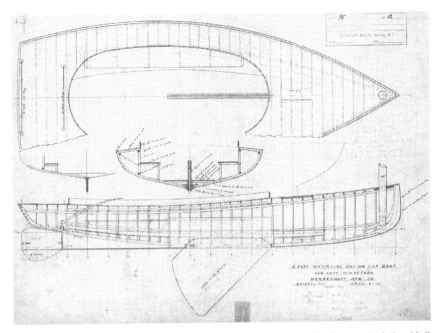

"She is of the lightest construction and finest workmanship," reported the Hull
Corinthian Yacht Club of *Mab* in June 1891. Every part was sized to provide the
needed strength at the least weight. Planks were 7/16" cedar screwed to 11/16"
x 13/16" white-oak frames. At a time when centerboards were typically made of
wood, *Mab*'s was made of 3/16" steel plate, permitting a centerboard trunk of
minimal width. *Mab* had the usual underhung rudder. Four other boats were built to
this appealing, practical design (Herreshoff Model 221), one for an owner on Lake
Minnetonka, Minnesota. (MIT Museum)

time. She's a reminder of the modest expectations, in terms of comfort, of
those who built her. They were sailors who went cruising with a chart, lead
line, compass, and bucket, and made seamanlike, coastwise passages. In the
end, *Sprite* seems to have been among the vessels that America's most revered
yacht designer remembered best, a simple catboat.

This story appeared in *WoodenBoat* No. 289, November/December 2022.

SEARCHING FOR
C. C. HANLEY

Recreating a Catboat
of the Golden Age

MY FASCINATION with boatbuilder C. C. Hanley eventually reached such a level of craziness that I began fantasizing about discovering one of his famous catboats in an old barn near Buzzards Bay. Quite unexpectedly, the next best thing happened. The Beetle Cat company received a commission to build a big, Hanley-designed catboat for Tim and Karen Fallon, both national- and world-champion-level sailors who'd grown up racing Beetles.

Today, some eighteen years later, it's clear that this rather unlikely project produced wonderful results. "I figured it would take about 10 years to become adept at sailing *Kathleen* and that proved to be about right," Tim noted. "Nowadays, we can do a lot more with our engineless boat than early on. Sailing on- and off-anchor has become second nature. Jibing the 1,000-square foot sail is still not easy but we have learned to control the 200' sheet with a wrap on the cleat as it pays out on the new jib. We've also learned to depower the huge gaff sail by pulling the board up some and easing the peak a little upwind or fully scandalizing downwind. We don't race *Kathleen* often but her hull shape somehow cheats her waterline length. She keeps up with 40-footers. On a dead downwind leg, she really shines. I can't imagine how fast the old cats were downwind when they set their big triangular spinnakers! Wood boats get a bad reputation of being maintenance intensive because most are old. I've been maintaining *Kathleen* myself and she ends up looking new each spring. She was designed and built well, doesn't have a modern boat's systems to break and so I expect she'll be sailing strong for the rest of my lifetime."

Spend enough time immersed in research and writing about bygone days and bygone boats, and one is prey to the development of some odd fantasies. One of mine goes like this. On a fine weekend morning, I attend an auction held in conjunction with the breakup of an old estate in one of those gracious villages that dot the shores of Buzzards Bay.

"What's down there?" I ask one of the appraisers, pointing at a distant, shingled building at the water's edge.

"Old boathouse," he answers. "Empty, they told us."

"Can I have a look?"

"Feel free," he says. "I'll come with."

The once-tended path is slippery with pine needles, dangerous with roots. Down at the boathouse, a rusty railway angles into the clear water from beneath padlocked doors. Oddly, the entry door is not locked. It opens with a few determined shoves. Inside, in sunlight filtered by the dirt-encrusted windows, we immediately see that the building is not empty.

"I'll be darned," says the estate appraiser.

"If you don't mind getting a little dusty," I say, "we could remove the cover."

"Hey, what the heck. Let's do it."

The canvas is tightly woven, a sort of gray-buff color, and it proves surprisingly light in weight. Still, getting the boat cover peeled off is a dirty job.

"What do you think?" my new friend says. "Looks like no one's bothered with this in 50 years."

"Maybe," I answer. "Maybe more years than that."

With the cover off, we find ourselves staring at a big catboat, perhaps as long as 27' or 28'. In the confines of the dim boathouse, it is hard to gain an overall perspective on the hull's shape. Standing on tiptoes, I can see the cabin has three oval portlights. A pair of opening round ports that won't be blocked when the mast is installed are mounted in the forward portion of the cabin coaming. There is a hint of artfully fashioned tumblehome in the stern sections. Freeboard is low. All planks are full-length.

I climb aboard. The first thing I see is a big wooden cleat mounted in the middle of the cockpit sole. Here, when racing, the mainsheet man, the crew's strongest, would have been stationed. The cabintop looks amazingly expansive, although it has only a slight crown. Down below, I know, there will only be sitting headroom. In the cabin, I discover an old newspaper, dusty, brittle, and dated July 21, 1897. Idly, I look around the boathouse. Lying in a spar rack built into one wall rests the black spruce mast. It looks immense, treelike. It is much longer than the boat, almost as long as the entire building. The boom seems just as long.

"So, what do you think?" says the appraiser, now genuinely curious.

"What do I think?" I answer, in some amazement. "I think this is an untouched catboat built by Charles Hanley sometime in 1896 or '97."

"Charles Hanley," says the appraiser. "Never heard of him."

Fanciful as it may sound, something shockingly close to this scenario actually happened, but not to me. Just after World War II, at Onset, Massachusetts, a 36' Hanley-built sloop was found in an old boathouse on what had once been a large estate. This boat, *Ramona*, was completely original, having been built in 1886 and stored away in 1908. "Seeing *Ramona*," wrote David A. Cheever Jr. in *Yachting* in July 1947, "is to be transported bodily into the 1880s. She is a perfect monument to the days when centerboards were as large as barn doors; rudders were only slightly smaller.... There isn't a single winch."

Why the fascination with C. C. Hanley and his boats, and especially the catboats? Because no living person has experienced the performance of a big catboat from the type's golden age in the late nineteenth century. Because a disturbing and general ignorance about such boats has persisted for almost a century with nothing to counter or validate criticism of the type. Because C. C. Hanley was, perhaps, the supreme master of the genre.

Once having accepted the fact that I would not be making a *Ramona*-like discovery, I developed a "what if" position. What if somebody who possessed a certain amount of money and, shall we say, a certain vision, decided to recreate a Hanley catboat? I had pretty much consigned this notion to the dust heap, too, when the phone rang one day about three years ago. On the other end was a woman who introduced herself as Florence Sauerbrey. In a musical, French-accented English, she asked me some very specific questions about C. C. Hanley. When I probed, she volunteered little but did suggest that her husband, a boatbuilder, might soon have a commission to build a C. C. Hanley catboat. We had a pleasant talk, but after it ended I filed our chat with my *Ramona* fantasy and got back to work.

There is nothing obvious in Charles C. Hanley's background that quite explains his intuitive touch for boat design and building. Once, in a tribute, MIT professor of naval architecture George Owen said that "Hanley had a genius for proportion which makes him worthy to rank with Nat Herreshoff among the great leaders in the development of racing yachts." Herreshoff himself recognized Hanley's great achievement. For his part, however, Hanley attributed his boats simply to "all guesswork, but somehow I usually guessed right."

C.C. Hanley was born in Damariscotta, Maine, in January 1851. His father Roger was then inspector of prisons in Maine but later became a

superintendent of lighthouses. He is said to have built the family home with
his own hands and to have passed on his tools to his son. After an apprenticeship with a Boston builder of piano cases, "Charley"—as people called
him—moved to Monument Beach, Massachusetts, in 1875. A year later, he
married Deborah Stevens of a well-established family in Sandwich.

There being little in the way of piano making on Cape Cod, Hanley
worked as a blacksmith, but at some unrecorded point he became interested
in boats. In an article that *The Rudder* published in 1919, Hanley claimed he
had made a half model for a 24' x 11'3" catboat forty years earlier and that
this "was the fourth boat I ever built, and I never built a better." He is said to
have entered his first race with the boat's name covered up and, after winning
the race, dramatically revealed the name—*Surprise!*

If Hanley's memory was precise, *Surprise* would have been built in 1879.
However, this is almost certainly incorrect because Hanley sold *Surprise* to a
member of the Beverly Yacht Club in 1885 and she became the club's champion for four straight years. Hanley never held onto a boat that long. The
chronology of the first boats may be as follows: The 23'6" *Eleanor* (named
for Hanley's daughter Sarah Eleanor, born in 1878) was perhaps his first
boat, built in 1879 or 1880. She was followed by the 20' *Dolly* in 1882, 22'
Tantrum in 1883, and *Surprise* in 1884.

When he was sixty-eight years old and looked back on his career, Hanley claimed it was *Surprise*, a boat shaped after he had gained experience by
trial and error, which established the "rules of thumb" that would guide his
later work. The hulls of C. C. Hanley's catboats were proportioned so that
the maximum beam was about 47 percent of the boat's overall length, and
the beam was carried noticeably far aft. He tinkered with deadrise angles and
overhangs while keeping his basic model unchanged. To minimize weight
and windage, freeboard was relatively low as was the cabin roof.

Hanley based his boats on 1" = 1' half models that he carved. (Despite his
design-by-eye genius, Hanley, as an old man, told a reporter that he believed
a designer required higher education that involved "scientific methods.")
When setting up, he is said to have erected mold stations at 4' intervals. The
finest white oak—seasoned in soft mud until it was "blue and hard"—was
typically used for keel and frames. (*Ramona*'s frames, though, were elm.)
Clear white pine was used for planking. Many of Hanley's larger boats, but
not the catboats, were double-planked. Fastenings were brass screws rather
than less expensive galvanized nails.

Following *Surprise* came a succession of catboats that included many
of the finest and fastest ever built, a kind of all-star roster that included the
26'6" *Mucilage* (1888), 28'6" *Harbinger* (1889), 26' *Almira* (1890), 33' *Thordis*
(1897), and many more. Once, in 1981, I met a tiny, very old man who had

Charles Hanley (left) and two of his crew (Harry Storms center)) pose aboard an unidentified boat at Hanley's Monument Beach yard circa 1895. Hanley is buried nearby in Gray Gables Cemetery. (Author's collection)

crewed aboard *Almira* and even singlehanded her as a teenager. But he didn't know what had become of that boat or of *Ramona* or if there might be a surviving Hanley catboat tucked away someplace. As a youth in Quincy, C. Willis Garey had idolized Hanley.

Charles Hanley soon became known to wealthy patrons from Newport to Boston to Chicago, from Texas to Canada. Such men could afford the best and they got it from Hanley, a prodigious worker who insisted that every detail of a boat be perfect before it left his shop. Hanley's success earned him the title of "the genius of Monument Beach," and Hanley built an impressive home on Shore Rd. where the Hanleys socialized with President Grover Cleveland and his family who summered nearby at Gray Gables. Cleveland, known for his honesty and common touch, had sold the presidential yacht but enjoyed fishing in a catboat in Buzzards Bay, often around what would be named Cleveland Ledge.

In 1897, apparently while Hanley was out harvesting timber, his shop burned down. Although details of the fire and its aftermath remain murky, the event set the course for the rest of Hanley's professional and personal life. Rather than rebuild on the Cape, Hanley reestablished himself in Quincy. John Cavanaugh, a top-flight racing sailor who became owner of one of

In this most unusual image, we see a nineteenth-century-style spinnaker pole being rigged aboard *Harbinger* on July 4, 1890. (MIT Museum)

Hanley's most famous yachts, the 44' *Meemer* built in Quincy in 1898–1899, claimed that Hanley moved to Quincy "since it was nearer demand for yachts. Also he wanted to get away from his wife." While details are scant, the Hanleys separated and, although there was sporadic contact, remained so for the rest of their lives.

Hanley's move to Quincy involved some level of partnership with the wealthy Lorenzo Baker. A man whose fortune had been built on the pioneering importation of bananas, Baker was a founder of what would become famous as the United Fruit Company. During 1897 and 1898, Hanley built a fine new 70' x 35' shop at Quincy Point. The shop had both electricity and steam heat. Here, Hanley turned to commissions for much larger yachts than those he had built on the Cape. Business was brisk, and in 1900 or 1901 Hanley and Baker incorporated the Hanley Construction Company, which became one of the country's largest yacht yards. Hanley, however, soon became unhappy with his role as chief designer and, in a financially ruinous move, he either quit or was forced out early in 1903. The yard itself was in receivership by January 1904 but was refinanced and then continued under the direction of Baker's son Reuben.

Essentially broke, Hanley now began an intensely difficult but ultimately successful two-year struggle to reestablish himself at his own two-acre facility across Quincy's Town River. There he built a few more boats but focused primarily on hauling, storage, and maintenance. In 1920, after another devastating fire, Hanley rebuilt. He sold out a few years later to his neighbor Fred Lawley and finally retired, enjoying gardening, brewing beer and distilling rum in his basement (although it was spoken of in hushed tones, Hanley's fondness for the bottle was no secret), playing poker, and freely sharing his colorful memories. He died on July 4, 1934, leaving behind a local reputation as a "merry old boy," a complete original who'd been one of New England's finest yacht builders.

One day, while visiting my boatbuilder friend Dave Birdsey in his West Barnstable shop, I noticed a dusty photograph of President Cleveland standing in the cockpit of a catboat with a fishing rod in his big hands.

"Did I ever tell you," Dave said, "that I used to own a catboat built by C. C. Hanley?"

"No way," I said. "You're kidding."

But he wasn't kidding. As a boat-crazy teenager in the mid-1950s, Dave had been given the remains of a 22' catboat that had been damaged in the hurricane of 1944 and then blown off its cradle and into the woods of the Sargent estate in Wareham by another hurricane a decade later. The rig was long gone and so was the 6-hp Lathrop that had been installed, but the hull, if hogged, was more or less intact. The full-length cedar planks were in good shape, as were many of the oak frames.

Somehow, working all by himself, Dave Birdsey got the old boat out of the woods on rollers and towed it with his outboard-powered skiff to Onset where he set about installing a new keel, rebuilding the decks, and eventually launching the boat, powering it with his twin-cylinder 5-hp Johnson and running it as a motorboat. Among the original features that remained untouched was what he still remembers as a "huge" knee that reinforced the maststep.

The man who gave Dave Birdsey the old catboat—it was eventually identified as *Cayuse*, built for F. W. Sargent in 1890—was named Henry Manamon, a caretaker on the Sargent estate in Wareham. Mr. Manamon, it turned out, had his own experiences relating to C. C. Hanley. As a youth, he had been cabin boy on none other than *Ramona*.

"Can you imagine," Dave Birdsey said, "*Ramona*! If only we could find her."

Because C. C. Hanley didn't draw plans for his boats, it was rare for the lines of a Hanley model to appear in print. The first and best to be published were

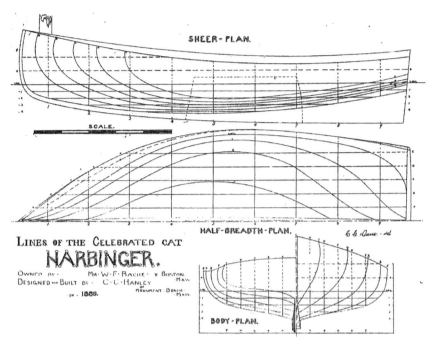

SHEER-PLAN.

SCALE.

HALF-BREADTH-PLAN.

LINES OF THE CELEBRATED CAT
NARBINGER.

OWNED BY -   MR. W. F. BACHE. x BOSTON.
DESIGNED AND BUILT BY -   C. C. HANLEY   MASS.
                          OF
        -IN - 1889.   MONUMENT BEACH-
                              MASS.

BODY-PLAN.

The shape of a champion: here are the lines of the 28'6" *Harbinger* (1889). They show "hollow" waterlines, modest deadrise (angle of the bottom from the keel outward) and some graceful tumblehome aft. The lines were drawn by Charles F. Davis (1870–1959) when he was design editor at *The Rudder* starting around 1898. (Author's collection)

those of *Harbinger* drawn for *The Rudder* by designer Charles G. Davis in 1897.

Twenty years later, in 1917, *The Rudder* published an article about renovations to *Almira* written by a regular crew member and Fore River Shipyard draftsman, the thirty-seven-year-old Norwegian-born Erland Debes. The Debes article included just enough of the lines for one to get a sense of the shapes. Finally, in March 1919, the magazine published an intriguing feature about Hanley (sans byline) that appears to have been written based upon direct contact with the builder. The story included both the hull lines and three construction drawings for a 28' catboat. These drawings, too, were made by Erland Debes who maintained a working relationship with Hanley for over a decade and eventually published several designs of his own.

The Debes drawings reflect Hanley trademarks: the hollow bow section, the great beam carried well aft, the modest deadrise, a raised forefoot, and a graceful stem that rakes aft slightly. The cabin is comparatively long but

A clean, graceful appearance was typical of Hanley's yachts. *Mucilage* was a race-winner from the day she was launched in 1888. A year later, wealthy New York yachtsman E. D. Morgan bought the boat for the purpose of winning a bet he made. Here *Mucilage*, renamed *Iris*, is seen in 1905 when she was a member of the D-Class fleet at Quincy. (See "The Cat Men of Quincy.") (Author's collection)

low-roofed. The centerboard trunk is a predominant feature. As if taunting those who decried the catboat's inherent lack of balance, the plans showed a tiller rather than a wheel. But this was not unusual, and some of Hanley's racing catboats such as *Mucilage*—Hanley rightly expected prizes would "stick to her like glue"—had a tiller.

The twenty-eight-footer was drawn up because it had been commissioned in 1917 by a prospective owner thousands of miles away. This man was George A. Sefton, a South African who then lived on a large, sandbar-strewn estuary off the Indian Ocean in Mozambique called Delagoa Bay. According to Mr. Sefton's nephew, Sheriff Saville, Sefton had once made a passage up the Intracoastal Waterway from Miami to New York in a catboat and never forgot the experience. When Sefton wrote Hanley, he included only a single specification for the catboat he wanted—its length.

Mr. Sefton's catboat was not built until the late 1940s or early 1950s in South Africa, but *Requisecat* then became an everyday sight in shallow Durban Bay. Dave Cox, who, as a youngster at the Point Yacht Club, sailed often aboard *Requisecat*, remembers that the boat "sailed well, but in certain conditions had quite a severe weather helm." Mr. Sefton sailed the boat into his eighties, stressing to guests that this was a "Cape Cod catboat." After his death, the boat was sold and converted to a sloop. The sole available photo of the sloop-rigged version suggests that liberties were taken with the cabin and some aspects of the hull shape, for the boat doesn't look much like a Hanley design.

Although my "what if" scenario had always envisioned someone building a boat to the Davis lines of *Harbinger*, or to lines taken directly from the boat's half model at MIT's Hart Nautical Collections, it was the twenty-eight-footer designed for George Sefton that had caught the eye of the mysterious potential patron of Florence Sauerbrey's husband. Gradually, details emerged.

At the 2003 Hog Island Tea, the seasonal award ceremony for the fall Beetle Cat race series at West Falmouth, Massachusetts, one of the racers let it be known that he was thinking of commissioning the building of a 28' Alden-design catboat. It was almost Halloween, an appropriate time for such a vision. The Beetle racer was named Tim Fallon. A software architect then in his late twenties, Fallon lives to sail. He grew up with Beetles and eventually became (and remains) a championship-caliber dinghy racer. At the Tea, Fallon bumped into Charlie York, builder of the Beetle. York said that perhaps Beetle Inc., which had recently been purchased by a new owner, might be able to help him realize his dream of a big catboat.

The man who bought Beetle Inc. is named Bill Womack. A compact, outgoing fellow with a dramatic mustache, Womack remains intent on bringing the customer service orientation and marketing magic he'd practiced in the heavy construction business to the building of wooden boats. After acquiring Beetle, Womack promptly made it a part of a company he named the Wooden Boat Center. Then he moved the operation inland from South Dartmouth to a big steel building in Wareham. "We were looking to expand on our core business and build some larger, traditional wooden boats when Tim came along," said Womack.

By the time Tim arrived, he had also met a thoughtful and highly skilled boatbuilder named Bill Sauerbrey, a man lanky enough to, like Tim himself, slip a big catboat's mast hoop over his shoulders, hula-hoop fashion, and slide it right down to his feet. "I said I was surprised he wanted such a cruising-oriented boat as the Alden design," Sauerbrey remembered. Fallon began doing research and promptly discovered C.C. Hanley. "He got excited about the Hanley from *The Rudder*," said Sauerbrey. "He thought it would have to be well-balanced because she had a tiller."

Quite suddenly, Bill Sauerbrey found himself working with Bill Womack and Tim Fallon on a project to build a C. C. Hanley catboat, the first such effort in this country in a century. Sauerbrey now faced the riddle of how to turn Tim Fallon's marvelous dream into reality. The first thing that Sauerbrey discovered was that Erland Debes's drawings had big problems. "To look at, they were okay," he said. "But you couldn't build a boat from them. I think he wrapped lead around a half model and used the resulting shape for lines without fairing them. If you tried to lay a batten over the various points in parts of the hull, you couldn't do it." The next step was to redraw and fair the lines.

Construction began in July 2004 with the arrival of a flatbed trailer loaded with timber from Suriname. A chainsaw was used to shape the angelique keel with its 8'-long centerboard slot. Unlike the keel Hanley would have built of oak, this one was made 2" wider aft to accept a shaftlog. Ultimately, the keel proved heavy enough that about 1,000 lbs. of the 3,500 lbs. of lead ballast would be removed after initial sea trials.

A grown white oak crook was used to join the stem and the keel, an area that would be subject to enormous stress and which Hanley always overbuilt. Because many of C. C. Hanley's construction methods died with him, Sauerbrey relied to some extent on his experience at Mystic Seaport. There he had worked with Barry Thomas during the latter stages of the building of the Crosby catboat *Breck Marshall*.

"We bent the frames similar to the way the Crosbys did 100 years ago," said Sauerbrey. "Teddy Crosby lent us a 'frame snake'—wooden blocks screwed together so the whole thing is flexible that we used to get the curve of the frames that were then bent around blocks screwed to the floor inside of a metal strap." After steaming, each 2"-thick white oak frame was secured inside of the metal strap and then bent around the form with a come-along. "That puts the whole frame into compression and fools the wood into thinking it's stronger than it is," said Sauerbrey who had examined fifty-year-old boats with compression-bent frames that were intact. "We didn't break a single frame despite some very tight curves, especially in the aft sections of the bilge area."

The frames were installed canted rather than vertically, another Crosby technique that eases the twist and curve of each frame in a shape as round as a catboat hull. The alternative, according to Sauerbrey, would have been to use smaller, weaker frames, or laminate frames and saw each frame's bevels, a comparatively inefficient method. Each frame had a dovetail cut at its inner end. The frames were fitted into notches in the keel where they were set in white lead and secured with a cypress wedge. This dovetail, along with steam-bent floor timbers screwed to the frames and lagged to the keel, then tied the boat together.

The hull, once framed out, was sturdy enough to permit the entire boat to be rocked from side to side. This simplified, among other things, installation of the tough wana garboard planks that had been pre-twisted in a jig. Planking was fastened with bronze screws. What Sauerbrey refers to as "very wide" wana planks were used at the sheer and the first broadstrake. "We found the old builders used wide sheer planks to strengthen the hull and resist the twisting imposed by the leverage of the rig."

The cypress sheer clamp, much wider than those typically used in other types of boats, was installed prior to adding the framing for the deck which was built Crosby-style of 7/8" x 1 1/8" silverballi strips screwed to the deck beams, edge-nailed together with bronze ring-nails and caulked with cotton. Air-dried angelique planks 16" wide were used for the steam-bent cabin coaming, while cedar formed the cockpit coaming, which was bent around cypress staving.

The cabintop was planked with cypress and covered with #10 canvas set in a rubber-based paint. Again following Crosby practice, the companionway hatch was not cut until the cabintop had been completed. That way, said Sauerbrey, "nothing moved at all." The centerboard was built of two sheets of 3/4" marine plywood bolted together and ballasted with 75 lbs. of lead. It is raised and lowered on a multi-part block-and-tackle, the pennant fed through a hole in the cabin bulkhead to one of several angelique cleats carved by Tim Fallon.

The reality that emerged from Tim Fallon's dream of recreating a Hanley catboat is named *Kathleen*, after Tim's mother. She is a slender, enthusiastic woman, a capable sailor who is now both crew member aboard her namesake and the principal caretaker of the orange Beetle Cat that has been in the family for many years. *Kathleen* was launched on a gray and chilly April morning some nineteen months after construction began. Both mast and boom are spruce, but the gaff, which Hanley would have built hollow out of spruce, is carbon fiber, although you'd never know it just by looking.

Sauerbrey, curious as anyone else about the boat's potential performance, has never forgotten his first impressions. "I was amazed the boat could carry her full 910-sq.-ft. sail in ten to fifteen knots and that she is so well balanced overall. I had the idea you'd feel like a mouse trying to sail a Beetle Cat, but that's not true at all."

Perhaps the biggest design change from Hanley's original is *Kathleen*'s provision for an engine. A shaftlog was bored, but a propeller aperture has yet to disfigure the boat's deadwood, so *Kathleen* may be as close as we'll ever come to learning the true performance of a racing catboat from the type's golden age. Currently, the "engineroom" is home only to a variety of lines and equipment.

As this is written in the summer of 2006, Tim Fallon has been living aboard in a laid-back, rather spartan fashion that entirely suits him. There is a comfortable double berth on the portside of the centerboard trunk and a composting toilet to starboard beneath the companionway step. Several wooden boxes screwed to a shelf hold a two-burner stove, foodstuffs, and necessities. A pleasant little painting of Tim's Beetle Cat hangs in the cabin.

My first glimpse of *Kathleen* afloat came on a foggy summer morning in Squeteague, a shallow bowl of a harbor within sight—on a clear day—of Cleveland Ledge. At first glance, I felt as if time had somehow been turned back a century, as if an old, much-studied black-and-white image had been reshot in color. There she lay, her boom extending well beyond the crutch, her hollow bow swelling dramatically a couple of feet aft of the stem. It is a shape that, when encountered with the boat out of the water, is shockingly beautiful. How *did* they get those planks to bend like that!

Kathleen's First Race

"This boat can clean up any cat he can find."

—Charles C. Hanley, *The Rudder*, March 1919

On July 21, 2006, *Kathleen* joined six eighteen- to twenty-four-foot boats for the Catboat Association's annual Squeteague race. By late morning, fog was lifting on Buzzards Bay but the wind was already gusting as high as twenty-five knots and maybe more. Even within Squeteague harbor, the gusts had power to them. With a displacement of around 14,000 pounds, *Kathleen* didn't dance about as the double-reefed battenless sail—beautifully cut by Squeteague Sailmakers—was fully peaked. Such behavior is a big plus for any catboat as it eliminates much drama when sailing off a mooring.

Concerned as he was about the falling tide, only an hour away from low, Tim jumped at the chance to have his friend John York (brother of Beetle Cat builder Charlie) guide us out. We fell off on a starboard tack, noting the increasing presence of sandbars all around while John plied the oars of his blue-painted and surprisingly fast pram dinghy.

"Head for the beach now, Tim. Tack *now*, Tim. Favor the port side, Tim. There's a little rock down there, Tim. Yup, *that* one."

Beating out of Squeteague's narrow, winding channel with moored boats in inconvenient places was a challenging endeavor. Small boys and fishermen stared saucer-eyed as *Kathleen* swept majestically and rapidly by, her crew working the centerboard and 200-foot main sheet while Tim handled the big tiller, quietly sharing his plans, seemingly unconcerned about the potential for mayhem.

Once out in Buzzards Bay, *Kathleen* immediately began answering long-held questions about C. C. Hanley's boats. "Experience has shown that Hanley cats carry their sail extremely well in a blow," reported *The Rudder* in its 1919 article about *Kathleen's* design. Now, she proved it, forging quickly upwind in the flatter water near shore but also show-ing the power to drive through silver-tipped, four- to five-foot seas that caused the smaller boats to labor. Upwind, the catboat was easily steered and nicely balanced.

Despite the big sail and thirty-six-and-a-half-foot boom, Tim had no worries at all about gibing around the downwind marks in the relatively heavy breeze—*whoosh*! Off the wind, in puffs, weather helm developed, though not excessive. Tim deftly lashed a small block to the tiller, ran a line through it to a comfortably graspable wooden "hiking stick" he'd crafted, and sat perched on the coaming, happily observing the rolling waves and guessing we were tacking through ninety degrees despite the head seas.

By the time the fleet—reduced in numbers because of the weather—returned to Squeteague, *Kathleen* had long since been greeted with the victor's welcoming horn. High fives had been exchanged and beer cans popped open. Tim Fallon's unusual twenty-first-century odyssey aboard the nineteenth-century *Kathleen* was well begun.

Kathleen spreads all of her 910 sq.-ft. sail. The twin opening front ports forward were a typical Hanley feature to improve ventilation. (Beetle Inc.)

This story appeared in *WoodenBoat* No. 193, November/December 2006.

THE CAT MEN OF QUINCY

The Rise and Decline of the D Class

All good things, it is often said, come to an end. So it was for the great catboats of the late nineteenth century. Those boats represented the ultimate expression of a type that had been developed from a pure working craft to race-oriented yachts owned by some of the sport's wealthiest men. Evolving hull design and rigs gradually eclipsed those boats, but there was to be a last act in the drama. It played out well away from New York, Newport, Buzzards Bay, and the Cape, long the home waters for such boats, and had as its focal point Quincy, Massachusetts.

In Quincy, a group of yachtsmen conceived the idea of acquiring some of the greatest catboats still in existence and forming a new association with its own rules that would govern racing. So, one by one, some of the best catboats ever built by the Crosbys, Herreshoff, and C. C. Hanley were bought at very good prices and refurbished by their enthusiastic new owners.

Although these boats had generally been skippered and crewed by professionals, this new era would see them helmed and crewed by amateurs, many of whom soon proved to be quite expert. What's more, families were also involved and a festive atmosphere surrounded the weekend races as the boats competed in regattas from Quincy to Marblehead. It is not an easy thing for today's catboat sailor, even the most experienced, to really comprehend what it took to sail boats like this. But enough information has survived to give insight into the judgement, muscle, and seamanship needed to handle a big racing catboat on the brink between maximum performance and some sort of disaster.

"Have a seat young man," the old-timer said. "You're here about the catboats we sailed years ago?"

"Yes," I answered. "I never thought I'd be lucky enough to meet a man who knew them, even in Quincy, Massachusetts, which seemed to be the heart of it all."

"Ah, well," he nodded. "Those were some days. All gone now."

Hanging on the walls were big, framed photographs that the old-timer had taken sixty years earlier of Boston's T Wharf crowded with fishing schooners, of local one-designs, and, of course, catboats. C. Willis Garey still had a sharp memory when we met in 1981 and he was eighty-eight. He could well recall boats he had known, and their dimensions and features, with no problem at all. After a while, when I had wearied him with questions and prepared to leave, he said, "Hang on a minute."

He walked, shuffling a bit and stooping slightly, to the staircase, where he removed a photograph from the wall. "This is for you," he said. "I took that in 1916."

And that is how, forty years later, I have a framed and matted print of *Almira*, among the greatest catboats designed and built by Charles C. Hanley at his Monument Beach shop on Cape Cod. Willis had taken the photo when he was twenty-three years old and *Almira*, built in 1890, was twenty-six.

On the matte beneath the image, Willis had neatly printed *Almira*'s specifications. He had noted the $85 (about $2,000 in today's money) that sailmaker H. Hamblin & Son, on Boston's Long Wharf, had charged for the 950-sq.-ft. sail with four rows of reefpoints. Willis also recorded *Almira*'s race results during 1916, when he was among the crew assembled by her then-owner, Dr. Horace Almon Jones, a dentist, of the Quincy Yacht Club (QYC): "19 firsts, 31 races, 7 boats racing."

There are photos of *Almira* by Willard Jackson and Nathaniel Stebbins, taken during the golden age of catboat racing, when she was new. But Garey's image recalls a different time. Starting in 1905, some of the finest catboats ever built, but by then abandoned in favor of newer types, suddenly got a new lease on life. For years, the old boats, long past their glory days at Rhode Island, Massachusetts, New York, or New Jersey, had been moldering under canvas tarps. But then appeared what Boston journalist Winfield M. Thompson called the "cat men" of Quincy.

It was these sailors who reinvigorated the sport. They joined the newly established Cape Catboat Association (CCA), acquired the old catboats, and competed hard in events all around Massachusetts Bay in a new class, Class D catboats. It was the last hurrah for some remarkable boats and sailors who really knew how to sail them.

This is the image of *Almira* taken by C. Willis Garey in 1916 and presented to the author in 1981. *Almira*: LOA 26'9", beam 12'2", draft 3', with centerboard 7'6", mast 40', boom 28' hoist 22', sail area 950 sq. ft., lead keel 2,300 lb., disp.13,000 lbs. *Almira* was renowned for balancing well. (Author's collection)

By the time the Cape Catboat Association was formed on January 23, 1905, the catboat's once overwhelming popularity had drastically diminished. Knockabout sloops and a growing list of one-designs and Universal Rule classes now dominated. But catboats had a good run. Thomas Fleming Day, editor of *The Rudder*, was so fascinated by the subject that in 1900, he published his own history of the catboat and the cat rig, which he properly defined as two different things. By the time Day had finished, "The Catboat" was so long that it had to be published in three parts.

Day concluded that small craft of a type that had a single sail set on a mast stepped right in the bow had first appeared in 1830 or 1840. The type developed in various forms in Barnegat Bay, Rhode Island, Cape Cod, Boston, and around New York, where, by the 1870s, marine artist James E. Buttersworth was painting evocative little canvases of plumb-stemmed catboats, each of which had an enormous sail, a big centerboard trunk, and the

Prior to the Cape Catboat Association, boats like *Hustler* competed in open classes. Here, on May 30, 1902, the Crosby-built *Hustler* races in "Class C" (25-feet) during a South Boston Yacht Club regatta. Few images reflect the use of the winged-out, self-tending jib as well as this one. Quincy Yacht Club commodore H. W. Robbins owned *Hustler*. (MIT Museum)

peculiarly long, "barn-door" rudder and tiller necessary for a strong man to keep things more or less under control.

In Massachusetts, from Buzzards Bay to the Cape and Boston, catboats of various sizes became staples among racing sailors. Boats were classed based on length, with five class divisions ranging from the First Class for boats over 23' to the Fifth Class for those under 15'. To cite but one example of the type's popularity, the 1885 roster of Hull Yacht Club in Massachusetts listed fifty-six catboats of from 17' to 28' in length.

The prime mover behind the CCA was a realtor and auctioneer named Frank Fessenden Crane, then commodore of the QYC. The first president of the association was Fessenden's fellow club member, thirty-six-year-old Ira M. Whittemore, a Quincy business owner. The measurer, responsible for verifying that boats complied with class rules, was nineteen-year-old Ralph Eldredge Winslow. Winslow had just completed an apprenticeship at a local boatyard and was commencing a distinguished design career.

The CCA's mission was "to keep boats of this type together and make interesting and instructive racing." While the nineteenth-century boats had typically been sailed by professionals, the cat men of Quincy would race as amateurs. The rules permitted one crew member for every 4' of waterline length.

The D-Class rules were crafted to explicitly eliminate atypical catboats with short waterlines, long overhangs, and a mast stepped well aft of the bow and supported of necessity with shrouds. While undeniably fast, sleek racing machines like Nathanael Herreshoff's *Merry Thought* of 1892 (31'2" x 25' x 11') or H. Manley Crosby's *Step Lively* (34'9" x 25' x 11'3") had so dominated more traditional competitors as to essentially end catboat racing as it had been known around New York and on Barnegat Bay.

D-Class rules limited overall length to between twenty-two and twenty-seven feet with overhangs not to exceed 20 percent of the waterline. Reverse curves at either bow or stern were prohibited. To eliminate overly low-sided boats, there were specific requirements regarding freeboard, and headroom was to be not "less than 2 ½ inches for every foot of waterline." There was to be no monkey business about where the mast was located. "The forward side of the mast shall not be more than one foot aft of the forward end of the waterline." That guaranteed the mast would be in the bow where it belonged. Boats had to carry cruising gear.

The rig of these D-Class catboats raised some discussion at the time and the subject has been a source of confusion right down to the present day. "Working sails only [meaning no spinnaker] were permitted," Winfield Thompson wrote, "but a jib is always carried, which off the wind may be poled out. The class thereby become sloops."

It is a useful reminder of how quickly knowledge can be lost that even historian William P. Stephens, who was forty-five years old when *Almira* was launched and closely watched yachting developments, was frustrated in his attempts to answer the question of whether a catboat was still a catboat when it carried a jib. He finally gave up, saying readers "may form [their] own conclusions as to when a Cape catboat is a sloop; the writer is unable to enlighten him further."

Research indicates that the Crosbys, whose boatbuilding on Cape Cod extended back to the mid-eighteenth century and continues today, were among those who with some frequency built catboats that carried a bowsprit and jib. When offered for sale as used boats, such vessels were typically advertised as a "jib and mainsail catboat." However, the desire to win races led to the over canvassing of top-echelon catboats. Serious prize money had a lot to do with this. The notice of a race at Newport during July 1885 was typical: "The catboat belonging to Scolford Hones of New York is being made ready for a race with the catboat *Cruiser*." The race was for $500—the equivalent of about $13,000 today.

Crowding on sail was the way to make a boat go faster. But when a catboat with an already generously sized mainsail added 100 sq. ft. to its area, a jib became necessary to restore some semblance of balance. The jib, in turn, required a long bowsprit, which was unsightly to a purist's eye. The response to criticism of this setup was that a catboat's chief feature, the mast location, remained "in the eyes" of the boat. Because neither bigger mainsails nor the addition of jibs were enough to get boats moving downwind in light air as fast as desired, spinnakers—then three-cornered sails set on long spars carried on deck—were adopted, too.

A catboat thus rigged could and did compete not only against similarly rigged catboats but in other classes, too. In one of the most dramatic such events, on July 15, 1889, the Eastern Yacht Club of Marblehead, Massachusetts, held a race in which the 28' Hanley catboat *Harbinger* (27'9" on the waterline) competed with two 30'-waterline cutters. *The Boston Globe* covered this race, which was sailed in a gale and heavy seas on Massachusetts Bay, in all its tack-by-tack, broken-spinnaker-pole, and parted-halyard detail. To the astonishment of all except her designer and builder, *Harbinger* won.

"When [two cutters] were defeated by an unknown craft, the interest shifted to the new type," Stephens wrote. It was this new type, the Cape cat with a long bowsprit and jib, that would find a second life in Quincy sixteen years after that Eastern Yacht Club event.

The CCA's promising 1905 inaugural season set a precedent for the future. Besides racing at Quincy or Hull, the boats journeyed elsewhere in Massachusetts, to Marblehead, Annisquam, Gloucester, and sometimes Provincetown, towing their tenders and racing each other along the way. Sometimes, crews were met by wives and kids.

"They race," journalist Thompson wrote, "in the same regattas with men who spend more in one season than they do in ten." The catboats were sailed hard, often on a delicate balance between top speed and disaster. If a boat heeled enough in a big gust so as to slice a wave with her lee cockpit coaming and scoop up fifty or more gallons of seawater, the crew bailed while the skipper remained focused.

The final 1905 points tally revealed that eighteen boats had competed in at least one of fifteen races. The champion was the 24'7" Herbert Crosby–built *Marvel* owned by QYC flag officer Ira M. Whittemore.* *Marvel* could sleep three in the cabin and accommodate fourteen in the cockpit, known

---

* A catboat named *Sunnyside*, which may or may not be *Marvel*, was purchased in 2020 by longtime catboat sailor John Conway. The boat is currently undergoing restoration as research efforts, always challenging when it comes to old boats, continue.

The Crosby-built *Marvel* was champion of the Cape Catboat Association's first season. *Marvel*'s mainsail has five sets of reef points to cope with all wind velocities. (MIT Museum)

in those days as the "standing room." Whittemore had spent the equivalent of almost $3,000 on *Marvel*'s Couzens & Pratt sails, with horizontal seams rather than the vertical seams of nineteenth-century sails.

In the association's 1906 season, however, Whittemore's average point score put him in third place. Businessman Henry C. Nickerson won with *Arawak*, built at Kingston, Massachusetts, by Hanley disciple George Shiverick. Crane was second with his newly acquired *Iris*, another Hanley-built boat that Hanley had named *Mucilage*. During 1905, Crane had sailed his Crosby-built *Dolly II*, but he sold her when he had the opportunity to acquire *Mucilage*, a catboat of great renown.

Under the patronage of the immensely wealthy yachtsman Edwin Dennison Morgan III, Charles C. Hanley had sailed *Mucilage* to Newport in 1889 and there defeated the fastest catboat in Rhode Island, almost certainly a Nathanael Herreshoff creation. In the parlance of those days, *Mucilage* had made her competitor "look like a dock."

Morgan then bought *Mucilage*, had her cabin reduced in size to save weight, and, according to Thompson, started the boat on a career that "for duration and victories has probably never been equaled among American small yachts." Subsequently, Hanley sold *Mucilage* to Elbridge T. Gerry, who served as the New York Yacht Club's commodore from 1886 to 1892, for use at Newport. When Crane learned that the yacht, renamed *Iris*, was lying idle, he promptly made an offer.

Selling one boat to buy another was not unusual for the enthusiasts of the association. Despite his success with *Marvel*, which included winning today's equivalent of $10,300 in prize money, Whittemore put her up for sale after the 1906 season. Like his friend Crane, Whittemore coveted Hanley's boats and, when the opportunity arose, he bought *Almira*. A few years later, Wallace W. Arnold, a shoe manufacturer who'd done well after buying the Crosby-built *Dolly II*, commissioned Daniel Crosby to build *Dolly III*, a typical, husky Cape Cod catboat but with a weight-saving hollow boom and gaff. When the time came to sell *Dolly III*, Arnold called her the "fastest cat in America."

The CCA rules adopted in 1905 anticipated that some revisions might be found necessary. In the August 1908 issue of *The Rudder*, Thompson reported what a likely revision would be. He wrote of the rules: "[W]hen they expire, the association will consider a suggestion that the next set abolish bowsprits. Bowsprit and jib do not belong to the catboat. . . . Boston has long employed them, thus debasing the cat, the simplest of all rigs, into a mongrel sloop."

Thompson's opinion about the bowsprit subject reflected a purist's sensibilities and personal experience. But he also had discussed the topic with Hanley himself, who was no fan of bowsprits. At any rate, when the association commenced the 1910 season, it did so with boats that were catboats in rig as well as name. In 1910, too, the single-sail policy—"Mainsail only shall be used"—was adopted by the Inter-Bay Cabin Catboat Association, which was intended to promote racing among the CCA's Massachusetts boats and those of the Yacht Racing Association of Southeastern Long Island, the Yacht Racing Association of Barnegat Bay, and the New Bedford Yacht Club.

The two Massachusetts yachts selected to compete at the 1910 inter-bay races hosted by the Edgewood Yacht Club in Cranston, Rhode Island, were *Iris* and *Dolly III*. All but one of the four races in the series were sailed in strong winds, and the sail-carrying ability of the Quincy boats, usually with one or two reefs tied in, was a revelation to their competitors. The reason, according to Thompson, who was a member of *Iris*'s crew, "was their perfect balance, the proper relation of sail to hull, which is obtainable in a catboat only by years of experience and by some men is never attained at all."

Thompson observed and explained the magic of boats such as *Iris*, *Dolly III*, and *Almira*. These yachts had avoided the pitfalls that challenged both

The "Big Six" of the Cape Catboat Association (1907)*

Yacht	Designer	Build Year	Dimensions	Sail Area (main/jib) sq. ft.	Owner	Notes
Iris	C. C. Hanley	1888	26'6" x 12' x 2' 6"	998/130	Frank F. Crane	Originally Hanley's own *Mucilage*
Almira	C. C. Hanley	1889	26'6" x 23'4" x 12'2" x 2'6"	1125 total	Ira M. Whittemore	Built to defeat *Mucilage*
Arawak	George Shiverick		27' x 23' x 11' x 3'6"	798/125	Henry C. Nickerson	
Dartwell	C. C. Hanley	1896	26'11" x 24'6" x 12' x 2'6"	940/150	George G. Saville	Ex-*Clara* of Walter Burgess. Shortened 6" for Class D.
Emeline	Crosby	1897	26'11" x 25'1½" x 11' x 2'6"	948/130	Herbert W. Robbins	
Busy Bee	C. C. Hanley	1896	25' x 21'	675/120	Walter S. Coombs	Built for actress Fanny Davenport and first named *Fanny D*

*Out of a fleet of approximately sixteen competitors, these six boats proved the most consistently competitive during the 1907 season.

Note: These boats had booms well in excess of their length. *Iris*'s boom was 39'6" long. Ballast varied. *Iris* carried 4,200 lbs. of copper dross; *Arawak* 2,600 lbs. of lead. It was generally believed that weight, whether in ballast or gear, did not hurt.

Table based on information recorded by Winfield Thompson and published in *The Rudder*, v. 20, 1908 and other sources.

the rule-of-thumb designer and trained naval architect alike. He was quick to note that *Virginia*, designed by the highly regarded naval architect Charles Mower especially for the inter-bay series, was no match for the highest development of Hanley or Crosby rule-of-thumb design.

"[I]f her centerboard is in the wrong place she will not sail properly," Thompson wrote. "If she is not ballasted to a nicety, all hope of winning is lost. If her stern is not the right shape, she will be thrown off her balance when taking a stiff angle of heel." Thompson noted that sloops or cutters might suffer from the same problems but that their headsails could cover the defect to some degree. But the catboat sailor "must work with his single sail [as] the only means of obtaining results."

Built by Daniel Crosby at Osterville, *Dolly III* shows all the design features of a classic Cape Cod catboat. Journalist Winfield Thompson described her as having "a very buoyant form, which took the sea as handsomely as a duck." (W. B. Jackson/MIT Museum)

While *Iris's* mainsail had been 998 sq. ft. when she raced with a jib, it was still around 900 sq. ft. after being recut in a quest to maintain balance. This, of course, was a huge sail for a 26'6" boat and, in Rhode Island, *Iris's* competitors half-expected her to capsize. By comparison, the 26' *Virginia*, representing the Island Heights Yacht Club in New Jersey, had a 765-sq.-ft. mainsail. Yet *Iris* stood up well to her sail, which was said to combine great driving power while having a shape superior to the others, several of which could not get their sails to set without wrinkles along the gaffs and booms.

Crane, an astute skipper, knew that *Iris's* 4,200-lb. ballast keel was about a ton more than carried by *Dolly III*. He had also assembled a crew that included two hefty men. His mainsheet man weighed 240 lbs., and another crewman weighed 210 lbs. Crane never begrudged the competitor who bested *Iris* in light air. But as he remarked to Thompson, "I'll tell you, my son, races aren't sailed in calms every day, and I'll hang onto my ballast." What's more, while other boats had crew lying along the windward rail, Crane kept his crew low in the cockpit, saying, "What's the use of putting your men up in the air to catch the wind?"

The popularity of the D Class is evident at the start of this race at Marblehead on August 15, 1908. (Historic New England)

By the end of the weeklong interbay matches, *Iris* and *Dolly III* had won ten of the twelve cups awarded, including the Thomas Fleming Day Trophy. *The Rudder*'s editor, "Skipper" as he was known, was present at the celebratory dinner in Bristol, Rhode Island, at the event's conclusion. He never lost his lifelong interest in what he recognized as a "pure, original American type . . . the boat our fathers cruised, fished, and raced in, and the best moderate-sized boat I know of for the purpose."

Having owned *Almira* for three years, Whittemore sold the boat after the 1909 season. He then purchased the Hanley-built *Dartwell*, first named *Clara* by her initial owner, yachtsman Walter Burgess, who'd had notable success with her. She was said to have no equal in windward ability and Burgess comfortably singlehanded her.

What led Whittemore to buy *Dartwell* and sell *Almira* is not known, but he may have had a sixth sense about the matter. *Dartwell*, sailing in 1910 under a cat rig, dominated her competitors and would continue to do so in the coming years. *Almira*'s new owner, however, had no success in the one 1910 race he entered. Essentially, *Almira* disappeared until 1915, when Garey's friend Dr. Jones bought her and undertook upgrades that included the new sail and a 2,200-lb., 17"-deep ballast keel that ran from forward of the centerboard back to her underhung rudder.

With her bottom coated with slippery melted lard, *Almira* immediately served notice that she would regain her former prominence, placing second to *Dartwell* in mid-August. But *Almira's* rejuvenation was much hampered when, on September 26, 1915, she was blown off her mooring and fetched up on the boulders of Grape Island in Hingham Bay, Massachusetts. She suffered a broken centerboard and other damage. Still, ten months later Dr. Jones had restored his yacht back to her winning ways. "*Almira* Continues Her Streak of Successes" was the *Globe's* headline on July 30, 1916.

Six months after that race, Crane died of a heart attack. His death was a shock to yachtsmen all along the coast and meant that the CCA had lost the visionary who had conceived it. There really was no 1917 season for the D-Class catboats. *Almira* soundly defeated *Dolly III* in a race on August 25, but by that summer most skippers had bought boats of a new type developed by C.R. Snow, who designed a fifteen-foot one-design catboat with a 250-sq.-ft. sail.

Things improved somewhat after World War I, but it was clear that both time and people were moving on. In the period 1919–1923, Class D racing drew only four boats: *Dartwell*, *Almira*, *Macushla*, and *Grayling* (see sidebar). The tide ebbed steadily for the class. On July 16, 1922, the *Globe* reported that only "two old-timers, the *Almira* and the *Dartwell*, had it out. H. Almon Jones of Quincy had a pretty fight on his hands, but won the race by 34 seconds."

By the time the QYC members gave C. C. Hanley a surprise seventy-sixth birthday party at his house on January 19, 1925—he'd long since moved to Quincy after his Cape shop burned down and his marriage collapsed—the D-Class fleet of the CCA had dispersed. But in the winter of 1926, a decade after Crane died in Quincy, came news about *Iris*. The boat had somehow found her way to Los Angeles, where she'd been purchased by two sailors named Fred Kohler and John Wallace. *Pacific Coast Yachting* magazine reported that the two men, along with Kohler's daughter, were planning to sail *Iris* to Miami.

It is testimony to the appeal of a catboat such as *Iris*, which is among Hanley's greatest creations, that she could inspire dreams for a long, coastwise ocean passage for which she'd never been intended. The magazine's editor cautioned against such a venture in a thirty-eight-year-old catboat. Presumably good sense prevailed over fantasy. As for the cat men of Quincy and the D Class, they had enjoyed excitement, good racing, and camaraderie that lasted longer than it had in many other classes. They demonstrated for all to see, both then and now, what a proper Cape Cod catboat could do as a racing and cruising yacht when handled by those who understood it.

Grayling—a D-Class Survivor

In 1913, a 22' newcomer named *Grayling* made her appearance in the D-class fleet. Thought to have been built in 1898 by Wilton Crosby, *Grayling* was purchased by Clarence V. Nickerson of Hull, Massachusetts, where he became superintendent of schools and also served variously as Town Treasurer and Selectman. On July 12, 1913, a windy, puffy day, *Grayling* won what might have been her first Association race. None of the five other catboats—including *Iris* and *Dartwell*—could make up their time on the smaller yacht.

Subsequently *Grayling* would enjoy other victories, mostly in light air, and Nickerson was still racing her in the Handicap Class as late as 1937. It seems likely that Nickerson owned the boat until a few years before his death in 1949. *Grayling* then passed through the hands of some five more owners until she fetched up on the south shore of Long Island. There, on a winter's day in 1981, all her years and indifferent care caught up with the old catboat. She sank in her slip at the Cedarhurst Yacht Club.

Doug Goldhirsch, who saw a "For Sale" notice for *Grayling* in *WoodenBoat*, has never forgotten his first sight of her in the club parking lot. "They had put a block of Styrofoam under each bilge to hold her up, and left her lying there." Despite *Grayling*'s condition, there was beauty to her and Goldhirsch, who was then working on a degree in naval architecture at the Webb Institute, recognized it right away. "She looked so good that I can only think that she had held her shape. Most of the rot in the frames turned out to be low in the bilge so I think the curvy parts were preserved."

But it was obvious that *Grayling*'s original mast position had not been preserved. "The mast had been relocated nineteen inches aft of the original step and chain plates had been installed," Goldhirsch said. "My theory is that as the boat aged, her bow was working too much due to the mast forces on the keel and deck. I've read accounts of old catboats beating to windward and the bow twisting so much that water would shoot through temporarily opened-up seams at the bottom of every wave. I think the mast repositioning was an attempt to keep sailing without rebuilding the hull. I also theorize that they replaced the deck at this time. The deck was fiber-glassed plywood with overly heavy framing. But whoever rebuilt the deck and moved the mast aft saved the boat from the scrap pile."

While Goldhirsch expected to replace the rotted frames (most of which had already been sistered), the discovery that a new keel was needed came as a disappointment. New floor timbers and centerboard trunk followed along with a new mast step, sternpost, bilge stringers and sheer clamps. Although the garboards needed replacement, many of the original bottom planks, ten or twelve inches wide and thought to be yellow pine, were in fine shape. The rebuilt *Grayling* was launched on a misty morning in June 1987. There was no interior or cockpit seating so, when Goldhirsch went sailing, he and friends sat on milk crates.

The 22-foot Crosby-built *Grayling* was the shortest D Class competitor permitted by class rules. Clarence V. Nickerson campaigned her from 1913 through the 1930s. Lovingly restored by Douglas Goldhirsch, *Grayling* still sails today in Maine. (Robert Mitchell)

Two more years of additional work saw installation of the cockpit, interior furnishings, and an ash ceiling in the cabin. A single-cylinder Yanmar diesel was installed off-center on the starboard side and a new water and fuel tank were fitted. So was a little galley, an electrical system, and a head mounted beneath the portside companionway step.

Grayling's rig retains what is believed to be the original gaff but a new boom was required and, more recently, a new mast built by Pleasant Bay Boat and Spar Company on Cape Cod. The boat's 470-sq.-ft sail is certainly smaller, probably by some 200 sq. ft., than the original but still requires the first reef when the wind exceeds ten knots and the second at fifteen. "She's a joy to cruise when reefed properly," Goldhirsch reports, "and she does great in light airs."

Doug Goldhirsch, who is proprietor of Southport Island Marine in Southport, Maine, and holds a Coast Guard 100 Ton Master license, is one of several maritime professionals I've met over the years who's found enduring challenge and delight in an old catboat rather than a modern, technology packed yacht. Today, 123 years after she was built and 108 years after she entered the Cape Catboat Association fleet, Goldhirsch has ensured that *Grayling* still carries D 27 on her sail.

This story appeared in *WoodenBoat* No. 279, March/April 2021.

"THE LITTLE ENGINE THAT COULD"

100 Years of Beetle Cats

Changing tastes and generations conspire to ensure that relatively few boats survive the test of time. Of one-design classes still being actively raced a century after their introduction, one might name the Wianno Senior and Herreshoff 12 1/2, both introduced in 1914, and the Beetle Cat, 1921. Of the three, it's only the Beetle that continues to be built in some numbers. The following story was published at about the same time the Beetle celebrated its 100th anniversary.

My introduction occurred many years ago during a vacation on Nantucket. At that time, there was a small boat rental business whose little fleet included Beetles moored in a shallow, grassy cove east of the town's wharves. The boat we rented was furnished with a couple of flotation cushions, a paddle, a bucket, and an anchor. Soon enough, we had lowered the centerboard, hoisted the blue sail, and threaded our way through the moored boats and out into the harbor. It was a day of sunshine, white dunes, and bright greenery and, with a fair morning breeze, we sailed out past Pocomo Head to Head of the Harbor and Wauwinet.

The trip back against both an increasing headwind and flooding tide was so wet that we anchored to await more favorable conditions. Eventually, we hoisted the sail and, in a dying breeze, made our way back to the little cove and picked up the mooring. It was a memorable sail in a wonderful wooden boat. With its gaff rig and centerboard, the Beetle is a fine boat to teach the neophyte sailor all the basics but, since its virtues never grow old, it's also a boat worth keeping for a lifetime.

"What we needed was a small boat, since we maintain them ourselves, one with plenty of room, since we all have families, but a boat fast enough to buck a four-knot tide and rugged enough to sail in the open ocean. There is only one boat that has these qualifications, the Beetle Cat."

—letter of Richard S. Borden, Westport, MA, to Waldo Howland, Concordia Company, 1948

"Every year since 1963, my mom went sailing in Quonochontaug Pond. At ninety-seven, she is happy we are still sailing a Beetle."

—Bill Boll, Weekapaug Yacht Club

Like a down-turned thumb, the peninsula known as Clark's Point projects south from New Bedford into Buzzards Bay. On the point's western side, bordering Clark's Cove, British forces came ashore in September 1778, and burned what was then known as Bedford Village. Hard times followed. But by 1787, when the village was renamed New Bedford, Clark's Point was home to salt works, woods, farms, and, in 1797, the first of several lighthouses. By then it was clear that whaling would power the growth of what became, for a time, the country's richest city.

The whaling fleet created a market for all sorts of equipment and supplies: barrels, blocks, pumps, sails, tools, rope, spars, and, of course, whaleboats. Among the spar makers were William Beetle (1787–1872)—a New Bedford street still bears the family name—and his son Rodolphus, one of the city's wealthier men. Another Beetle, James (1812–1886), established a boat shop and developed a method for the rapid, volume production of whaleboats.

Sometime after 1877, James moved the shop from downtown Eddy's Wharf to Clark's Point where he and his wife Ann Amelia Hathaway had a little house on what is now East Rodney French Blvd. Here, James worked with his sons John Henry, Charles Darwin, and James C. Beetle.

Sailor and author Llewellyn Howland, who knew Clark's Point well and got his first job at Beetle's putting bungs in whaleboats, witnessed the production system. In *Sou'West and By West of Cape Cod*, published in 1947, Howland—whose family of whaleship owners had a long connection with the Beetles—described the system.

"There were molds, battens, clamps, and special tools. . . . There were knees, applewood crotches, loggerheads, rubbing strakes, tholepins, rudders, tillers, mast steps—all segregated [for ease] of access." Howland recalled orderly stacks of cedar, pine, and oak, much of it pre-shaped into boat parts. A whaleboat could be produced and delivered in forty-eight hours.

The Beetle boat shop prospered with the rise of New Bedford whaling, but the Civil War, dwindling demand, and competition resulted in steady decline. James Beetle's response was to focus on the growth of yachting. James and his sons James C. and John H. joined the New Bedford Yacht Club in 1878, a year after it was formed. On April 15, 1878, the *Boston Globe* reported: "The three best cat-rigged boats in the fleet . . . are those owned by James Beetle and his sons John H. and James C. all of whom are widely known as skillful boat builders."

Although John H. Beetle took a day job as a lumber surveyor in 1883, he maintained a close connection to the shop. A forward-thinking, adaptable man, Beetle was installing gasoline engines in catboats by 1905. His son Carl was advertising a line of standardized twenty-two- and thirty-foot flush-decked power cruisers by 1922.

Waldo Howland related the Beetle Cat's conception this way. "In 1920, as a fill-in project for the yard, John Beetle and his son Carl modeled a 12-foot Cape Cod–style catboat . . . a safe, useful, and pleasurable boat for young members of the Beetle family and, they hoped, for other youngsters as well."

In May 1921, *The Rudder* published a brief feature about the "Twelve Foot Club Catboat." "She is a typical Cape cat form with slightly overhanging bow. The mast is far enough abaft the stem to get a good lead for the headstay. The Construction is fairly heavy. . . . This boat is being built in quantities by Carl N. Beetle." The $225 price was raised to $250 in the thirties. *The Rudder* article included profile and plan view drawings presumably done by the magazine. There were no Beetle Cat lines or construction drawings until postwar, and the whereabouts of a half-model, if one ever existed, are unknown.

The "Club Catboat" didn't attract a single order in 1921 from the New Bedford Yacht Club. However, the Duxbury Yacht Club promptly added the "catboat class" to its fifteen-foot one-designs and Baybirds. A 1923 pictorial in *The Rudder* showed a fleet of Beetles in "Downeast water" together with photos of seven other one-designs, all now long-forgotten.

At Nantucket, where thirteen- and sixteen-foot catboats had been raced since 1916, the Beetle was adopted in 1926. A Nantucket Yacht Club tradition of different-colored sails was continued. Around 1930, a staged photo by pioneering Nantucket photographer H. Marshall Gardiner showed the "Rainbow Fleet" sailing single-file past Brant Point Light. By 1938, the fleet numbered eighty boats.

The New Bedford Yacht Club adopted the Beetle in 1927. In August 1934, when twenty-six Beetles raced, the *Globe* reported they represented "the largest number to race in a single class in the [Club's] history." On Cape

Perhaps Concordia's first Beetle Cat ad appeared in *Yachting* in March 1946. The black cat logo, reminiscent of the one created by the Cape Catboat Association before World War I (see "The Cat Men of Quincy") didn't last. (Beetle Inc.)

Cod, the first Beetle appeared at the Bass River Yacht Club and at Barnstable in 1927, at Narragansett Bay in 1930.

As time passed, Clark's Point became a fully developed part of New Bedford. The Roosevelt Junior High School had been built on Frederick St. a couple blocks from the Beetle shop and Leo Telesmanick never forgot how, as a student, he daydreamed about boats. "John Beetle used to let us go down there to make models after school," Telesmanick remembered in a 1999 interview. "We'd go down there and watch them build boats and stuff like that."

In 1928, when John Beetle died at age seventy-three, his brother Charles took over the shop and Charles's son-in-law John Baumann became the master builder. John Beetle's daughter Ruth, a New Bedford elementary school teacher, served as treasurer and bookkeeper assisted at times by her sister Clara who later became a librarian at the Library of Congress. In 1930, with fifteen-year-old Telesmanick still regularly hanging out at the shop, Baumann offered him a job as an apprentice.

"I was damn lucky," Telesmanick remembered of that time during the Depression. Telesmanick's father, who had seven kids and worked in one of the big cotton mills that became New Bedford's primary industry after

The Duxbury Yacht Club was likely the first to adopt the Beetle Cat. Here, young crews set out. From left to right are *Cricket, Queen Bee, Tick,* and *Greenhead.* (Frank E. Lawson and Beetle Inc.)

whaling's decline, suggested his son accept. The pay was six dollars for a forty-eight-hour week.

"For three years all I did was clean the shop or straighten nails. . . . Then I took care of the steam boiler which was nothing but a pot-belly stove with a copper kettle on top."

The Beetle Cat of that period was built, as were the whaleboats, upright over a mold, starting with the placement of keel and skeg. "You planked before you framed," noted Telesmanick. Holes were drilled in the pre-positioned planks and galvanized clench nails were inserted so the boat, as Telesmanick said, "looked like a porcupine." After the boat was turned over, Telesmanick's job was to get underneath and hold a weight against the newly installed steam-bent ribs while the clench nails were set.

Gradually, the young apprentice's education expanded. "We'll teach you all about wood our way," Charles Beetle told him. But, for four years, he was sent to night classes in machine shop, math, blueprints, and other subjects. "They guided me," Telesmanick said, "to everything I did."

Charles Beetle died in March 1936 and, recognizing the need to plan ahead as his own health quickly declined that year, Baumann tutored twenty-one-year-old Leo Telesmanick. "John taught me" Telesmanick remembered, "where to get the best oak, when the pine you buy should have been cut. . . . I watched every move he made."

After Baumann's death, New Bedford boatbuilder Palmer Scott made Ruth Beetle an offer for the business. "I've got my man," Ruth replied. She kept the business and made Leo Telesmanick foreman.

"The real story of the Beetle Cat," opined the late Llewellyn "Louie" Howland III, Waldo's nephew, "is it's the little engine that could. There were several times when the story could have taken a wrong turn."

Each morning before she drove to school, Ruth Beetle went to the shop where goals for the day were discussed. During the late thirties, Telesmanick recalled building forty to forty-eight boats per year with two assistants. But it wasn't all work. Telesmanick was given the use of Ruth's Beetle Cat and went camp cruising with friends.

"We would leave the Acushnet River Friday afternoon and sail to the Elizabeth Islands," Telesmanick wrote in a *Catboat Association Bulletin* article. "We did all our cooking on shore. We put a piece of canvas over the boom for shelter. After sundown we . . . put a little church candle right on the centerboard trunk, and that candle would dry out the blankets and the dampness in the boat. . . . We always brought a gallon water jug."

Telesmanick and his friends never ventured beyond Edgartown and were careful about weather. In September 1938, however, having sailed to Cuttyhunk, they were confronted with the trip back in twenty- to twenty-five-knot winds, more in the puffs. But Telesmanick had told his wife Alma that he'd be home that day. Against the advice of islanders and the Coast Guard, he set off on the twelve-mile trip across rough Buzzards Bay.

"We made it in an hour-and-a-half. That was one of my last cruises. The 1938 hurricane was the next day."

A Wind to Shake the World was the title that New Bedford *Standard Times* writer Everett S. Allen gave his book about the 1938 hurricane. Everything the storm touched was destroyed or damaged. Photographs of the Beetle shop show it engulfed by water, the walls coming apart. In the aftermath remembered John H. Beetle's great-granddaughter Betsy Adams, "the business was moved to the Beetle house's backyard, and the shop was rebuilt as two buildings, a barn and a tumble down-workshop."

The building mold had survived and new Beetles were built until the December 1941 attack on Pearl Harbor. "That was it," Leo Telesmanick recalled. "We had to close the shop. Couldn't get material. I had everything put in a big safe—turnbuckles, stays, castings, all that stuff, for after the war."

Telesmanick spent the early years of World War II in the New Bedford shipyard established by Carl Beetle and, after Beetle's government contracts ran out, at Palmer Scott's yard. In August 1945, vandals set fire to the Beetle shop at Clark's Point. But although the building mold survived, there would be no need for Telesmanick to return. The Beetle Cat had no place in Carl Beetle's vision of the future.

"Carl was twenty years before his time," remembered Leo Telesmanick. At war's end, with financial backing from prominent New Bedford businessmen, Carl Beetle formed the Beetle Boat Co. and began producing a pioneering line of "rot-proof, leak-proof" fiberglass small boats including the twelve-and-a-half-foot B.B. Swan (Beetle Boat Swan) catboat.

When he returned from Navy service, Waldo Howland immediately began searching for a small wooden boat that his Concordia Company could produce. He vainly pursued several possibilities. In *A Life in Boats, The Concordia Years*, Howland recalled that he was preparing to move ahead with production of the Buzzards Bay 14, designed for Concordia by L. Francis Herreshoff, when he made a surprising discovery.

"[There was] a growing demand for new Beetle Cat Boats. This unanticipated development prompted me to visit Carl Beetle." At first, Beetle was not interested in either building new catboats for Concordia or in selling Howland the business. After more discussion, however, Beetle relented.

"In essence," Waldo Howland wrote, "Concordia acquired the original Beetle Cat Boat business for nothing, and Carl had his shop cleaned up for free." The deal included several half-finished hulls, parts and patterns, lumber, and the mold. Louie Howland remembered that "everyone laughed at Uncle Wally [and called him] an old fart. But he said 'you can go to the New York Boat Show [with your fiberglass boats]. I'll build Concordias and Beetles.'"

Carl Beetle's "plastic" boats were unveiled to much enthusiasm at the 1948 New York Boat Show. Compared to the Beetle Cat, the B. B. Swan had a shorter foredeck, longer cockpit, and was lighter (300 lbs. vs. 450 lbs.) with the weight distributed differently. It was a sturdy boat with an aluminum mast and Marconi sail but, as Waldo Howland noted, all the differences "upset the sailing qualities."

At the same time, rather to his own surprise, Howland learned that instead of the anticipated annual demand for eight or ten boats, he was receiving orders for many more. Such volume was far greater than Concordia could fulfill at its facility in Padanaram. In response, Howland turned to his long-time acquaintance Palmer Scott.

Like Carl Beetle, Scott, too, was pioneering fiberglass boats and the key employee he had hired as plant superintendent happened to be Leo Telesmanick. Now Telesmanick would oversee Beetle Cat production in addition to his other responsibilities. It was also decided to improve the boats' uniformity and eliminate the occasional complaint that a particular Beetle possessed an unfair advantage.

"Leo built one boat with special care," Howland wrote, "checking out every measurement against a number of older boats." New Bedford naval architect Ben Dobson took the lines of this special hull and drew up plans. Leo Telesmanick then built a precise new mold on which the hull would be constructed upside down with the pre-shaped planks screwed onto white oak ribs. But there was no change to the specifications, contributing both to fair competition and to maintaining older boats' value. The original upright mold was taken to the dump.

By the time Concordia had its drawings and mold in 1947, new regulations were under development by the New England Beetle Cat Boat Association (NEBCBA). The association traced its history to 1937 when the Barrington Yacht Club had initiated championship races for crews of two boys or girls under sixteen years of age. Postwar, the Beetle's real potential would be recognized with racing in seven classes: Juniors, Seniors, Men's, Girl's, Women's, Mitey Mites, Tired Fathers. Although it would take some time before sail dimensions were finalized, all other dimensions and equipment were specified. By 1964, the association had thirty-four member clubs and today remains the class's governing body.

The Concordia–Palmer Scott arrangement saw production of about thirty boats yearly and continued until Scott's retirement. In 1960, the operation was moved from Clark's Point to Smith Neck in South Dartmouth where a new shop was built on land owned by Waldo Howland's accomplished partner Martin Jackson. Leo Telesmanick moved close by and, as time passed, became as much a New England legend as the boat. A *New Yorker* writer who visited the Smith Neck shop in 1981 described Telesmanick as "a spare, reserved man of medium height, with forceful eyes, fine white hair [who] looks like the senior partner in an old Yankee law firm."

Telesmanick was still presiding over the Beetle Cat in 1969 when Concordia was sold to businessman William W. Pinney Jr. who'd been born the same year the Beetle was launched. In 1971, celebrating the boat's fiftieth anniversary, Pinney—an avid sailor and conservationist—noted that "over 3,000 Beetles" had been built. A decade later when Pinney sold Concordia to yachtsman and businessman Robert A. "Brodie" MacGregor, who was then working for the company, Beetle Cat production continued. But with Telesmanick's retirement impending in 1983, MacGregor knew a succession plan was needed.

Action at a Beetle race: Tim Fallon of North Falmouth, Massachusetts, is first to round the mark in West Falmouth harbor at the Annual Fall Hog Island series in September 2022. (Emily Ferguson, Land's Edge Photography)

"Mr. Brodie hired Charlie York and told me Charlie was coming into the business," Telesmanick remembered. "But Charlie knew what he was doing . . . I [just] wanted to show him some of the tricks."

York, a young boat builder who had grown up sailing Beetles, understood the challenge. "I told Brodie there's no way I can build those boats unless Leo shows me how." What Telesmanick showed him was that "the genius the Beetles had for doing this work . . . is really astonishing, even for an accomplished boat builder." Looking back on that time, York called it "the best six months of my life." The student and his teacher built twenty Beetles in 1983.

A decade later, the Beetle Cat faced a new day of reckoning. Brodie MacGregor recalled: "Charlie York was working full-time for Concordia, managing the Beetle Cat operation which included storage, maintenance, repair, and new boat construction. In addition, he spent many evenings and weekends marketing and selling Beetles. There came a time when the Beetle operation could no longer afford to pay Charlie what he earned. This led to the idea of Charlie buying the Beetle operation, so he would be able to directly control his own future and that of the Beetle Cat business."

After the sale, from October to March, the "retired" Telesmanick spent four hours each morning at the shop. He made centerboard boxes, stems, and other components, thus creating a parts supply while York built the boats.

As years passed, Leo and York became recognized, even by non-sailors, as representing an ethos that had largely disappeared from American life. Yet while an understandable romanticism attached itself to the Beetle shop with its neatly arranged old hand tools and sweet aroma of cedar, the business reality was sobering. When folklorist Steven Matchak visited Smith Neck, he found the hard-working York struggling "to keep the business viable . . . since the value of his seaside land has become more valuable for building lots: causing his rent to rise and his lease to become tenuous."

That was the situation when Leo Telesmanick passed away in January 2001. By then, Leo had been involved with building every Beetle Cat. He had won dozens of trophies, and had served as secretary of NEBCBA. The class's championship regatta is named in his honor. Engraved on the back of Leo and Alma Telesmanick's tombstone is a fine rendering of a Beetle Cat.

In the winter of 2002, a civil engineering consultant and Vietnam veteran with multiple tours in the Seabees named Bill Womack ordered a new Beetle to replace his forty-one-year-old boat. During visits to the shop, Womack recognized the challenges that York faced in terms of both building boats and managing the business. An offer to help get the shop organized led quite unexpectedly to a brief negotiation.

"Well," Womack said, "I bought the franchise." The agreement stipulated that York would remain for five years as the master builder, passing on to a new apprentice what Telesmanick had taught him.

To manage the business on a daily basis, in 2004, Womack hired Michelle Buoniconto, a civil engineering colleague who initially knew little about boats but a lot about management, number crunching, and planning. "The biggest challenge when Bill first bought the company," she remembered, "was the logistics of then having three locations, and having no designated office/accounting person to hand off to me."

Those initial challenges were met by moving the business to a Wareham industrial park where Womack and Buoniconto worked together setting up an accounting system and getting a handle on inventory and production costs. There was also the need, as Womack put it, "to find the next Charlie York." The new apprentice, who signed on in 2004, was Jonathan Richards, a small boat sailor who had been brought up in the construction trades.

"We lost money the first two or three years getting out of debt but then turned it around," Womack remembered. Orders for new boats numbered some twelve to fifteen per year but the service aspect soon revealed its potential. "The Beetle community was starving for some place to take care of the

At the Beetle shop in Wareham, Massachusetts, boatbuilders Manny Palomo (kneeling) and Seth Arenholz install the seventh of the eight planks necessary on each side of a Beetle Cat. (Beetle Inc.)

boats that had the expertise at a fair market price," Womack said. From initially caring for some twenty-five boats, Beetle now stores and maintains around 250. (See *WoodenBoat* No. 216 for the story on maintenance.)

Shortly after the move to Wareham, it became apparent that opportunities existed in the realm of custom wooden boat building. When Tim Fallon, a longtime Beetle owner and racer, mentioned he was looking for a shop to build a 28' catboat, Womack bid on the project. He then hired Bill Sauerbrey as the lead builder. Born into a family of Beetle Cat owners, Sauerbrey had, among other achievements, won the Mitey Mite championship at the Wild Harbor Yacht Club at age twelve. His genius for traditional building methods and materials resulted in the shop's extraordinary C. C. Hanley–designed *Kathleen* (see "Searching for C. C. Hanley").

"My goal became always to have a side project," Womack noted. *Kathleen* was followed by a Herreshoff Alerion, faithful to Capt. Nat's drawings, and an authentic whaleboat for Mystic Seaport's *Charles W Morgan*. Sauerbrey also designed three new production boats for the shop: the Beetle 14 and two attractive and practical skiffs.

As for the Beetle Cat, Womack tells customers it's "a forty-year boat." He has never compromised on the quality of Atlantic white cedar, western fir, or any other material even as costs increased as much as tenfold. Galvanized screws had been replaced in 1973 by silicon bronze, but only high-quality domestic fasteners are used although they cost about twelve cents each more

The proprietor: Bill Womack stands amid a few of the more than 200 Beetle Cats that the shop stores and services. (Stan Grayson)

than less sturdy imported fasteners. There are over a thousand screws in a Beetle Cat.

The mold built so long ago by Leo Telesmanick is still in use but planks are now full-length, a nice feature that eliminates the previous need for butt blocks. The proprietary hardware is still cast to Beetle's specs in a domestic foundry. "The boat is handmade in the USA," said Womack, "and people know they are getting quality. That is something people still recognize and appreciate."

Many Beetle owners also appreciate what the boat represents to their families for Beetles have often become a tradition linking generations. "My grandparents had one in West Falmouth," said writer Nathaniel Philbrick. "One of my first memories was being under the foredeck with mildewed kapok life jackets. My father raced one at the Barrington Yacht Club."

When Philbrick and his wife Melissa moved to Nantucket, they bought a Beetle that Melissa raced with their kids. Eventually, they bought a new Beetle from Charlie York. "Our kids are now 35 and 38," Philbrick said, "and the Beetles are part of family lore."

The Beetle is part of yachting lore, too. In 1953, when NEBCBA added its Women's Series to the schedule, the *Globe*'s Leonard M. Fowle reported: "For the yachtsman south and west of Cape Cod, [the Beetle] is THE class."

Over the decades, the Beetle survived the coming and going of many small one-designs including some intended to replace it. After failing to acquire Beetle, Palmer Scott turned to Phil Rhodes for the cat-rigged 13.5' Wood Pussy, a boat with a narrow rather than full bow and a tall Marconi mast. Those features, Waldo Howland wrote, made "the boat somewhat prone to capsize when her anchorage became rough [and] made conventional reefing underway difficult."

Carl Beetle's belief in fiberglass boats and the Beetle Swan was not rewarded with financial success. After Beetle's death in 1952, the Carl N. Beetle Plastics Corporation, producer of fiberglass components for industry, was acquired by others. Beetle was inducted into the Plastics Hall of Fame in 1977. The B. B. Swan is now rare, although a beautifully restored example resides at Mystic Seaport.

But a century after John and Carl Beetle built the first "Club Catboat" at Clark's Point, the Beetle Cat sails on, giving adults pleasure and lucky youngsters lessons for a lifetime in how to hand, reef, and steer. Trained in a Beetle, they acquire skills and an appreciation for craft and responsibility well beyond those accessible to young Optimist pram skippers. Then too, the inter-generational nature of a post–Beetle race get-together remains something very special to all involved.

After a century, the Beetle Cat is the only one-design of its era still in production as a wooden boat.

This story appeared in *WoodenBoat* No. 276, September/October 2020.

OSCAR AND *VANITY*

Remembering New England's
Last Catboat Fisherman

It's been forty-one years since I journeyed to Martha's Vineyard to meet with Oscar Pease, who was to be the focus of a chapter in a book called *Catboats*. Oscar was the last in that long line of fishermen still using a catboat for his work. By 1982, though, Oscar was no longer a full-time fisherman. He kept at it, more or less, out of habit. His old wooden boat was as much a part of him as his sturdy arms and legs.

Oscar was one of those rare individuals who represent a strong connective figure between the old days and the new. Even Oscar's language was sprinkled with wonderful words from another time. To this day, when seeking some odd bit in my collection of old bike parts or model-making scraps, I say—"Maybe I'll find the right gumpwitch in the cultch."

I well remember my surprise when, after a delicious dinner prepared by his wife Nellie, Oscar asked if I'd served in the military. I was then twelve years removed from Army service in Vietnam. When I shared that with Oscar, he insisted I accompany him that evening to the local American Legion post. That was the first and almost the only time that I found myself among men and women who really understood, without discussion, the lasting impact of war and loss.

The following morning, which I spent with Oscar aboard *Vanity* in Cape Pogue, remains indelible in my memory. Twenty-five years later, long after the passing of Oscar and Nellie, and having learned the troubling story of what befell *Vanity*, I shared an updated tale about Oscar in *WoodenBoat*. I suppose that if I had to choose a personal favorite story, it would be this one.

In the winter of 1982, I found myself at work on the outline of a book called *Catboats* and, early in the project, it became apparent that a visit to the island of Martha's Vineyard would be highly desirable. There, I knew, lived a man renowned for his knowledge of the old days. His name was Oscar Pease and he was the last working catboat fisherman in all New England. I had no way of knowing that my time with Oscar would lead to what many would regard as the book's most memorable chapter. Neither did I anticipate that I would remain in touch with Oscar as the years passed or one day follow with dismay the story of what became of his beloved boat. That story is ongoing. The latest chapter, but not the final one, was crafted in part by an ocean storm barely eighteen months ago.

Although I'd managed to meet Oscar on Cape Cod and go sailing with him during the summer of 1982, we had some trouble coordinating the all-important trip to Martha's Vineyard. That visit was planned to give me insights into the "working" part of Oscar's life, which had always been lived according to the season, wind, and tide. Finally, Oscar suggested the best thing would be to hope for decent weather and come in time for the early part of scalloping season. That plan worked and the chilly morning of November 17, 1982, found Oscar and me walking to his car at 5 a.m. The brittle rattle of a northwest wind shaking bare branches was the only sound to be heard in Edgartown, Massachusetts.

"You build that?" I asked as he hitched a small utility trailer to his car.

"Yes I did," was the answer. "The springs are off a Model T Ford and the wheels and axle are off a Model A. This trailer is 46 years old."

I was taken aback by this statement, because the trailer appeared to be brand new. Before the day ended, however, I discovered that everything Oscar owned, no matter what its age, was maintained in immaculate condition. There wasn't even any sand on the floor mats of his Dodge Omni. We drove through Edgartown's silent little streets, past the shingle and clapboard houses and soon came to a crunching halt in a driveway paved with crushed scallop shells.

"If you cart the stuff onto the dock," Oscar said. "I'll fetch in the boat." With that, he launched his eight-foot skiff by pushing it across the beach on a wooden roller. Later, I learned he had built the skiff in 1939 but fifty-three years later, it would almost have passed for new. After I had moved all the gear, I stood on the dock and watched Oscar pull up alongside his catboat and clamber aboard. In a moment, there was a puff of white exhaust smoke. He walked forward, paused to lower the centerboard just so, secured the skiff to the mooring, and headed in.

Once, this harbor had been full of boats more or less like the one now motoring straight toward me. In Edgartown alone, there had been dozens of such vessels, beamy centerboarders perfectly adapted to the area's shoal waters. For seventy-five years or more, starting about the late 1850s, these boats had provided a living for their fishermen owners.

The Edgartown boats were just one of several working fleets. Others existed at Newport, at towns bordering Buzzards Bay, at Nantucket and, of course, on Cape Cod. Now, all those men and all those boats had long since gone. Only this one man remained. Within him were values, skills, even a vocabulary passed direct from his grandfather, a whaling skipper by age twenty-one, to his father who had taught him beginning when he was just four years old in 1916.

It took only a few minutes to emerge from the inner harbor and, when we passed Edgartown Light, we met a stout, three-foot swell. Everything was unlovely. The cloudy sky, the water, the exposed part of Sturgeon Flats just off the Chappaquiddick shore—all were the color of lead. At some point, Oscar handed me the tiller and said we could steer pretty much straight for the very narrow entrance—"there's lots of current and an unmarked rock right in the middle of it"—to Cape Poge Bay.

We let our knees flex a bit as the boat shouldered her way through the seas. Occasionally, the wind carried spray back to us and it rattled against our yellow slickers like gravel inside a fender well. The boat felt solid, but Oscar said she was a bit wetter than expected thanks to something that happened during her construction. Still, there was no need, on that day, to shelter beneath the inside steering position that Oscar had invented for the companionway.

The boat was on her third Lathrop engine, this one a four-cylinder that could produce as much as forty-five horsepower. Oscar had fitted a 16" x 10" propeller with two wide blades shaped to shed seaweed. That prop generated both a lot of thrust and a lot of torque. Even with the centerboard mostly down, it took some pressure on the helm to keep a straight course.

Precisely at 7 a.m., the officially permissible starting time, Oscar lowered two dredges from each side of the galvanized framework he had designed. In the old days, Oscar had towed dredges attached to a one-and-a-half-inch diameter "curb line" that ran from the stub mast entirely around the boat's coamings. Now, the painted cap rails atop the cockpit coamings were protected from the dredges' lines by unfinished wooden strips. In the spring, Oscar would remove the strips, fill the nail holes, and repaint the coamings to look like new.

With the tiller between his legs, his foot tapping the throttle as necessary, Oscar guided us on our first drag. We were in the southwest side of the bay, somewhat in the lee of the Chappaquiddick shore, in about eight feet of water. Ten minutes later, Oscar took a turn of line around a winch driven

Here is *Vanity* in Edgartown Harbor. She's in her winter rig and ready to drag for scallops. (Stan Grayson)

off the Lathrop and the first dredge came home. Oscar lowered it onto the culling board that ran across the boat's wide cockpit and we began chucking stones, clumps of grass, and an occasional small eel back overboard. Hidden in the remaining grass were the scallops, their plump, fan-shaped shells a variegated beige color. We tossed them into the first of the wire baskets. There, the scallops began opening and closing their shells, making a small symphony of clicking noises.

Because I was a "novice"—which he pronounced "no vice"—Oscar instructed me in how to tell a live scallop from an empty or mud-filled shell. Mostly, I got it right. When I didn't, Oscar assured me that "it isn't just a 'no vice' that makes mistakes." He winched aboard the second dredge, and we repeated the routine, then came the third and fourth. It occurred to me that all this could become hard work. Before I could say anything, Oscar reported that, up until about 1977 when he turned 65, he had still hauled his dredges by hand. He was a big-boned man and remained impressively powerful. He turned the boat 180 degrees and we headed back for our second run.

Oscar's father Thomas bought his first catboat, a Crosby-built twenty-three-footer in 1900 when he was eighteen years old. As was then common,

Thomas Pease took out parties of island visitors during the summer and used the boat for commercial fishing the rest of the time. Rather than do needed repairs on the Crosby in 1905, Pease sold it and bought a newer seventeen-footer with a big fish well. He kept that boat until Oscar was sixteen and he reckoned that the two of them—father and son were, islanders said, seldom more that "a fathom apart"—would soon be fishing together. Thomas Pease ordered a new catboat in the fall of 1928.

The man who built the boat was named Manuel Swartz Roberts, although he didn't regularly use his last name—anglicized from its original Azorean Portuguese "Roberto"—until late in life. As for the name Swartz, it was pronounced "Swas" by Manuel's Portuguese friends. Manuel had two signs hanging over his shop door. One read "M. Swartz Boat Builder." The other read "Manuel Swartz Roberts, Boat Builder." This business of Manuel's names, and their derivation, merely added a tinge of mystery to one of the island's great characters.

The way Manuel aka Manny told the story, he had started working at age seventeen, constructing houses. Soon, however, he became convinced that he was always assigned the coldest corner in winter and the hottest one in summer. He talked his way into the West Tisbury boat shop of William King, asking the builder if he "would teach me to put two pieces of wood together so they will be watertight?" From King, Manuel learned to leave some "leeway" when rough fitting two pieces of wood but to "pinch into the wind" when exactness was required. Two years later, when King called it quits, he told Manuel to start his own shop. "I've been watching you," he said. "You'll do all right."

In 1905, Manuel Swartz moved into an old building that had housed a Dock Street sail loft on Edgartown's inner harbor. Other sail lofts had blown away in hurricanes but this one was reinforced by iron tie rods. Here, Manuel fine-tuned the design of his boats in a then rather unusual method, for he had learned from William King not how to carve half models but how to draw hull lines using a French curve on paper ruled with one-inch squares.

Manuel's shop soon became a magnet for the island's watermen and for summer visitors who delighted in the boat builder's ability to chat amiably and work at the same time. Joseph Chase Allen, the great columnist for the *Vineyard Gazette*, described the shop as "a place where the deep sea colloquial was commonplace. For someone was forereaching on someone else, someone else had been hove down with bilge trouble, and Manuel was laying a great circle course to follow with his band saw."

It was Allen who came up with a nickname for Manuel. He called the talkative boat builder "the Old Sculpin" after a species of large-headed, large-mouthed fish. (Today the shop survives as the Old Sculpin Gallery replete with a bronze historical plaque.) "There was only one thing," said Oscar, "that Manuel wouldn't talk about—his work secrets. Those you had to be sharp enough to learn by watching."

A Manuel Swartz–built catboat was generally thought to be more heavily constructed and therefore a bit slower than a boat built in Osterville by the prolific Crosbys. "Father said Manuel built too strong of a boat," Oscar remembered. "But they didn't have any flex to them." As for Manuel, he never forgot the time that Manley Crosby told him, "Manuel, you build better catboats than we."

How did a fisherman order a boat from the Old Sculpin? "Father said to him," Oscar reported, "'Well, Manuel, I've got a thousand dollars interest money and I think I'd like you to build me a 20-foot boat. I want a centerboard, a fish well, a six-horsepower Lathrop engine. Will you do it?'"

"Well," Manuel said, "I'll build you the boat as you state for a thousand dollars."

By 1928, Manuel had built some 140 boats and Thomas Pease had seen a twenty-footer with notably full bow sections that he especially liked. Manuel said he still had that boat's molds and that he could duplicate just what was wanted. It was not until the hull—cypress over oak with iron fasteners—was planked up that Thomas Pease realized something was wrong. The bow was too sharp. Standing in the wood shavings beneath the boat in his signature baggy pants, Manuel evaluated his work. "Now that I think of it," he admitted, "I believe I added to the forms originally to fill her out forward but the damn pieces must have got knocked off the molds."

"Oh," Oscar remembered, "Father was unhappy about it!"

The result was a boat that was wetter than it should have been but also faster, the fastest boat of her type in Edgartown. Manuel, the island's Lathrop dealer, installed a two-cycle, six-horsepower Lathrop with the old-fashioned make-and-break igniter instead of a spark plug. Such a low-tension ignition system would keep sparking even if the engine was soaking wet. Whatever the shape of the boat's bow sections, this was a handsome vessel, with a gracefully swept sheer, single, oval port lights, a 10'4"-long cockpit, and nicely balanced proportions. "Father said the bow sections weren't Manuel's only mistake," Oscar told me. "He had built some homely damn boats. This wasn't one of them."

Because of her handsome looks, Thomas Pease named his new boat *Vanity*.

On the night of my arrival, Nellie Pease served up a wonderful dinner of roast chicken, mashed potatoes with gravy, and a homemade strawberry and rhubarb pie. Afterward, Oscar asked me a surprising question. "Would you be a veteran?"

"Well," I answered. "I spent a year in Vietnam."

"Good," said Oscar, "tonight is the American Legion meeting. There are people who will want to meet you."

As we drove over to American Legion Post 186, Oscar told me about the most important thing in his life besides his parents, his wife, his catboat, and fishing. He'd been drafted in 1941, seven months after his father's death. Then, he hauled *Vanity* and covered her up under a tree in his mother's yard. There *Vanity* rested safely through the hurricane of 1944, an immense storm that destroyed a number of the island's remaining catboats. Oscar Pease was assigned to the Army's 82nd General Hospital unit and served as a ward master in France and in Iscyod Park, a stately country house in Shropshire near the Welsh border that served as a hospital for American forces. That is where he met Nellie, whom he married in September 1945.

There were just five legionnaires at that evening's meeting but they were accompanied by their wives as it was "ladies' night." The modest turnout didn't keep Oscar, who was the post adjutant, from running the meeting as if an entire company, or at least a platoon, had shown up. The old vets shook my hand. A decade after my return home, still with painful memories of friends who didn't, I was stunned to be warmly greeted by men who understood what a later generation of veterans, many unwilling draftees, had felt. Oscar, who was a perennial co-marshal of Edgartown's July 4th parade, seemed pleased.

At the time Thomas Pease ordered *Vanity*, the entire scalloping fleet of catboats in Massachusetts had long since been converted to power. "Maybe here and there a fisherman of the school of Noah still depends upon the variable winds," wrote Clarence Hall in *MotorBoat* in November 1924, "but for every one such there are scores and scores of gliding motorboats." Hall had visited New Bedford and Mattapoisett where he met these catboat fishermen. It was a good business and two scallopers, each bringing in the then limit of ten bushels per day could earn some $18 apiece, the equivalent today of about $206.

It was not until 1938 that Thomas Pease decided to rig *Vanity* for sailing and begin taking out summer visitors who wished to go fishing alongshore or bathing at Chappaquiddick. The spars were fashioned from a spruce log salvaged from Vineyard Sound where it had washed off the deck of a coasting schooner. When *Vanity*'s new mast was stepped for the first time, it was obvious that there was too much rake, a "piratical" rake according to Oscar. "Manuel measured from the deck down to the keel and made some marks,"

Oscar said. "He did a few quick figures and cut that mast step back and then the mast was plumb. Not a gumpwitch was needed."

"Gumpwitch?"

"That's what you call the little piece you might need to fill a space between a rib and a plank or some other little gap."

If the sight of *Vanity* was enough to evoke nostalgia, even in people who might not really know what they were looking at, sailing with Oscar was a lesson in attitude and technique that nobody who experienced it ever forgot. Prior to going scalloping with Oscar, when I joined him in Osterville's West Bay during the summer, the first thing I noticed was the boat's color scheme. It was not quite the white hull with buff decks and cabin top that one traditionally associates with catboats.

"She was sort of buff originally," Oscar said. "Then father was able to buy from Sears and Roebuck a paint called 'dove.' So the buff became gray, and that included the cockpit floor."

Vanity had more than a hint of folk art in her. All the trim was painted and there was only one varnished component on the boat. That was the wheel that replaced the painted tiller—the latter replete with a multifaceted carved knob on its end—when Oscar rigged the boat for sailing. Oscar was not above changing his boat's color scheme if it suited him. The cockpit sole was now painted dark green instead of gray. At some point, Oscar went back to what he called "Crosby colors." He mixed burnt umber with white to create a sort of "buff" that had just a hint of pink or gray in it depending on the light.

I noticed that *Vanity's* anchor rode ran through an unusual wooden snatch block belayed to the forestay. Oscar had invented and made the block himself, of course. It permitted him to haul and lower the anchor from the cockpit and avoid going forward to the boat's cramped foredeck. There, the boom was mounted just abaft the mast on a pedestal or "boom crab." On deck, forward of the cabin were fittings for the scalloping rig. Also, a big sweep oar was secured on deck on the starboard side of the cabin, the blade neatly fitted into its own custom mount beside the mast.

"Quick as a tick," Oscar pointed out when the Lathrop fired at the first touch of the starter. The engine was painted gloss gray and probably looked better than it had when it left the factory. Oscar had a little mirror that helped him see out-of-the way nooks and crannies so he could touch them up. Originally equipped with a six-volt ignition system, the Lathrop had been converted by Oscar to twelve volts. The conversion involved making a new mount for a new generator and even a new manifold to accommodate it.

"How is it," I asked, "that you seem to have all these bits and pieces, Model T springs, metal for generator brackets, all the right bits of wood?"

"Oh well," Oscar said, "I can usually find what I need right in the cultch in my shop."

"Cultch?"

"You know, all those odds and ends."

Vanity provided a stable platform as Oscar moved slowly along the boom, casting off the sail gaskets. He took up on the topping lift and I removed the boom crutch. Then, slowly but surely, Oscar hauled away on the throat and peak halyards. The gaff and sail rose neatly through perfectly positioned lazy jacks. Even these displayed a special touch. The eye of each line coming down from the mast contained what Oscar, who had carved them out of teak, called a "lizard" —a wooden grommet in which the lazy jacks themselves rode smoothly, eliminating line-through-line chafe.

When fishermen learned their gasoline engines were reliable, the once expansive rigs of the working catboats began to be dramatically reduced in size. *Vanity*'s sail may have been about 275 square feet. Needless to say, this was not the marginally built item that sometimes passes for a sail today. It had been beautifully cut and seamed in the old vertical manner, had three sets of reefing pennants and was without battens. Because the boom overhung the stern by several feet, the first two cringles at the clew were permanently rigged with reefing lines. These could be hauled tight and cleated from the safety of the cockpit.

There was no need for a reef that summer's day. There was just enough weather helm to be comfortable and *Vanity* forged ahead with vigor. Always, Oscar was two or three steps ahead of events and everything proceeded pleasantly no matter what the circumstances. Later, when I photographed Oscar as he sailed, he was perched atop the steering gear box. From a distance, the man appeared to be as much a part of his boat as the mast or a gumpwitch.

Three months after that sail with Oscar, as we filled our last basket with scallops, the sun finally emerged and the waters of Cape Poge Bay turned from pewter gray to emerald green. The other boats, I noted, observed where *Vanity* was dragging but they kept off. Oscar's ability to find what he called "good quality stock" was well known. Twice, his scallops had been sent to the JFK White House and at least one of those occasions had been noted in the *Vineyard Gazette*. "[A] select order of bay scallops destined for the Presidential table at the White House" is how *Gazette* reporter Mark Alan Lovewell described that catch.

Now, we headed back for Edgartown. Oscar assured me that Nellie, who had served up a breakfast of scrambled eggs, homemade bread, and moist cake on white china, would have an equally good lunch waiting. The seas had

Vanity's sail set perfectly and Oscar knew how to get every ounce of performance out of his boat. (Stan Grayson)

subsided as the sun came out, and *Vanity* made her way easily back toward Edgartown. Our speed was half that of the rough-looking outboard-powered skiffs passing us but Oscar, of course, had a different conception of time than a latter generation of fishermen. "They want to go down there in three minutes and go back in two and a half," he said. "It takes me 15 minutes or more to go down to Cape Poge and the same to come back. But I don't mind. I'm cleaning the boat all the time I'm coming back so I'm not losing any time. Here, take the tiller." With that, Oscar produced a mop from its proper place and began washing up. By the time the catch had been unloaded, my job, Oscar had the boat back on her mooring and finished tidying things up. When he rowed ashore in his skiff, *Vanity* glistened in the sunshine.

It always comes as a shock to hear of accidents that befall capable people who are masters of their craft. One day, many years after my last visit with Oscar,

I was stunned to hear that he'd been plucked from Edgartown harbor by a house builder who just happened to look up and notice someone floating facedown in the water. "He was taking the carburetor out to the boat," said Steve Gentle, who grew up thinking of Oscar and Nellie Pease as a second set of parents. "Something happened and he got knocked unconscious. They revived him. He was a very strong man."

A few years later, on July 28, 1995, Oscar Pease died at his home in Edgartown. Tributes poured in from those who'd known Oscar and Nellie, who had died previously. The "Steward of the Island," the "craftsman of all craftsmen," the "soul of friendship," the "unflappable individual" was gone.

With Oscar's passing, *Vanity* began her most dangerous voyage. Of course, Oscar had given thought to his boat's ongoing care. *Vanity* was, after all, irreplaceable. In 1986, a Mystic Seaport film crew went to Martha's Vineyard to record New England's last working catboat. That experience, together with some prompting from Catboat Association founder John Leavens, got Oscar thinking about Mystic as a potential home for *Vanity*. Curator Peter Vermilya remembers that "we were pretty interested at one time. We were waiting for Oscar to get set in his mind to let it go. But, we should have courted him more."

Ultimately, Oscar left the boat to what is now the Martha's Vineyard Historical Society. In the Fall 1995 *Catboat Association Bulletin*, Townsend Hornor, a man thoroughly qualified from a technical, historical, and executive standpoint to comment on the situation, reported: "They have established a fund in his memory to be used to preserve her at the museum in Edgartown. The boat has been out of water and covered with tarps for the last two years. There is considerable evidence of rot in various places from the entrapped moisture. This must be attended to immediately before the permanent exhibit can begin."

There were many people who recognized the importance of promptly conserving and then displaying *Vanity* exactly as Oscar had kept her. Steve Gentle envisioned *Vanity* as a centerpiece of island history and donated various items that Oscar had given him—eel spears, blocks, dredges, life preservers, skiff—to the Historical Society. "I pushed for an 'Oscar Pease' building so people could appreciate the way of life as it was on this island," he said.

According to one source, however, an abutter objected to a planned building to house the boat. As months and then years passed, the boat was not effectively conserved until an appropriate resolution could be achieved. By the fall of 1999, *Vanity* was in "desperate condition" according to the Society's Maritime Heritage Committee. Bids were then solicited for a complete rebuild, the work to be paid for with funds contributed by then anonymous donors.

Oscar at the wheel: he seemed as much a part of his boat as its mast or cleats. (Stan Grayson)

The winning bidder was Gannon and Benjamin in Vineyard Haven. "My proposal," Nat Benjamin told me, "was to keep the original and build a new boat. In a shed, that boat could have lasted forever." In the end, the boat builder complied with instructions that *Vanity* be made seaworthy and he turned out a predictably beautiful piece of work. What remained of the original were a few topside planks and the keel.

The Historical Society still faced the question of what to do with its new boat. There would be liability issues if the vessel was launched. Also, reported the Maritime Heritage Committee, "if the boat is kept in the water on a mooring, the public, for whom after all we have restored the boat to be seen and appreciated at close hand, will not have the opportunity to see her except as a speck in Edgartown Harbor."

A plan to house the rebuilt boat in a purpose-built shed on the society's premises failed to materialize. With that, the vessel was launched in the summer of 2000 and, if a speck in the harbor, was made available to small charter groups. In April 2007, heavy seas broke through the barrier beach at Norton Point on the island's south shore. Overnight, Chappaquiddick became an island. Katama Bay was now open to the sea and this increased the swift currents in Edgartown Harbor. For that reason, the rebuilt *Vanity*, which had not been equipped with its engine (or engine beds), wasn't sailed during the 2007 season. Only time will tell the existing boat's fate.*

This story appeared in *WoodenBoat* No. 203, July/August 2008.

---

* In April 2023, I spoke with Mark Alan Lovewell, long-time staffer at the *Martha's Vineyard Gazette*. He reported that *Vanity* has been well-cared for by the Martha's Vineyard Museum. Moored during the season in Edgartown, she is the Museum's "only floating exhibit." She is available to take charter parties sailing in the waters Oscar knew so well.

PART II

YACHTING

THE "YANKEE SLOOP"

Puritan and the 1885 *America*'s Cup

Writing about nineteenth- and early twentieth-century *America*'s Cup races presents a particular challenge, namely determining which of often conflicting primary source materials can be trusted. There have been times when I felt that writing a single accurate paragraph was a real problem. Yet the subject is fascinating for one is dealing with evolving theories of yacht design, rig developments, and construction methods. The yachts themselves became the subject of dramatic paintings both then and now.

What's more, the races were deemed nationally newsworthy. If the general populace had no particular interest in yachting, many did feel a pride of country. Well into the nineteenth century, Americans were well aware that their forbears had been battling the British to gain their independence barely a century earlier. Many became, for a little while at least, a bit boat crazy.

The crowded spectator boats that followed the dueling yachts were so numerous that they could, and occasionally did, get in the way of the competitors. The races themselves were recounted in a detailed way with tacks, jibs, and sail changes all noted in a play-by-play manner. Adding to the drama was the fact that the contestants included some of the world's wealthiest people. Inevitably, there was a clamoring for insight into the lives of "the rich and famous."

Puritan's tale is as fascinating as any story in Cup history, perhaps more so given that she was an "outsider" not from the New York Yacht Club, her designer's background, and the fact that her professional crew included, for the first time in Cup history, wealthy amateurs, "Corinthians," from the Eastern Yacht Club in Marblehead.

On a cold, gray day in December 1884, the New York Yacht Club received a letter from thirty-five-year-old Irish-born naval architect John Beavor-Webb who announced that two yachts of his design intended to challenge for the *America's* Cup. The first challenger would be the cutter *Genesta* owned by Sir Richard Sutton, a baronet, sportsman, and member of the Royal Yacht Squadron (RYS). Should *Genesta* fail, Lt. William Henn and his wife Susan, owners of *Galatea*, would then try.

Beavor-Webb's letter prompted a nine-month period that would pit *Genesta* against an American yacht which, in December 1884, didn't even exist. That vessel, *Puritan*, would in due course be recognized as the fastest American yacht yet built. What's more, at a time when the first iron yachts had appeared along with "composite" vessels of steel framework with wood planking, *Puritan* would be the last *America's* Cup defender built entirely of wood until *Columbia* in 1958.

The Background

In 1857, six years after the schooner *America* won what was known in English yachting as the RYS £100 Pound Cup (among other things), the trophy—renamed the *America's* Cup—was donated by its owners to the New York Yacht Club of which they were members. Thirteen years later, on August 8, 1870, the first effort to recapture the Cup was made. Yachting writer J. D. Jerrold Kelley presented the situation: "[T]he fair fame of the country was at stake, and all classes of our citizens were assembled to greet the foreign yacht which had pluckily sailed 3000 miles of stormy sea to redeem a national defeat."

That foreign yacht was the British schooner *Cambria* owned by James Lloyd Ashbury, commodore of the Royal Harwich Yacht Club. Ashbury knew the odds were against him. His competitors were fourteen American schooners. (In 1851, *America* had defeated fifteen English yachts to win the cup.) Fouled during the race, *Cambria* ultimately finished eighth. Yet Ashbury wanted to try again. After heated letters with the NYYC about event format, he entered his new schooner *Livonia* in a best-of-seven match race series. What ensued were arguments about rules and more defeat. Racing against the schooner *Columbia* and, after she suffered damage, *Sappho*, *Livonia* never won a race.

The injustice of having to sail against two different defenders did not go unremarked. Author Kelley noted: "[T]hanks are due for progress towards more intelligent consideration of the claims of challenging yachtsmen." In 1876, when the Royal Canadian Yacht Club challenged, the format was a best-of-three series against one NYYC defender. But the Canadians' schooner *Countess of Dufferin* had no more success than *Livonia*. Neither, in 1881, did *Atlanta*, built at Belleville, Ontario, and towed through the Erie Canal by mules. She was trounced by the NYYC's iron-built sloop *Mischief.* Thus ended the "first epoch" of the *America*'s Cup. In December 1881, the races were reimagined in a new Deed of Gift crafted by George L. Schuyler, the last survivor of those owners who had won the Cup in 1851. Among other things, the new deed stipulated that challengers must come from a club with premises adjacent to salt water and sail to New York.

NYYC's Response to the Challenge

Genesta's record in England had been mixed but she was considered the best all-around boat in the United Kingdom and dominant in heavy weather. So Sutton's challenge was recognized as formidable. To ensure the most capable American yacht would face *Genesta*, the NYYC planned its own new contender but also invited other clubs to build a potential defender.

Up in Boston, the Eastern Yacht Club (EYC) accepted the invitation. Eleven members formed a syndicate managed by General Charles Jackson

Entomologist-turned-yacht-designer Edward Burgess (1848–1891) drew *Puritan*'s lines during the winter of 1885. (Author's collection)

Paine, great-grandson of a signer of the Declaration of Independence, Civil War hero, and stock market investor. Paine promptly asked EYC member Edward Burgess to design the new yacht.

Then thirty-seven, a Harvard-trained entomologist and amateur yacht designer, Edward Burgess had enjoyed a life of affluence until the failure of the family sugar business in 1883. That forced Burgess to leave his modestly paid teaching post at Harvard. Although he would still refer to himself with some humor as a "bugologist," Burgess opened a yacht brokerage and design office in Boston. Self-taught, Burgess had designed a number of successful boats, ranging from catboats to big cutters. Now, Burgess began making sketches for what would become *Puritan*.

Design and Construction

By the mid-1880s, the extremes of yacht design were represented by the shallow, beamy, centerboard "skimming dish" favored, to one degree or another, in the United States and the excessively narrow, deep-keel cutters prevalent in England. These "lead mines" were a result of the English Yacht Racing Association's rule of measurement that taxed the beam severely.

A man of instinctively moderate tendencies, Edward Burgess set out to design a compromise between the extremes. Burgess drew *Puritan*'s lines on linen-backed paper that he himself prepared after which his wife Caroline applied a layer of paste that was lightly sandpapered to produce a surface of beautiful smoothness. "All his lines," wrote yachting historian W. P. Stephens, "were faired to a degree which was not possible to reproduce on the [shop] floor." According to Burgess's brother Walter, the design work was completed within a month's time, probably by early March 1885.

Journalist Winfield Thompson described the result this way: "*Puritan* was a radical departure from the old-time American sloop, and a type in herself, combining the beam, power and center-board of the American sloop with some of the depth and outside lead of an English cutter. . . . In this respect she was the first of her kind."

Puritan was built by George Lawley and Sons of timber of such quality that today's boat builders can only fantasize about. A perfect specimen of white oak 53' x 26" square served as the basis for the keel, which was laid on March 16. By April 12, two-thirds of the frames were in place. Planking stock was of "immense lengths and of fine quality." (See table for *Puritan*'s materials.) Planking was complete by about May 3, after which the decking was laid. While black was the typical color for a big, formal yacht, smaller boats had been painted white for some time. So was *Puritan*, setting a trend.

Puritan: Her Bill of Materials

Component	Material and dimensions
Keel	Oak 53' x 22" x 26"
Frames	White oak spaced 22" on centers
Planking below waterline	Oak (2 ¾" thick)
Planking above waterline	Hard Pine (2 ¾" thick)
Fasteners below waterline	Copper and treenailed
Fasteners above waterline	Galvanized
Deck	White pine laid straight
Deck Beams	Yellow pine 8" x 10" at mast, 6 ½" x 5 ½" elsewhere
Hanging Knees	Hackmatack, 12 pairs
Stanchions	Locust, 16" forward and 14" aft
Rail	Oak
Centerboard	Hard pine with oak upper and lower planks, lower plank faced with knife-edge iron shoe weighing 900 lbs.
Rudder Head	Locust, 10" diameter
Rudder	Oak tapered to 2 ½"
Companionways and skylights	Mahogany
Mast Step	Cast iron, 1,000 lbs. bolted to keel
Main Cabin	Finished in mahogany and pine, 16' x 12'
External Keel	Lead, 45' long x 2' wide x 16" deep, 27 tons
Keel Bolts	1 ¼" Muntz metal*
Standing Rigging	Crucible-steel wire
Sail Material	Plymouth Duck (cotton)

*Alloy of 60% copper and 40% zinc with a trace of iron patented by George Fredrick Muntz, Birmingham, England, 1832. Also referred to as "yellow metal." First used as below-water sheathing as it possessed anti-fouling properties at 2/3rds the price of copper sheathing.

Note: Table based on *The Lawson History of the* America's Cup, the *Boston Globe*, April 12, 1885, and other sources.

From laying the keel in mid-March to launch on May 26, 1885, Lawley's had made a beautiful job of *Puritan*. Said the *Boston Globe*, she "has sprung up like a mushroom in the night . . . a large and beautiful sloop."

Break-In

Puritan's spars were built by H. Pigeon and Sons in East Boston. The standing rigging was crucible steel wire, which offered greater strength than manilla rope and minimal stretch. Sails were made in Boston by J. McManus and Son of "Plymouth duck" tightly woven in Plymouth, Massachusetts, by the Russell Mills. Paine considered the Plymouth canvas to be "the best ever put in a yacht in the United States." June 16 saw the bending on of the 5,000 sq. ft. mainsail.

On June 17, it was decided to take *Puritan* on a brief trial spin in very light air. When the wind increased, however, the yacht was promptly headed back for the mooring rather than risk overly stretching the new sails. On this three-hour sail, *Puritan* proved stiff and well-balanced. After further work, she was judged ready for a maiden voyage to Marblehead where the EYC had built its new clubhouse a few years earlier.

The skipper selected by *Puritan*'s owners was Capt. Aubrey Crocker, a highly regarded professional from Cohasset well-known for his many successes with the remarkable Herreshoff sloop *Shadow* (see *WoodenBoat* No. 43–44). Under Crocker's skillful command, on Saturday, June 20, *Puritan* departed Boston. Breaking in a wooden yacht with cotton sails and hemp running rigging required experience and favorable weather. *Puritan* headed for Marblehead under her main and jib in a light westerly breeze that freshened to ten knots. When the big balloon jib was set, *Puritan* accelerated to nine knots. A towboat skipper who watched her prophesized astutely: "When that boat gets a breeze, she'll puzzle the best of them."

But much remained to be done. The *Globe* reported: "She is not now in fair trim. Her halyards need stretching: the head of the mainsail does not fit as well as it should: the sail has got to be stretched out on all sides before it will be what is required. The jibs fit well but also like the mainsail, they need stretching and hauling out. The ropes being all new, do not work through the blocks as they should, but this will be remedied by constant use."

Down in New York, the EYC's new boat had critics. While most referred to her as the "Yankee sloop," some called her the "bean boat," deriding her Boston heritage. Cornelius McKay, son of clipper ship builder Donald McKay, labelled *Puritan* a "brick boat." A common term in New York then, a brick boat was a slow yacht best suited to freighting bricks on the Hudson River. By contrast, NYYC member A. Cary Smith, who had designed the

A well-tuned *Puritan* sails off Marblehead, Massachusetts, on June 30, 1885, a month after her launching. She carries her No. 1 jib, forestaysail, mainsail, and enormous club topsail that required great skill to handle safely. At the mainsail's peak flies the private signal of designer Edward Burgess. (MIT Museum)

New Yorkers' new candidate as he had *Mischief,* never disparaged *Puritan.* *Priscilla* represented the latest technology. She was built of flush-plated iron over steel frames.

Trial Races and Selection

On June 30, 1885, *Puritan* entered her first race, the thirty-mile EYC annual regatta. Arrayed against her were some of the finest sloops and schooners extant. Among the schooners was EYC Commodore Henry Hovey's renowned *Fortuna* designed by A. Cary Smith and the old *America*, now owned by Civil War general-turned-politician Benjamin Butler. The *Boston Daily Advertiser* reported the result: "Standing up like a church, the *Puritan* out pointed and out sailed everything, and although at times she was closely pressed by the others, she easily won, leaving time allowance out of the question."

Ten days later, *Puritan* sailed to Gloucester to compete unofficially in a race held to determine which of four big schooners was the fastest. *Puritan,* "looking very neat with her white hull and spotless white sails," as the *Globe* noted, rather easily outpaced all the schooners. "Well," said one observer, "that there *Puritan* is sailing faster than any craft we've seen around here."

Puritan's next race was at Newport where she competed on August 3 for the Goelet Cup established—one cup for sloops and one for schooners—by New York real estate mogul Ogden Goelet. The race would, for the first time, bring *Puritan* into direct competition with *Priscilla*. The New York boat was named for Priscilla Mullins, said to be the first "maiden bride" in New England when she married John Alden, the youngest Puritan colonist. Painted the traditional black, *Priscilla* was assumed in New York as the boat most likely to defend the Cup.

The forty-five-mile course took the yachts from a start off Beavertail Light in Jamestown past the Sow and Pigs, Hen and Chickens, and Brenton Reef lightships and back. Although the wind that day didn't blow more than about fifteen knots, the seas were unaccountably running as high as if a gale was blowing.

Puritan's start was hampered when her gaff topsail got entangled with her peak halyard. But once things had been squared away, *Puritan* put in a memorable performance. The race had started at 10:25 a.m. An hour later, *Puritan* was a mile ahead of *Priscilla*. She appeared to tack as if on a pivot while *Priscilla* required two minutes to come about.

In the rough conditions, *Puritan* surged easily to eleven knots. "Greased lighting," was the term applied. She demonstrated much superior pointing ability and ultimately defeated *Priscilla* by some eleven minutes on both real and corrected time. In fact, *Puritan* came home well ahead of the larger schooners. She won the Goelet Cup, which, renamed the Puritan Cup, remains to this day one of the EYC's most coveted trophies.

Priscilla's resounding defeat was diminished as a fluke by the NYYC, which then prepared to hold trial races to select the Cup defender. These were contested by four boats: *Priscilla*, *Puritan*, and two older yachts, *Gracie*, an 80' centerboard sloop built in 1868 and *Bedouin*, an 84' on deck, three-year-old English-style cutter. The first of the races was held on August 21 and won handily by *Puritan*. *Priscilla* won the second race, thanks to a fortunate wind shift. On August 25, 1885, in a splashy front-page story, the *Boston Globe* reported the result of the final race. "Never in the history of yacht racing was there a more magnificent race held than the third trial [to choose an *America*'s Cup defender] between the New York and Boston champions."

The race had been close, with *Puritan* winning by less than two minutes on elapsed time and about the same on corrected time. But *Puritan*'s consistent superiority upwind had been obvious. What's more, her decisive win in the heavy-weather Goelet Cup race figured heavily in her favor. One old salt labelled *Priscilla*, which sailed best in light air, as a "water cask with a stick in it." Frustrated by the whole experience, A. Cary Smith was, by the end, referring to *Priscilla* as "that damned steel scow."

Organizational Matters

Throughout the trials, *Puritan* had flown the private signal of designer Edward Burgess, technically signifying him as the vessel's owner. This created a problem because *Puritan* couldn't compete in races conducted under the NYYC's rules unless enrolled by a club member. The matter was resolved by entering *Puritan* under the name of General Paine who was both an EYC and NYYC member.

The NYYC regatta committee now either suggested or imposed some changes in *Puritan*'s personnel. It was felt that having aboard a captain and pilot with experience in local waters was required. Capt. Crocker would handle the wheel but under Capt. Joe Ellsworth's direction. Capt. Terry, skipper of the renowned New York centerboard schooner *Grayling* was named pilot.

Although there would later be some second-guessing about these moves, it may have been advantageous to have a brain trust that included men familiar with the shoals and currents around New York Harbor, Sandy Hook, and the waters outside. Also noteworthy was the fact, noted in the *Boston Daily Advertiser* on Sept. 19, that "Seven amateurs trod the decks of *Puritan*." Among them were the EYC syndicate's Paine, Burgess, Hovey, J. Malcolm Forbes, *Shadow*'s owner Dr. John Bryant, and two more. For the first time in a Cup event, Corinthian sailors—unpaid amateurs—would be involved in working the yacht.

Genesta

Built on the Clyde in 1884 at the D. and W. Henderson yard, *Genesta* was of the composite construction—steel frame with elm and teak planking—that John Beavor-Webb had developed. She became the first composite yacht to compete for the Cup. Prior to her Atlantic crossing, *Genesta* got a thorough going over and a newly coppered bottom. To improve the yacht's light-air performance, Beavor-Webb designed a new mast with three feet more hoist than the original, which he later stated was too much. The taller mast required the addition of ten tons additional ballast to the keel. She had the loose-footed mainsail typical of English cutters and believed to provide better airflow and more power than a sail attached to the boom.

Puritan and *Genesta*: Their Specifications

	Puritan	Genesta
Owner	Eastern Yacht Club Syndicate	Sir Richard Sutton
Designer	Edward Burgess	John Beavor-Webb
Builder	George Lawley & Sons (South Boston)	D & W. Henderson and Co. (Glasgow, Scotland)
Type	Centerboard Sloop	Keel Cutter
Dimensions	94' LOD x 81 ½' WL x 22'7" B x 8 ½' draft (board up)	96'9" LOD x 81' 7 ½" WL x 15' B x 13'6" draft
Ballast	47-ton keel, 27 tons internal	70-ton keel, 2 tons internal
Centerboard	22' L x 11' deep x 4" thick (900 lb. iron shoe)	NA
Bowsprit (outboard)	36'6"	39'7"
Mast (deck to hounds)	60'	52'
Topmast	44'	44'6"
Boom/Gaff	76'/47'	70'/44'
Spinnaker Boom	62'	64'
Sail Area (NYYC Rule)	7,982 sq. ft.	7,387 sq. ft.
Sailmaker	J. H. McManus & Son	Ratsey & Lapthorne

Note: dimensions based on *The Lawson History of the America's Cup* by Winfield M. Thompson and Thomas W. Lawson, Boston, 1902.

Genesta's racing spars and canvas were shipped to New York aboard a steamship while she made the crossing under jury rig and storm canvas. She departed Greenock, Scotland, on June 16, encountered a gale on July 8—"riding over the waves like a swan," according to a crewman—and arrived in New York on July 16. Once *Genesta* had her racing rig installed, she participated in the NYYC cruise. But skipper John Carter did all he could to mask the yacht's performance. She towed a tender to slow her down, pinched too close to windward to offer observers a true sense of her ability, and never set all her sails at once.

Such tactics made Sir Richard Sutton an easy target for the press, which interpreted them as reflecting the snooty superiority many associated with the English upper class, not to mention being unsportsmanlike. That image would soon change in a remarkable way but a certain precedence of secrecy regarding competing yachts' designs would endure in future Cup events.

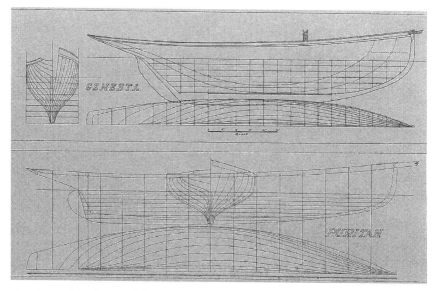

The lines of *Puritan* and *Genesta* show substantial differences in hull form. The body plans (cross sections), especially, contrast the English cutter's narrow beam and "wall side" with *Puritan*'s beamier hull. (*The Lawson History of the* America's *Cup*)

Puritan vs. Genesta

Prior to the first Cup race on September 7, *Puritan* was taken to Brooklyn where, at the C and R. Poillon shipyard, her gaff jaws were reinforced and many of her iron fittings were replaced with heavier ones. She got a new jib topsail taken from *Priscilla* and a new club topsail that "fit to perfection." Finally, *Puritan*'s hull was sandpapered smooth, cleaned with chamois cloths, and coated with pot lead (powdered graphite) up to within two inches of her gold cove stripe. The centerboard received the same treatment, believed to create the slickest surface possible. Once resplendent in white, *Puritan* was now, as noted in the *Globe*, "a dull leaden color."

The first race was sailed in baffling breezes that came and went and shifted about. An enormous fleet of steamers, yachts, and tugs followed *Genesta* and *Puritan* as each yacht dealt with the fluky breeze. When the race was finally called off because there was no hope of finishing within the allotted time, *Puritan* was two miles ahead of her rival.

The following day, September 8, brought blue sky, fleecy white clouds and a south-southeast breeze that increased to about 10 mph. The yachts had their club topsails set and were moving fast as they approached the starting

The foul: this drawing by illustrator W. G. Wood captures the moment that *Puritan*'s bowsprit pierced the mainsail of *Genesta* resulting in a foul that forced cancellation of that day's race. (*The Lawson History of the* America's Cup)

line with *Genesta* on starboard tack and having right-of-way. Aboard *Puritan*, it was thought they could pass safely in front of *Genesta*, luff up and blanket her, thus gaining a starting advantage. But they were wrong. At *Genesta*'s helm, 137 feet aft of the bowsprit's tip, Capt. Carter held his course. *Puritan* almost made it past, but not quite. *Genesta*'s bowsprit speared a hole through the leach of *Puritan*'s mainsail, snagged the 4" diameter leech rope and broke.

This foul meant that *Genesta* could claim victory. Sir Richard Sutton, however, declined to do so. Reflecting a level of sportsmanship applauded by all, he not only refused to claim the race but also declined General Paine's offer to pay for the damages. Now, instead of being criticized as a snobby nobleman, Sutton was praised for his magnanimity. *Genesta* was taken to the Poillon yard where Beavor-Webb supervised the creation of a new bowsprit. Built of seasoned yellow pine, it was 54' long overall and tapered from thirteen inches inboard to six inches at its tip. The broken bowsprit was spotted by visitors who cut off bits of it as souvenirs.

Although *Puritan* outsailed *Genesta* in the races on September 11 and September 12, loss of wind prevented either from being completed. Finally, on the fifth attempt, on September 14, a day of light wind, no wind, and finally a fresh southerly of fourteen knots, *Puritan* defeated *Genesta* by some sixteen minutes. It was noted that *Genesta* was driving her new bowsprit into the green seas while *Puritan* pitched a bit but seemed steadier.

After the race, Sir Richard Sutton had *Genesta* towed up alongside *Puritan* where he and his crew gave their rival "three rousing British cheers." The gesture was returned by *Puritan*'s crew, each of whom now sported a red rose in a buttonhole, the flowers tossed aboard by women spectators. During the race, *Genesta* had suffered damage to the iron upper cap on her mast. Again, good sportsmanship prevailed and the NYYC race committee called off the next day's race so their challenger could make repairs.

September 16 brought just the sort of windy "cutter weather" *Genesta* was hoping for. At the start, it was sunny with a west-northwest wind of fourteen knots. The starting gun went off at 11:05 a.m. and *Genesta* was first over the line and, on a downwind run to the first mark, pulled out a 1:21 lead. By 12:20, dark clouds had gathered and the wind was blowing twenty knots. A *Puritan* sailor was sent up the weather shrouds to lower the topmast. An hour later, the wind was gale force and *Puritan* was outdoing the English yacht, which began making her own sail adjustments.

The weather next deteriorated further into a thunder squall with heavy rain leaving in its wake a thirty-six-knot wind. Capt. Carter had elected to keep *Genesta*'s topsail up and, as a result, frequently had to luff to keep from carrying away the yacht's topmast. By 2:30, off Point Pleasant, New Jersey, *Puritan* was a quarter-mile in the lead and well to windward of *Genesta*. Ultimately, it was a closer race than it needed to be according to some of the EYC crew who felt Capt. Ellsworth had sailed in an overly cautious manner.

Still, Ellsworth's knowledge of local waters had also proved valuable. In the first race, with *Genesta* closing on *Puritan* on the final leg, Capt. Ellsworth told a reporter how they maintained their lead. "We saved our distance by hauling up the centerboard and steaming along Flynn's Knoll in water where [*Genesta*] could not go."

In the final race, *Puritan* finished 2:38 ahead of her rival. The Cup was safe and, overnight, Edward Burgess became the country's most celebrated designer.

Afterward

In answer to a reporter's question following the races, EYC crewman Charlie Welch responded: "I am of the opinion that the *Genesta* can beat any other boat in America." Before departing for England in October, *Genesta* convincingly won three important races and, in 1887, the first Round Britain race. *Genesta*'s owner, Sir Richard Sutton, died of peritonitis four years later in 1891 at age thirty-eight.

After celebrations in New York, *Puritan* was promptly put up for auction so that her syndicate could recover something of its investment. General Paine made the winning bid of $13,500 (about $335,000 today.) Upon *Puritan*'s arrival in Marblehead she was visited by crowds of enthusiastic people who kept Capt. Crocker busy answering questions. After the victory, *Puritan*-branded products, ranging from cigars to tissue paper, appeared.

In 1886, Paine sold *Puritan* to fellow EYC member J. Malcolm Forbes who successfully raced her and sailed her as a trial horse against Paine's new Burgess-designed, composite-built (twelve iron floor timbers) *Mayflower*. *Mayflower* was a somewhat larger, fuller boat than *Puritan*. She was 100' on deck with an 85' waterline length and slightly beamier—23.6' vs. 22.7'. Burgess believed correctly that she would have "a little more initial stability and ought to carry sail better." *Mayflower* easily defeated the steel-built challenger *Galatea*.

John Beavor-Webb, who sailed aboard *Galatea*, remained in New York. He would design more yachts including J. P. Morgan's *Corsair II* and *III* before dying, a wealthy man, in 1927.

In 1887, the Burgess-designed, steel-built *Volunteer* defeated challenger *Thistle*. Four years later, in July 1891, Edward Burgess died of typhoid fever at age forty-three. He was widely mourned. His multitalented son Starling would become a well-known designer as well.

In 1896, Forbes sold *Puritan* to a yachtsman who installed a schooner rig more practical for cruising. In 1902, the EYC's Charles H. W. Foster, avid sailor and yachting photo collector, bought *Puritan* and had a new deck put on. But *Puritan*'s luck ran out in 1905 when she was sold at auction to owners who valued her mainly for what her external lead keel and fittings would bring. Hauled at Lawley's until December 1907, the bedraggled *Puritan* was sailed to Providence, Rhode Island, where she was eventually sold for under $3,000 and then used to seasonally transport Cape Verdean fishermen to New Bedford.

Pronounced unseaworthy in 1911, *Puritan* became floating quarters for Providence River dredging crews. But in 1926, the *Scientific American* reported that *Puritan* "was doing good service as a motor fishing boat, taking parties out for deep-sea fishing off the Atlantic coast." In 1932, the *Globe* published an unverified report that *Puritan* had returned to the Cape Verdean trade and was lost at sea with all hands.

This story appeared in *WoodenBoat* No. 283, November/December 2021.

SEARCHING FOR
CHARLES D. MOWER

"He Designed Some of the Best"

An important part of my career has been devoted to chronicling automotive history and, at a later time, working in the industry as a marketing and product-training consultant. From time to time over the years, I had access to a place normally off-limits to outsiders, the design studio of the Ford Motor Company. For a car guy, such visits were incredibly exciting and informative. In the studio, one could discuss with designers their concepts for new vehicles, always several years ahead of their introduction, and view the colorful sketches for vehicles that represented the future.

The designers embodied a unique blend of intellect and creativity. The same, I soon learned, is true of the yacht designer. Some of my most memorable interviews have been with yacht designers and I've never tired of posing questions and listening to their responses. At the same time, it was inevitable that I developed an abiding curiosity regarding designers of the past, men who based their work on carved half models or, by the later years of the nineteenth century, upon drawings.

Among the most prolific of those designers was Charles D. Mower who was born only a few miles from where I write this in Marblehead. His story proved challenging to piece together but the process was highly rewarding and I knew that Mower's name would be familiar to many *WoodenBoat* readers who shared my curiosity about him. Bit by bit, Mower's story emerged from the past. After this article was published, I learned that, indeed, many folks had long been interested in Mower and some readers responded to the story with thanks that they finally had the opportunity to learn about the man himself.

A long time ago now, at a cluttered used-book shop on the New Jersey Shore, I acquired the 1945 edition of *Sailing Craft, mostly descriptive of smaller pleasure sail boats of the day*. First published in 1928, *Sailing Craft* had been conceived and edited by a wealthy Philadelphian named Edwin J. Schoettle. Although he'd gained considerable success as a manufacturer of cardboard boxes, Schoettle's real passion was sailing. It was this boat obsession, centered on but not limited to Barnegat Bay, and his impressive social connections, that gave Schoettle access to the best-known yachtsmen and designers of his time.

Thus it was that Schoettle persuaded a cast of characters as diverse as Sir Thomas Lipton, Cornelius Vanderbilt Jr., and designers Edson B. Schock, Maurice Griffiths, and Francis Sweisguth—who designed Schoettle's great catboat *Silent Maid* (see *WoodenBoat* No. 214)—to contribute, gratis, the sixty-five articles that make up *Sailing Craft*. As I began reading Schoettle's book, I encountered one yacht design after another credited as "Designed by Charles D. Mower."

I'd heard of Mower, of course, and readers of *WoodenBoat* magazine will almost certainly have encountered his name, too. Although I didn't know much about him, I did learn that Mower was someone Schoettle counted as both a friend and sailing companion. Mower, who was always more interested in designing, building, and sailing than money, contributed many drawings to his friend's book. Among them were an R-Class sloop, the Long Island Sound Interclub, the first of Barnegat Bay's A-Cats, a schooner, one-design sneakboxes, and a 6-Meter. Whoever Charles D. Mower was, I thought, he was demonstrably versatile.

The Mower boats in *Sailing Craft* represented only a small portion of his work. One day, I attempted to total up Mower's designs. I counted 124 published in *The Rudder*, 50 more created during his partnership in Philadelphia with Thomas D. Bowes, Jr., and 29 in *Motor Boating*. But over time, I stumbled upon other Mower designs as well. To name but one, there was the Winthrop Hustler, a buoyant-looking, 18' marconi-rigged catboat adopted by the Winthrop (Massachusetts) Yacht Club in 1925, and whose popularity continued well into post–World War II years. The *New York Herald Tribune*'s Pulitzer Prize–winning yachting journalist William H. Taylor noted that Mower's designs "were too many and too generally successful to attempt a list of even the best. He designed some of the best in all types."

When I checked the dates of all these creations, it became clear that for some three decades, from 1899 until the 1930s, Charles D. Mower was responsible for a prodigious output. Then, suddenly, and years before Mower's death in 1942, it all came to an abrupt end. What, I wondered, had happened? And who was this C. D. Mower, anyway?

Early Days

Broad Street in Lynn, Massachusetts, was, particularly in the nineteenth century, among that city's most gracious avenues. Shaded by tall trees, it was bordered by wide sidewalks and big homes owned by many of the city's more prosperous citizens. One of them was Charles F. Mower, a pioneering shoe manufacturer. It was in Mower's house at 73 Broad St. that his son Charles was born on October 5, 1875.

There's no record of when Charles Drown Mower became interested in boats. But the Mower house—it turned out I'd passed the address many times either on a bicycle or in my car—was located about a mile from the Lynn Yacht Club and even closer to the Lynn shore overlooking Nahant Bay.

Mower came up, as the *Boston Globe* yachting writer Leonard Fowle Jr. wrote, "the hard way." What that usually meant for a yacht designer in the nineteenth century was a public-school education coupled with creativity, a head for numbers, and a boundless work ethic. At age twenty in 1895, Mower was accepted as an apprentice by the Boston naval architect Arthur Binney. Between his work at Binney's and sailing aboard local yachts, Mower soaked up information quickly and he designed his first boat in 1896. He built her himself, of half-inch pine planks on oak frames, in the backyard of the family's Broad St. home.

The *Boston Globe* published a plan and profile view of this boat, a 25' LOA sloop named *Vitesse* (French for "speed"), calling it "a smooth-looking piece of work for an amateur to turn out." *Vitesse's* specifications suggest she would have been fast and challenging to handle. The boat drew 4" with her board up, had moveable ballast (sandbags), and a sail area of 550 sq. ft. Under the burgee of the Lynn Yacht Club, Mower won the 15' waterline (Fourth-Class) championship in her, in 1897.

Vitesse's performance so impressed yachtsmen from Quincy to Marble-head that she found a buyer who continued her winning ways. Mower then designed, built, and sold *Duchess*, an enlarged version of *Vitesse*, for the 18' waterline class, and she was also a winner that brought more favorable press attention to her designer. By now, Mower had become Binney's chief drafts-man and, on the side, he designed and built his third yacht, the 21'-waterline *Heiress*.

"Well," remembered Mower's granddaughter Mildred "Holly" Pastula, "grand-dad always wanted seven letters and a double-S in his boats' names."

Heiress, owned and capably sailed by Mower himself, proved so fast that on June 17, 1899, off Nahant, she not only won her class but also outdid on actual time the thirty-footers including the C. C. Hanley–built *Meemer*. It was an extraordinary performance.

In 1897, at age twenty-two, Charles D. Mower designed his first boat, *Vitesse*, a 17'-waterline racing yacht that reflected the extremely shallow-draft "skimming dish" hull form popular in the United States in the late nineteenth century. (Historic New England)

By now, Mower had joined the Boston design office of Bowdoin "B. B." Crowninshield and worked on a variety of projects with another bright apprentice named W. Starling Burgess. At age twenty-five, however, Mower was ready for a new challenge. On January 14, 1900, the *Globe* reported that Mower had moved to New York City where Thomas Fleming Day, founder of *The Rudder* magazine, had hired him to be design editor.

When he considered Mower's career in his biography of Starling Burgess, *No Ordinary Being*, Llewellyn Howland III summed it up like this: "In no way constrained by a lack of academic grounding in naval architecture, Mower gave as good as he got as a designer of open-class racing sloops . . . and of a wide range of handsome and competitive yachts. . . . However, it may have been as *The Rudder*'s youthful design editor that Mower most directly influenced American yachting."

Design Editor

Soon after he began publishing his "monthly journal of aquatic sport" in Watertown, New York, in 1890, Thomas Fleming Day found himself in the unhappy position of having to tell subscribers that he could not give permission to build a boat from the drawings in *The Rudder*. Instead, he referred readers to the designer who owned the drawings. Boat plans and commentary were a popular feature of the magazine and hiring Mower meant his plans could be sold direct.

Mower's very first design in *The Rudder*, which had by now moved to 9 Murray St. in Manhattan, was for a 24' "racer" published in November 1899. It was followed in February 1900 by a one-design Swampscott dory, a round-sided boat distinct from the Banks fishing dory. The Swampscott dory was fast gaining popularity as a racing class on Boston's North Shore. Mower's dory, named *Swampscott*, predated his joining *The Rudder*. It had been commissioned by the Swampscott Club, which still occupies an eighteenth-century building fronting the ocean. A variety of designs followed the dory: a 35'6" yawl, 24' and 28' sloops, a 10' tender, and many more.

When Capt. Joshua Slocum showed up at 9 Murray St., Day assigned Mower to go up to Bridgeport, Connecticut, where Slocum's famous *Spray* was then moored, and take off the boat's lines. Of course, Mower would have expected to find the *Spray* high and dry but, instead, the yacht was afloat. Mower measured the Spray from the waterline up, hoping to complete the job when the boat had been hauled. Instead, Slocum loaned Mower a scale model of the *Spray* which, Mower soon discovered, had discrepancies with his own previous work. None of this seems to have bothered Thomas Fleming Day. When Slocum's *Sailing Alone Around the World* was published in March 1900, Day advertised the book in his magazine, noting "Lines and Plans of the *Spray* by C.D. Mower."

Mower's job also included reporting. By 1901, he was covering the Seawanhaka Cup races, describing in fascinating detail the bending on of sails aboard the *America*'s Cup hopeful *Independence* ("the mainsail was fearfully big and heavy"), and writing an article explaining how to calculate center-of-lateral resistance. But his design work remained central. Day had Mower develop a catboat featured in a multi-part article called "How to Build an 18-foot Racing Cat." Each step was described by Mower who, of course, had his own experience to draw upon. "The frames must be 'cooked' until they become soft and pliable, and they must be quickly bent into place before they cool."

Day also had Mower design boats with the intent of publishing their plans and building instructions in books that would be sold through the magazine. "[H]ere for a small price a man can have the plans and full instructions for building a thoroughly able and good-looking launch," Day wrote in a 1902 issue about *How to Build a Motor Launch*. After one of *The Rudder*'s subscribers built a knockabout according to Mower's plans and instructions, he wrote to thank "Mr. Mower sincerely for putting us in possession of such a good set of plans and building instructions." Charlie Mower had become a kind of early twentieth-century, one-man WoodenBoat School.

Within three years of joining *The Rudder*, Mower was so firmly established on the New York yachting scene that, on August 18, 1903, the *Boston Globe* published a photo of the earnest-looking, bespectacled twenty-eight-year-old with the caption: "Charles D. Mower, Former Lynn Yachtsman. Now Measurer of the New York Yacht Club." The occasion was the upcoming *America's* Cup between the Herreshoff-designed *Reliance* and the William Fife-designed *Shamrock III*.

Interest in the event was so high that even the measuring of the yachts became a spectator sport and the trolley line that led to the Erie Basin dry-dock where the measuring was conducted broke records for the number of passengers carried. "Charles D. Mower . . . will be the man around whom the entire interest of Erie Basin will be focused tomorrow," the *Globe* reported on August 18. Spectators were treated to the site of Mower perched in a bosun's chair atop *Reliance's* 157' mast, said to be the world's tallest, with his steel measuring tape. When waterline measurements were taken and a ripple disturbed the water's surface, Mower redid the task under the watchful eyes of designers Herreshoff and Fife, because the yachts could not exceed, even by a fraction of an inch, a 90' waterline limit.

In March 1905, Mower entered and won a competition sponsored by *Forest & Stream* magazine for a 40' waterline cruising sailboat. This boat was one of some two dozen cruising yawls and sloops Mower designed before 1910, all reflecting what one observant yachting writer later called, "the approach of an artist." But it was the comparatively small yawl for *Forest & Stream*, created with functionality and the amateur builder in mind that garnered Mower national publicity.

"Size has little to do with a boat's ability to live at sea," Day told his readers. Soon after Mower joined *The Rudder*, Day began discussing with him ideas for a bare-bones sailboat that offered bluewater cruising potential. Mower translated Day's ideas ("I was concerned in her making," Day later wrote) onto paper. Day called the 25'5" result, which he named *Sea Bird*, "a safe, handy cruiser . . . not a fast boat . . . so well balanced she will work under any grouping of sail."

In the November 1901 issue of *The Rudder*, Mower published an article about *Sea Bird* typical of his how-to-build pieces. It began with instructions for lofting and was illustrated with a photograph of the keel, centerboard trunk, and stem setup with the station molds in place. Day took *Sea Bird*, a V-bottomed, hard-chined boat, on a trial sail from New York to Nantucket and found the little yacht met all his expectations. In 1911, Day and two friends—Theodore R. Goodwin and Fred B. Thurber—sailed *Sea Bird* to Italy.

During the time when Mower was building his first boat in the backyard, the revolution that the gasoline engine represented was also commencing. There is no doubt that Mower recognized the potential impact of internal combustion and he dedicated himself to learning about the new technology. Between 1900 and 1909, he designed a dozen 20' to 60' motor launches including the 28' "Number Boat" runabout/racer for the Thousand Islands Yacht Club (see *WoodenBoat* No. 220) and his own 27' x 4' *Express*, which he used both for work and pleasure on Long Island Sound.

Mower took every opportunity to gain sea time aboard a variety of sailing yachts and he did the same regarding power boats. When the *New York Herald* publisher James Gordon Bennett Jr. offered a trophy for the winner of the first powerboat to win a race from New York to Bermuda, T. F. Day took up the challenge. He skippered the Cary Smith–designed 60', 50-hp *Ailsa Craig* in a race against the 59' 25-hp W. B. Stearns-designed-and-captained *Idaho*. Both boats carried modest rigs in case their engine irrevocably broke down.

Ailsa Craig arrived first in Hamilton, thanks in part to a time-consuming clogged carburetor aboard *Idaho*. *Ailsa Craig*'s eight-man crew included Mower. When an igniter—a mechanical precursor to the spark plug—in the *Ailsa Craig*'s engine failed and the powerplant was shut down to replace it, Mower's watch-mate, the yachtsman Walter M. Bieling, reported that "Mower claims he sailed her, but if he did it was not forward. . . . Our jib-header wasn't worth a whoop." Mower's motorsailers would never suffer that problem. His first, in 1909, had a practical gaff-schooner rig.

There were no sailing problems with the Sonder boat that Mower designed on private commission for Bensonhurst Yacht Club commodore William H. Childs for the 1909 German-American races (see *WoodenBoat* No. 284) at Marblehead. *Joyette* was beautifully built by Gil Smith (see *WoodenBoat* No. 177) at his shop in Patchogue, New York. Competition to be selected to represent the United States was fierce because it included twenty-two Sonders from top designers. *Joyette* was among the three Sonders chosen, and she ultimately won the event trophy, the Taft Cup, which was presented by the president himself to Childs. In attendance in addition to Childs were the skipper, yachting writer William W. Swan, Butler Whiting who handled the mainsheet, and designer and jib-trimmer Charles Mower.

Job Change and His Own Shingle

In 1910, Mower moved to Philadelphia where he joined naval architect Thomas D. Bowes to form Bowes and Mower. It could be that Mower thought it advantageous to affiliate himself with men who possessed a college degree.

Arthur Binney had earned a two-year degree from MIT. Crowninshield had graduated Harvard. Although Bowes was nine years younger than Mower, he had a mechanical engineering degree from Cornell.

After this move, Mower continued to contribute designs to *The Rudder*. With the exception of two catboats, including a twenty-two-footer for a popular class that raced at Toledo and Detroit, the majority were for big cruising powerboats and launches. With the United States entry into World War I in 1917, Bowes and Mower both joined the Naval Reserve. As a lieutenant commander in the Construction Corps, Mower supervised the building of a fleet of 110' submarine chasers.

During or before his time in Philadelphia, Mower met and married Frances Hollingsworth Petrikin with whom, in December 1920, he'd have a son. By then, Mower had returned with his wife to New York where he opened his own office on Madison Avenue. *The Rudder* reported Mower's new venture, noting his experience designing successful racing yachts and that when it came to power boats, he was "a firm believer in a wholesome type of cruiser . . . of moderate speed and comfortable cruising accommodations in place of the so-called express cruisers, which have had a short term of popularity." The first of more than twenty Mower power-cruiser designs began appearing regularly in *Motor Boating* beginning in December 1919.

Barnegat Bay

One July day in 1982, I found myself seated in a most unusual two-bedroom apartment overlooking the Toms River. Beneath the apartment was a 40' boat-slip and on a marine railway outside was a sleek, racing sneakbox. This was the boathouse built in 1916 by yachtsman Edward Crabbe, who had contributed an important article to Schoettle's book called "The Toms River Cup." Now, sitting in the wood-paneled living area of the boathouse, I remarked to Crabbe's son, also named Ed, about the impressive model schooners on display. They were *Windjammer* and *Shellback*, both Charles Mower designs.

"*Windjammer*," said Ed, "was designed in 1924 and was one of the first shoal draft schooners of any size here that could handle offshore work. She drew a little over four feet board-up [useful in shallow Barnegat Bay] and was very successful. Mower proved you could design a safe centerboard boat." Ed had a nice photo of *Windjammer* docked alongside the boathouse with the transom of an A-Cat visible in the background. That was *Bat* built by Morton Johnson and launched in 1923. She was Mower's second A-Cat, the first being *Mary Ann* a year earlier. These were innovative catboats with tall, well-stayed Marconi rigs.

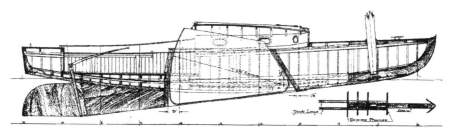

Mower designed the first A-Cat, *Mary Ann*, in 1922. When this drawing was published in *Yachting* in August 1923, the accompanying text noted that her "Marconi rig was something of an experiment but proved very successful as she handles nicely and is fast on all points of sailing." *Mary Ann*: 28' x 22'4''' x 10'9" x 2'6". Sail area: 605 sq. ft. (*Yachting*)

"Originally," said Crabbe, "the A-Cats had to have heads and mattresses. I've sailed down to Beach Haven and back. They were supposed to be cruising catboats, not for the ocean, but for Barnegat Bay." By the time I visited Crabbe, though, the A-Cats (see *WoodenBoat* No. 171) were, and remain, essentially a much-loved racing class whose popularity is, if anything, higher today than during the 1920s, thanks in large part to the efforts of yachtsmen Nelson Hartranft and Peter Kellogg. Five of the original seven were Mower designs, two by Francis Sweisguth.

As for the family schooners, Ed had cruised to Bermuda with his father and Mower aboard the 61' *Shellback* and never forgot the time he spent with the designer. "[He] was the nicest man you ever met, very quiet and unassuming, very knowledgeable about boats and yachting without pushing it at all. He was a top-grade gentleman."

The Top-Grade Gentleman

One day recently, while looking through a research file I'd compiled for a book called *Catboats* in 1982, I discovered a too-brief interview I'd had with Mower's son, Charles Mower Jr. who, after working for Sparkman and Stephens, had started a marine construction business in Greenwich, Connecticut. I learned from Mower Jr. that his father didn't stay long at his Manhattan office. Within a year or two, he relocated to Plandome on Long Island where he built a fine new house, indulged his love for chow chow dogs, and continued his membership in the nearby Manhasset Yack Club where he served as measurer. "He also became," Mower Jr. told me, "great friends with Herb Stone who was editor of *Yachting* magazine."

Mower flourished in the 1920s. In *Yachting*, William H. Taylor wrote that "Throughout this period, Mower-designed craft were among the outstanding yachts of many different types." He designed and sometimes skippered-to-victory a number of Class R boats including *Alert IV*, in which he won the Eastern Yacht Club's prestigious Ladies Plate in 1928. Another Mower R-Boat, *Ardelle*, which was pictured in *Sailing Craft* and built in 1926, was still winning fiercely competitive R-class races on Lake Michigan in 1940.

When the International Rule began generating interest in the 6- and 8-Meter classes in this country, Mower designed competitive yachts to both rules, among them the 6-Meter yachts *Ace* for investment banker Adrian Iselin, and *Priscilla*, whose lines appear in *Sailing Craft*. At least five of the first 6-Meters in 1922 were Mower designs. One of them, for a Larchmont Yacht Club syndicate, would be sailed by the redoubtable Long Island Sound racer Cornelius Shields. Mower's 8-Meters included *Mab*, designed for Robert N. Bavier, and *Sally*, for E. Townsend Irvin, both of which won trophies.

This volume of work did nothing to deplete Mower's creative energy. Regarding the M-Class, which reached its peak in 1929, William H. Taylor wrote that the Mower-designed *Windward* was "the most beautiful and [in heavy weather] the fastest." Mower also produced many one-designs including what Taylor called "one of the most successful one-design classes that ever raced on Long Island Sound, the Sound Interclubs . . . which were the inspiration for two other one-design classes, the Vineyard Interclubs and the Great South Bay Interclubs, also from his board." The Sound Interclub was replaced on Long Island Sound in 1936 by the International One Design (IOD); much of the Sound Interclub fleet then moved inland to Lake George, New York, where it remained active for decades, and has been revived in recent years (see *WoodenBoat* No. 242). At the same time, Mower was also designing cruising boats that competed well in the Bermuda Race and other offshore contests, and a 36' sloop named *Duckling*. Owned by New York attorney Charles W. Atwater, *Duckling* was awarded the Cruising Club of America's Blue Water Medal in 1937 after a voyage from New York to Reykjavik, Iceland.

Mower's interests included the design of model yachts, too, and he was an expert modelmaker. In January 1921, *The Rudder* advised that the famous New York City model-making firm of H. E. Boucher was offering Mower designs for 22–30" waterline model yachts with either gaff or marconi rigs. Modelmakers could acquire the hull of their choice in either finished or "rough blocked form."

Throughout his life, as busy as he usually was, Mower was recognized for his personal warmth and interest in others. One yachting journalist who knew the great designer well described him as overflowing "with the milk of human kindness."

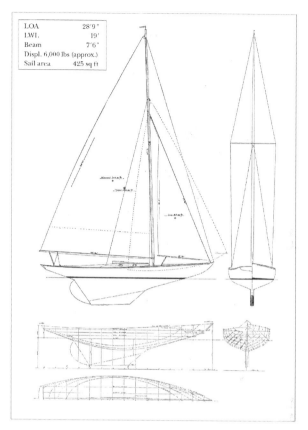

LOA	28'9"
LWL.	19'
Beam	7'6"
Displ.	6,000 lbs (approx.)
Sail area	425 sq ft

The 28' Sound Interclub was one of many delightful Mower designs. Yachting journalist William W. Swan lauded the yacht's comfortable cockpit "where one can handle his boat with only thumb and forefinger on the tiller under average conditions." (*Yachting*, December 1925)

Changing Times

At some point, probably just before or soon after the 1929 stock market crash, Charles Mower and his family left Plandome and moved to Pelham, New York. Pelham was some six miles away from City Island, and Mower's son recalled that his father "had an office in the house [but] worked as a naval architect at the Nevins Shipyard on City Island." There, Mower immediately became involved designing the 120' *Analgra* for Lewis Pierson, president and CEO of the Irving Trust and president of the United States Chamber of Commerce. This, the largest yacht ever built by Nevins, still sails today in the exclusive charter trade.

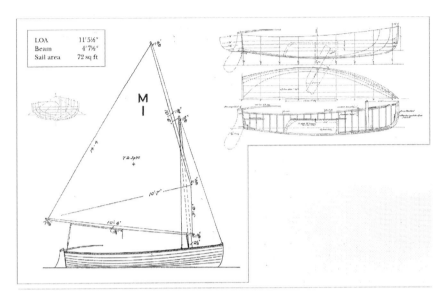

LOA	11'5½"
Beam	4'7½"
Sail area	72 sq ft

Ever versatile, Mower designed large yachts and dinghies including the 11 ½' *Snow Bird* for frostbite racing in 1933. Mower's own *Snow Bird* was built at Kretzer Boat Works on City Island. The boat offered two sail plans: the more popular gunter rig shown here, and an alternate lug rig. (*The Rudder*, April 1933)

At the opposite end of the design spectrum, Mower took personal note of the beautiful little sailing dinghies used for the new Depression-inspired sport of frostbiting, Mower designed a boat he called *Snow Bird* and, during the early 1930s, he proved himself in highly competitive racing at Larchmont and elsewhere against the region's best skippers.

In 1932, Mower designed a stout 34' cutter named *Jubilee*, built in Maine at the Hodgdon yard in 1933. By then, however, the once prolific designer's work was no longer appearing in yachting magazines. In 1934, *Motor Boating* published an article by Mower on rigs and in 1935, the designer wrote a brief, unpublished reminiscence that harked back to the early 1900s and the extreme, lightly built and very successful racing catboats of his early days. It was called "Mower Boats on Barnegat Bay."

What had slowed Mower down?

"Well," Mower's granddaughter told me, "C. D. Mower had Parkinson's disease."

This was, of course, devastating to Mower who could no longer precisely draw the beautiful lines so eagerly studied or commissioned by the

Mower often lit a pipe when sailing, finding that the smoke gave a useful guide to the wind direction. (Holly Pastula/Author's collection)

yachtsmen of his day. "It is doubtful," wrote William H. Taylor in *Yachting*, "if any designer ever accumulated more, or warmer friends, or a greater number of men who, not knowing him personally, admired him for his work."

Charles Drown Mower died at age sixty-six on January 17, 1942. He was buried in Pine Grove Cemetery in Lynn, Massachusetts, about two miles from the Broad Street home where he'd built his first boat. It's peaceful there, and is the resting place of a number of famous men and women, and there's a memorial to Lynn's fallen in the Civil War. At Pine Grove, I found the granite monument to the man the Boston newspapers always called the "Lynn boy."

"Say, Charlie," I said, "how I wish we could have a little chat."

This story appeared in *WoodenBoat* No. 287, July/August 2022.

THE SONDER CLASS

Germany vs. America, 1906–1913

Although international sailing competitions have long since become an integral part of the sport—think the Olympics and various one-design world championships to cite but two—this wasn't always the case. For much of the twentieth century, such events were held but were comparatively rare. The most notable of course, were *America*'s Cup events. These competitions were big news that involved men of great wealth and big boats manned for the most part by professional crews.

The German-American races of 1906–1913 were different. By design, they involved much smaller, more affordable boats than *America*'s Cup yachts and they were manned by, as the saying then went, "gentleman sailors." Such sailors were, generally speaking, successful in a variety of professions—often the law, business, manufacturing, or stock investing—who viewed sailing as their chief leisure activity. The Sonder sailors competed for the sport of it and the honor of their countries.

The concept of the German-American races generated a surprisingly high level of interest, particularly in Boston newspapers. In August 1906, when the first German Sonders arrived, the *Boston Daily Globe* was on hand and published a detailed story and several big photos. Such coverage continued for the life of the contests and less-detailed news items appeared in papers across the country. Conceived during a period when major European countries were building up big navies and armies, the Sonder races also had a laudable goal—to increase understanding and friendship between two peoples. Three American presidents and the German kaiser agreed to award the trophies, garnering further public interest. All in all, the races were a great story but with a tragic ending, the advent of what we now refer to as World War I.

This is a story that began well over a century ago and has yet to end. It's a tale that involves a forward-thinking yachtsman from Massachusetts, European royalty, three American presidents, the top names in early twentieth-century yacht design, and amateur sailors whose accomplishments are remembered still in the clubs they once represented.

As for the boats involved, each was alike yet different—varied interpretations of a simple class rule. These were the yachts of the German *Sonderklasse* (Special Class). From 1906 to 1913, Sonders from Germany and the United States competed in regattas organized to foster international friendship and, in Germany, to train a growing number of sailors who might someday advance Kaiser Wilhelm II's naval ambitions. Ultimately, it fell victim to the political failures that resulted in the Great War but, for those involved, the German-American races represented an experience they remembered all their lives.

The Key Man

Although Shooters Island is now a bird sanctuary, the island, which straddles the border between the states of New York and New Jersey in Newark Bay, was once home to various industries, including the Townsend and Downey Shipbuilding Co. There, on February 25, 1902, a new 161' steel schooner, *Meteor III*, was launched. Designed by A. Cary Smith, the boat was special in itself, but it was her owner who made this occasion an international news event. Thomas Edison sent a cameraman to film what would become one of the earliest newsreels. President Theodore Roosevelt was in attendance. In fact, his eighteen-year-old daughter, Alice, would do the christening.

Meteor III had been built for the kaiser, who was represented at the ceremony by his brother, Prince Henry, a naval officer and yachtsman. Among the 2,000 people who attended this launching was a sailor from the Eastern Yacht Club (EYC) in Marblehead, Massachusetts, named Henry Howard. An MIT-trained chemical engineer, Howard was a proponent of cruising and racing in much smaller yachts than were considered fashionable.

The good feelings evident at *Meteor III*'s launching inspired Howard. Years later, in his autobiography, he wrote: "It . . . seemed to me that an international race arranged with Germany in which small boats should be used and in which the helmsman and crew on both sides should all be amateurs would appeal to the public in both Germany and the United States and would also be very good for the yachting reputation of the Eastern Yacht Club."

The races would have three goals: to promote good feeling between the German and American people, to increase public interest in yacht racing by bringing into it the spirit of international competition, and to enable yachtsmen of moderate means to participate thanks to the use of boats that were smaller and less expensive than those typically associated with big-time regattas.

During the next few years, both on business trips to Germany and as chairman of the Eastern's Regatta Committee, Howard oversaw the necessary arrangements. In creating a list of eleven regulations, he sidestepped the potentially thorny matter of what boat would be used. Regulation 7 stipulated: "Size about 27-33 ft. rating or about 30 ft. (9 meters) waterline length." Regulation 8 stipulated: "Measurement and classification that of the challenging club."

When he looked back at this critical aspect, Howard wrote, "in the first match at Marblehead, we would use the German system. This was so liberal and so sportsmanlike that they simply could not refuse it." Ultimately, "the German system"—the Sonder Class—would remain for the life of the contest. Class rules required that the boats be designed and built in their respective countries and be "owned, manned and sailed by native-born citizens of the country they represent." Helmsman and crew were to be amateurs.

Howard also accepted stipulations made by the prestige-conscious Germans. President Roosevelt would present the first cup for the races in the United States as would the kaiser in Germany. The Kaiserlicher (Imperial) Yacht Club in Kiel—the club officially representing Germany—could select its entries from all of Germany's yacht clubs.

The Sonder Class

Sonder Class rules were finalized in 1899 with the intent of having boats ready for what remains Germany's premier regatta, *Kieler Woche* (Kiel Week) in June 1901. Among the eleven boats built or ordered during 1900 was one for the kaiser, who was a strong Sonder supporter. On December 19, 1900, his representative concluded a detailed contract with the highly regarded Hamburg yard of Max Oertz and Harder for *Samoa II*. Finish was to be bright with dark blue sheerstrakes. Nineteen items of equipment were listed, including a boathook, anchor and rode, boom crutch, cradle, and even a marlinspike.

It is almost certain that Howard was aware of the Sonder. In 1902, the American Sonder *Uncle Sam*, designed by B. B. Crowninshield, won the Kaiser Cup at Kiel Week. The boat was owned by Francis J. Riggs of the New York Yacht Club and skippered by J. Hopkins Smith Jr., who'd grown up and learned to sail in Portland, Maine. Smith attended Harvard and graduated in 1902 after just three years. *Uncle Sam*'s victory so impressed the kaiser that he bought the yacht. Renamed *Niagara*, she was used to train young German sailors.

The class design rules stipulated that the waterline length, plus breadth, plus draft not exceed 32'; the weight could not be less than 4,035 lbs.; and the sail area was limited to 550 sq. ft. No centerboards or leeboards were permitted. The Sonders had fin keels, which were then a reasonably "modern" development that had been introduced in the United States by Nathanael Herreshoff in 1892. The yachting writer Winfield Thompson summed up the various designs of the first fleet in 1906 this way: "The boats varied as much in form as in dimension, some being purely scows while others were normal and harmonious in their proportions."

The Germans, who considered the racing scow, with its flat or nearly flat bottom and extreme overhangs, to be undesirable boats, were semi-incredulous, yet impressed, by the scow-shaped American Sonders. "My, my, my," was a typical reaction. Thomas Fleming Day, editor of *The Rudder*, was critical of the "Sonder scow," calling it a "freak." But the Sonder was always an open, hotly contested development class of pure racing yachts, nothing more and nothing less. "Freaks" were inevitable.

Construction specifics were spelled out. No double-planked hulls were allowed. Hulls were to be fore-and-aft planked of cedar, mahogany, or heavier wood, and copper-fastened. Planking was to be not less than 5/8" thick, a rule that on more than one occasion tripped up an American Sonder. Metal interior trusses and braces were allowed. Cockpit length could not exceed 8'. Hollow or bamboo spars were not permitted. Although a couple of cat-rigged or sliding-gunter Sonders were tried and found wanting, the most successful were gaff-rigged sloops. A Sonder's sail inventory could be extensive. The E. A. Boardman–designed *Spokane III* of 1909 had five mainsails, two jibs, a storm jib, two ballooners, and three spinnakers.

Class rules included a cost restriction to encourage more Germans to become sailors, which was one of the kaiser's goals. In the United States, the limit was $2,400 (roughly $61,000 today). While a Sonder was affordable to well-off yachtsmen, the class remained out of reach for working people, whose annual wages in 1914 were $627. A new Ford Model T cost $490. On the other hand, a Sonder's cost was far removed from that of a big Herreshoff one-design or, of course, an *America's* Cup yacht.

Writing about the Sonder Class in *The Rudder* in December 1906, Winfield Thompson noted: "[Y]achting, as expressed in the contests for the *America's* Cup ... was not representative of the bulk of the yachting fraternity of either country but expensive contests paid for by millionaires and executed by professionals, between sailing machines of huge proportions, which no yachtsman could attempt to operate."

B. B. Crowninshield designed *Sumatra* as a light-weather Sonder. Dimensions: 33'8" x 20'4" x 6'8" x 4'11", 4,150 lb. displacement. Planking was Spanish cedar over ¾" x ¾" oak frames spaced on 6" centers. *Sumatra* shows that, when not racing, a Sonder could be a spirited daysailer. (MIT Museum)

The 1906 Contest

In mid-July 1906, the Eastern held selection trials in which seventeen Sonders competed to be among three to face the Germans. The boats represented eight yacht clubs and nine designers. The Germans had their own selection trials, and their three Sonders were shipped to Boston and then towed to Marblehead, where they were given a rousing salute by the EYC's signal cannon. Henry Howard arranged for the visitors to stay at the Eastern clubhouse and the Germans were immediately charmed by Marblehead both as a colonial-era town and yachting venue.

It is easy to imagine the fascinating scene the Sonders created as they were rigged, weighed, and measured by the EYC's measurer, designer W. Starling Burgess, at his boatyard on Marblehead Harbor. Winfield Thompson noted such interesting details as "The *Glückauf* [*Good Luck*] has a balance rudder while the *Wannsee* is of the common (attached to the fin keel) type." Burgess shared his opinion on the German boats with *The Boston Globe*: "If we get strong winds, the Roosevelt Cup will go to Germany." More moderately proportioned than the American boats, though probably excessively narrow, the German Sonders had roller-reefing gear and sails made of comparatively heavy cloth that were longer on the foot and shorter on the hoist than the American sails.

The Germans were deeply impressed by the knowledge of the American sailors. "The comments on our boats show intelligence and thought," one told the *Globe*. The friendliness of the Americans also came as a pleasant surprise to the Germans, who were accustomed to strict formality. On August 5, at a 200-person dinner at Marblehead's Corinthian Yacht Club, Otto Protzen, the Germans' top helmsman and skipper of *Wannsee*, thanked his hosts and proposed a toast to President Roosevelt. Reciprocation came as a toast to the kaiser.

The first race—twice around a seven-and-a-half-mile course—was held on September 3, 1906, a day of puffy winds that ranged from about 11 mph at the start to 30 mph at the finish. The event, like those that followed, made front-page news in the *Globe*, whose reporter noted aspects of the German Sonders' performance that must have surprised Burgess. "Their boats were practically over-powered by the wind and though they shortened sail, they dragged around the course, displaying less sail-carrying power than the American boats. . . . Their low and sharp bows constantly dipped under the waves in the windward work, sending solid water back to the cockpit coaming."

Charles Francis Adams, the finest amateur helmsman of his generation, owned a Sonder named *Auk* that had not been thought the best design for heavy weather. Yet Adams's skill and seamanship more than made up for any real or perceived deficiency. Although *Wannsee* made a perfectly timed start, she could not hold the lead. Adams, who paused to tuck in a reef, was brilliant to windward, forging ahead with his trademark technique of letting the mainsail luff shiver just a bit.

Both *Auk* and *Caramba* had opened some hull seams in the heavy going and needed recaulking. Otto Protzen took note of this and expressed his belief that the German boats were "superior in strength and workmanship . . . one could see that at a glance." Winfield Thompson called the German Sonders "beautiful little ships."

The next races were held on September 8 after repairs had been made and celebratory dinners consumed. In a fresh southeasterly wind, and short, green seas, Otto Protzen sailed *Wannsee* to victory, defeating C. H. W. Foster's *Caramba* by over a minute and earning a great round of applause from his hosts. This expression, too, came as surprise to the Germans, accustomed to applauding only close friends or the very famous.

The final races were held on September 10, when the William Gardner–designed *Vim* proved to be the best boat in all conditions, especially

This Willard B. Jackson image most likely shows the elimination race sailed on August 11, 1910, to select the three American Sonders that would compete against three Spanish boats starting on August 17. The ultimate winner of the Spanish-American contest was C. H. W. Foster's *Beaver*, recognizable here by her unusual batwing sail. The Sonder was designed by Starling Burgess who also served as a crew member. (MIT Museum)

to windward. The event concluded on Friday, September 14, aboard the presidential yacht *Mayflower* anchored off Roosevelt's Oyster Bay home, Sagamore. Roosevelt had been unable to accept Henry Howard's invitation to attend the races, but Winfield Thompson wrote: "[T]he president of the United States received victors and vanquished and expressed to them his gratification over the happy results of the first yachting contest between America and Germany."

The American Sonders made a profound impression on the Germans. They acquired the lines of *Auk, Caramba, Marblehead,* and *Sumatra* which, after being published in *Die Yacht* magazine, would influence German design. But what made the most lasting impression on German yachtsmen were the American sails. The subject was well-presented in the *Die Yacht* article written by Erich Meisner, who had crewed aboard *Glückauf IV*. Meisner noted the flat German sails were less powerful than American sails with their fuller curve and draft in the correct place. He recommended that the Germans study American sails before the 1907 races.

German-American Contestants, 1906

Name	Owner/Club	Designer	L.O.A.	L.W.L.	Beam	Draft	Weight (lbs)
Auk	C. F. Adams 2nd/Eastern	Edwin.A. Boardman	37.77'	19.87'	6.9'	5.12'	4,037
Caramba	C. H. W. Foster/Eastern	Edwin A. Boardman	37.0'	19.25'	7.18'	5.50'	4,220
Vim	Trenor L. Park/American	William Gardner	35.55'	19.85'	6.68'	5.00	4,485
Glückauf IV	G. Stinnes/Imperial and A. S. V.	Wilhelm von Hacht	32.41'	20.51'	6.0'	4.90'	4,185
Tilly VI	C. Dollmann, R. Krogmann, Prince Henry of Prussia / North German Regatta Club	Max Oertz	32.80'	21.10'	5.94'	4.55'	4,095
Wannsee	Seglerhaus am Wansee	Max Oertz	32.35'	20.35'	5.95'	4.95'	4,290

"Any sailmaker can make a flat sail," reported Winfield Thompson in the *Globe* on February 24, 1907, "but only an artist can make a full sail with the flow in place to give the greatest speed."

While the Germans could improve their sail design, their sail cloth remained wanting. American cloth, made of upland Texas cotton rather than the Egyptian and Sea Island cotton used in Europe, was recognized by the Germans as superior to their own. The Boston Yarn Company touted the "Lowell Duck" fabric it wove as "the closest [weave], strongest, best setting canvas for yachts."

Kiel, 1907

By December 1906, it was clear to Henry Howard and his associates that having an American team in Germany in time for Kiel Week in June 1907, as the kaiser hoped, was impractical. It would have required launching boats in April and holding trials in May, a problem given New England's spring weather. Neither was it practical for the amateur crews to leave their jobs before the yachting season. As a result, the races were scheduled to be held at Kiel beginning on August 12. Before departure, Henry Howard received a letter from President Roosevelt expressing his "hearty good wishes."

Right from their arrival, the Americans were dubious. They quickly perceived that the new German Sonders had benefited from study of the American designs. They were longer—around 37' vs. the 32' of the 1906 German boats—and had greater overhangs and freeboard. What's more, the German sailors had also absorbed lessons regarding sail design. Their new sails were not the equal of the American sails but were more than good enough.

The American team's real worry was the wind. The royal observatory at Kiel reported average winds in August of 25 mph, significantly more than prevails in summer on Boston's North Shore. In fact, during the time available to tune the boats, the winds ranged from 20 mph to a squally 50 mph. The American team's three Sonders included *Marblehead*, designed by B. B. Crowninshield, which was judged to be the team's best all-around yacht; *Chewink VIII*, designed and built in Boston by Small Brothers which was best in light air and smooth water; and *Spokane*, a Clinton Crane design, which was the best heavy-air boat. But heavy, in this regard, was 15 mph, not 25.

On the second day's racing, Prince Henry, at the helm of *Tilly VI*, took first place, well over four minutes ahead of *Spokane* and over thirteen minutes ahead of last-place *Marblehead*. The American Sonders didn't win a single race. "[A] weakness of our yachting," reported the *Globe* on August 18, "is to design and rig our boats for light air only."

The kaiser presented the Kaiser Cup to Otto Protzen, skipper of *Wannsee VIII*. As it had at Marblehead, good sportsmanship prevailed. Prince Henry acknowledged the design lessons the Germans had learned from the American Sonders in 1906. He received an honorary degree from Harvard, applauded by the Americans who were mainly Harvard men themselves.

Henry Howard, meanwhile, was a close observer of German naval technical developments—German warships were present during the regatta—which he passed on to contacts in the U.S. Navy. The British, suitably wary of Germany's naval build-up, had objected to the German-American races in the first place. The Irish writer Erskine Childers's influential spy novel, *The Riddle of the Sands*, had been published in England in 1903, foretelling the danger of German naval ambitions.

The Americans had another date in Europe in 1907. On a business trip, Howard had made contacts that resulted in an invitation to Madrid, where he was introduced to Spain's twenty-one-year-old King Alfonso, a yachting enthusiast. That meeting led to an invitation to compete at San Sebastian for what was billed as the Hispano-American regatta, the prize being the King's Gold Cup.

Howard recalled later: "The American yachtsmen, still suffering from their defeat at Kiel, felt no doubt about their ability to win with ease in Spain, especially as they saw the Spaniards use the then unheard-of technique of carrying a balloon jib to windward in light breezes, a custom later adopted throughout the yacht racing world under the improper name of 'Genoa jibs.'"

In contrast to Kiel, the wind at San Sebastian was light and fluky, and local knowledge may have given the home team an important tactical advantage. *Spokane* won a race, but the Spanish dominated. "We were as badly beaten by the Spaniards as we had been by the Germans at Kiel," Howard said.

The Americans Rebound

On June 13, 1908, the *Globe* reported: "This is an off-year in the Sonder class, and there is no match with the Germans." But with the races on for 1909, the *Globe* noted that twelve new Sonders had been designed and built. The Germans were pleased to learn that President Howard Taft would present the Taft Trophy. What's more, Massachusetts governor Eben Sumner Draper sponsored his own trophy for the second-best boat. By the eve of the first race, August 29, 1909, the *Globe* was calling the event "the most important international contest in the yachting world."

Most unfortunately, the German helmsman Protzen suffered torn knee ligaments when he slipped on a gangway. Howard responded that if only two

German boats could race, the American team would start two rather than three. Protzen would sail, however, persevering through his injury, which would later help keep him out of the German army. On September 2, in a gusty northwest wind, *Hevella*, sailed by Protzen, won. Not only did he sail a fine race, but the roller-reefing gear of his boat allowed him to quickly remove a reef that had been needed during the early stages. Second place went to the German Sonder, *Margarethe*.

But that was the Germans' only victory. It was evident that their boats were slower and that their fastest point of sail was downwind. That was not enough to make up for their windward deficiency. The winner, *Joyette*, had been designed by Charles Mower and beautifully built by Gil Smith at his shop at Patchogue on Long Island, New York, for owner William H. Childs, commodore of the Bensonhurst Yacht Club. *Joyette's* first skippers were lukewarm about the yacht, but Mower believed in her. Mower arranged for William W. "Billy" Swan, one of New York's top amateur skippers, to helm *Joyette* while he himself would handle the jibsheets and another capable sailor tended the mainsheet.

Tuning up during the selection races in August 1909 is the eventual winner of the Taft Cup, *Joyette*. Her designer, thirty-three-year-old Charles Mower, is lying to leeward. (See also "Searching for C. D. Mower" and "Gilbert Monroe Smith.") (MIT Museum)

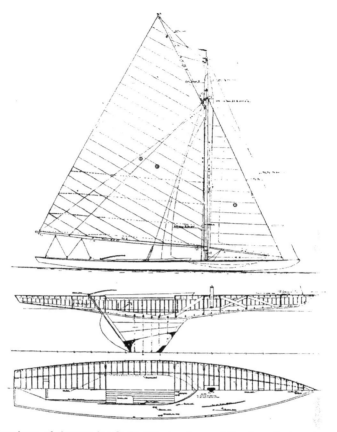

These drawings of *Joyette* by C. D. Mower show all the key design aspects of a champion Sonder: long overhangs and low freeboard, a fin keel with attached rudder, a slender beam, a four-part main sheet to aid trimming (no winches), and running backstays. *Joyette*: 37'4" x 19'9" x 7'8" x 4'9". (*Forest and Stream*, November 27, 1909)

The Germans remained good sports. The kaiser's representative at the races, Vice Admiral Barandon, told the *Globe*: "Your designers have made wonderful progress. Your boats are faster than ours, so we have nothing to complain about. We shall learn something from defeat." In a gesture of good sportsmanship, Charles Francis Adams, the American helmsman, donated to the Germans his Boardman-designed *Crooner*. A favorite to make the 1909 team, *Crooner* ultimately had been edged out. In Germany, *Crooner* was studied, and she became a trial horse for the latest German boats.

The following year's Sonder races at Marblehead involved not Germany but Spain. This 1910 event also attracted wide attention. The arrival of the

Spaniards was noted briefly in sports columns as far away as Oregon. This time, the tables were turned by the Eastern boats that included Adams's *Harpoon*, Guy Lowell's *Cima*, and Charles Foster's *Beaver*, the thirty-first of a long line of yachts he would own. Even on days when the wind was light and shifty, what the *New York Times* called "typical San Sebastian weather," the Spanish Sonders were dominated.

Final Races

To help ensure there would be no repeat of sending inappropriate boats to Kiel in 1911, Howard held the selection races in Buzzards Bay, where conditions are typically windier and rougher than at Marblehead and where an active Sonder fleet had existed for several years. (In 1909, the tennis great Dwight F. Davis of Davis Cup fame bought *Sally VIII* to race in Buzzards Bay.) The result, reported the *Globe*, was a sweep at Kiel, "a source of considerable satisfaction at the EYC."

The Nathanael Herreshoff–designed *Bibelot*, his best Sonder, proved to be the fastest boat at Kiel, edging out *Beaver*, a Burgess design. Afterward, speaking of *Cima* with the Eastern's Guy Lowell—a Boston architect when he wasn't sailing—the kaiser blamed the 1911 losses on poor design rather than the German sailors. Wilhelm and a group of German yachtsmen then bought *Bibelot* for use as a training boat. *Cima*, Lowell's second Sonder to bear the name, was sold to an Austrian yachtsman.

Augustus Eustis, who with two friends had bought *Beaver* from Adams, her original owner, shared his thoughts regarding the sport in Germany. "I gained the impression that the interest in yachting . . . was shared by a very much smaller number of people in Germany than in this country [and] that the International Race played a very unimportant part in the general racing which was going on at Kiel."

The next contest was held in 1913 at Marblehead, and its trophy was named for the third president to be involved, Woodrow Wilson. Race preparations for the Wilson Cup, noted the *Globe*, included two piano polishers who spent an entire day on the topsides of the Boardman–designed *Sprig*. An inherent oddity of the races that had existed from the first contest was noted by the *Globe*: "In order to allow for the difference in specific gravity between the Baltic water at Kiel and at Marblehead, the measurer, when measuring the American boats, must place in each boat a weight equivalent to 1/64 of the displacement." This was for measuring purposes only; the weight, which accounted for the Baltic's lower salinity, and therefore less buoyant water, was not carried during races.

The series, sailed in disappointingly light, fluky winds, was another sweep for the American yachts. *Ellen*, the top American boat, was sailed

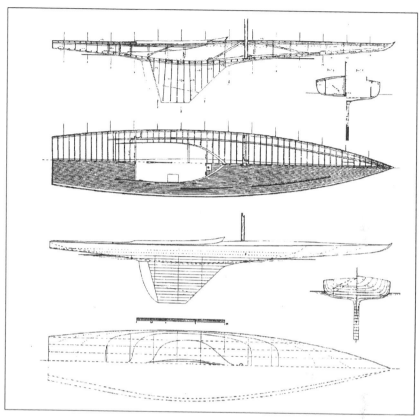

Launched in 1910 and the winner of the Kaiser's Cup in Kiel that year, *Bibelot* was narrower, longer, and had more deadrise than most Sonders and was N. G. Herreshoff's most successful Sonder design. *Bibelot*: 38' x 19'4" x 7'5" x 5'3". Sail area: 550 sq. ft. Displacement: 4,241 lbs. outside lead. (*Segling* [Sweden], September 28, 1911)

by sixty-one-year-old Charles P. Curtis, a distinguished Boston lawyer, and his two sons. Two days later, at a ceremony on the south lawn of the White House on September 11, 1913, President Woodrow Wilson, addressing the American and German yachtsmen and officials, said, "I think that one of the most delightful things about modern sport is that it brings the men of different countries together and I hope that the German representatives present will not consider it an international discourtesy on our part that the American boat won."

Nine months after that ceremony, while the kaiser was cruising in the North Sea off Norway, Austrian archduke Franz Ferdinand was assassinated in Sarajevo. Most historians agree that the kaiser, a grandson of Queen

Victoria, was the one man who could have prevented the outbreak of war on July 28. At first, there were hopes that the war might be over by Christmas. Howard and his fellow yachtsmen made skeptical preparations for a selection series in which five boats, including two new ones, took part in August. Those were the last American Sonders to be built in that era.

As the war dragged on and the trenches were dug, thoughts of resuming the German-American races ended. When Germany announced unrestricted submarine warfare on April 2, 1917, President Wilson asked Congress to declare war. With that declaration, the *Boston Globe* reported that "Kaiser Wilhelm was formally expelled," from Eastern Yacht Club. "As an honorary member, his name will be stripped from the rolls, and in this year's club book it is already missing."

The Eastern then offered its clubhouse for use as a naval training center. The irony was lost on nobody. The *Globe* headline for May 6, 1917, read: "Sailors Drill Where German Admiral Was Once A Guest."

The Sonder Sails On

Sonder racing became a regular feature of the Massachusetts yachting season and it continued after the international races ended. The prestigious Quincy Cup was a Sonder trophy until, in 1915, the Sonders were replaced by P-Class yachts. Still, a core group of boats raced in the newly formed Sonder class of the Interclub Yacht Racing Association. Twelve clubs were involved. At least ten Sonders found homes at the Eastern Point Yacht Club in Gloucester, Massachusetts, where they were actively raced well into the thirties. Eastern Point also established a cup for women Sonder skippers.

The total number of U.S. Sonders numbered around sixty-five yachts. That compared favorably with the universal rule or meter-boat classes of the era. The Atlantic One-Design, which Starling Burgess biographer Llewellyn Howland III noted was "not unlike the open-class Sonder boats that they could be said to have replaced," totaled about ninety-nine.

In Germany, at the time of the armistice in November 1918, the kaiser abdicated and departed for exile in Holland. The post-1918 years brought crushing inflation, violent political strife, and a diminished yachting scene. In *Segeln für den Kaiser, Die Internationale Sonderklasse (Sailing for the Kaiser, the International Sonder Class)*, Klaus Kramer noted only five Sonders were built postwar, three in 1920 and two in 1921. However, older boats survived and some racing continued on the

Starnbergersee and Bodensee in Bavaria. Fleets were also established in Austria under the auspices of a union of various clubs. Austria's Wolfgangsee and Attersee became the principal venues.

The Nazi takeover in Germany cast a grim shadow over everything, including yachting. "After Hitler's annexation of Austria into the German Reich in 1938," noted Jutta Boergers of the Berlin Sailing Club, "all Germany's yacht clubs including the old *Kaiserlicher* (Imperial) were merged to become the Yacht Club of Germany." The sportsmanship of prior days was now replaced with a single thought, noted Klaus Kramer: "Sport is battle."

This was a sad contrast to the good feelings that developed among the German and American yachtsmen. Before he returned to Germany after the 1906 racing, Otto Protzen told the *Globe*: "I am proud of the fact that three of my American opponents are my best friends." In some cases, the relationships formed would survive both world wars.

The first post–World War II Sonder race took place in 1948 when eleven Sonders gathered on the Wolfgangsee not far from Salzburg, Austria. Those races continue to this day as surviving Sonders were restored and upgraded. According to Klaus Kramer's research, 150 Sonders were built in Germany between 1899 and 1921. Thirty boats are known to exist today.

Among the surviving boats in Europe are the Mower-designed *Cima* and *Tilly XV*, both beautifully restored. *Tilly* XV, designed and built in Hamburg in 1912 by Wilhelm von Hacht, has even returned to Marblehead where she competed in the 2017 Panerai Corinthian Classic Yachts Regatta. (Videos of *Tilly XV* may be viewed on YouTube. Search Sonderklasse segeln.) The fleet also includes *Bibelot II*, a state-of-the-art version of the Herreshoff original engineered by the gifted Steve Barnes of the Rockport Apprenticeshop where it was beautifully built by Todd French and John England in 1992.

Once in the hands of her owner in Bavaria, *Bibelot II* inspired the creation of a second new and more radically modernized Sonder, *Fima*, designed by Barnes and completed in 1994. In a postscript to his well-told story on the new Sonders in *WoodenBoat* No. 131 in 1996, Art Paine reported: "*Bibelot II* has proven to be especially efficient in light airs, but *Fima* probably has created the greatest sensation after having been clocked at 18.6 knots on the Attersee."

This story appeared in *WoodenBoat* No. 284, February 2022.

GILBERT MONROE SMITH

The Wizard of Great South Bay

The following story about Patchogue, New York, boatbuilder Gilbert Monroe Smith represents, I believe, the longest piece of mine published in *WoodenBoat*. It exceeded the usual 4,000-word maximum length by over a thousand words. Nor were the accompanying illustrations reduced in number or size to squeeze things in. That said, I don't recall any discussion about seriously cutting the manuscript. Smith's story is so rich, his place as a designer and boatbuilder so important, that editor Matt Murphy decided that Smith must get his due.

In truth, the story could have been twice as long, or easily expanded to book length. Unlike so many designers and builders about whom very little has survived, there is a substantial printed record about Gil Smith. Plans and models exist as do the published recollections of those who knew him. Often Smith's boats appeared in *Manning's Yacht Register*, thus preserving basic information.

By dint of good timing, Smith found himself in the right place on Long Island at the right time. Wealthy men in Manhattan were building homes on the water, wanted sailboats, and word soon got around that Gilbert Monroe Smith was a boatbuilder with a special touch. The indisputable beauty of his boats, the quality of his construction, racing successes, and the wealth and influence of his clientele led to one referral after another. The majority of his boats were his own designs but he sometimes built to plans provided the New York firm of Gardner and Cox or others. Local sailors invariably fell under the spell of the slender, blue-eyed artisan and some devoted themselves to seeing to it that his name was not forgotten.

The story is told, in the villages beside Long Island's Great South Bay, of the time that Capt. Wilbur Corwin, from Bellport, chanced upon a stranger lying beneath a boat built by the locally famous Gil Smith. It was March and the boat's topsides were covered still against rain, wind, and the lingering threat of snow.

"What are you doing under there?" Corwin asked of the figure who seemed intent on examining the bottom's curves.

The stranger, wearing a black overcoat against the chill day, slowly unfolded himself from beneath the hull. Years later, when he told the story, Wilbur Corwin, well known as a skipper of yachts and ferries, admitted the surprise he got when he saw the stranger's face.

"I was just lookin'," said Nathanael Herreshoff, "and tryin' to find out how he made 'em draw so little water and go so fast."

The date of this encounter went unrecorded, but there is no reason to doubt its basics. We do know, thanks to Gil Smith's son Asa, that Edwin Bailey, proprietor of the big lumber mill by the Smith boatyard, once went up to Bristol to see Capt. Nat about a new boat. Bailey was angry. Although he had owned Smith boats, the builder had recently refused to sell him his creek-front yard so that Bailey could expand. But when Herreshoff learned the boat was to be a centerboarder for Great South Bay, he promptly suggested that Mr. Bailey return and talk to Smith. Perhaps Capt. Nat was thinking of one of his boats that had been renamed *Question*. While successful on Long Island Sound, it did not fare well on Great South Bay against the Smith sloops. The boat raced in a class known locally as P-class (which had no connection to the P-Class of the Universal Rule).

Such incidents became tantalizing fodder for the passed-down legend of Gil Smith's life and work. Each episode would take its place in the cherished oral history and collective memory of those who revered the slender old boatbuilder. Here was a man who emerged somehow from that profusion of once remote bays and pine barrens and villages on eastern Long Island to become recognized as an artist who happened to build boats. His was a life lived fully, for he spent it doing what he learned that he was born to do, and the legacy he left behind was one that would ripple down through time to mesmerize those of our own era. Let there be no doubt—sixty-four years after Smith's death, his capacity to inspire is very much alive.

The Man from Good Ground

Gilbert Monroe Smith was born in July 1843, in Manorville, New York, a woodsy Long Island hamlet where rivers fed cranberry bogs and powered a variety of mills. Barges served the mills and it seems likely that Smith's father

Gil Smith at the wheel: the photo was probably taken circa 1921 when Smith was seventy-eight. (Author's collection courtesy of Al Terry Jr.)

John, who described himself then as a "boatman," may have worked those flat-bottomed craft. The Smith family left Manorville shortly after Gil's birth and relocated to a succession of villages within the town of Southampton. Probably by 1850 they had settled in what is now known as Hampton Bays but was then called Good Ground.

The story is told that a two-year-old Gil Smith made a toy boat out of a piece of bark and a stick and sailed it in a rain puddle while protected by an umbrella held by his father or older sisters.

Details of Smith's life at Good Ground are sketchy. They derive primarily from what little he shared with local newspapers or from the memories of his adoring youngest daughter Jennie. Between the ages of seventeen and twenty, Smith worked first as a fisherman, then as a deep-sea sailor, and then sailed coastwise on vessels supplying the Union Army. Upon the occasion of a family reunion in his eightieth year, Smith told the *Brooklyn*

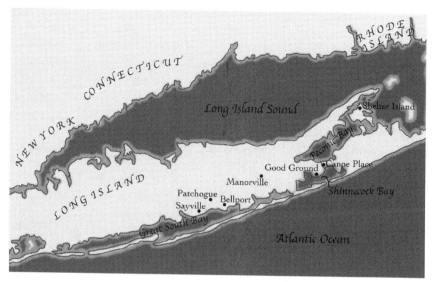

Gil Smith's Long Island: Smith's move from Canoe Place to Patchogue in 1876 gave him access to what would become a growing market for fine yachts purchased by wealthy New Yorkers. (*WoodenBoat*)

Daily Eagle that "I built my first boat when I was 17. Going to school, I passed the shop of another boat builder, and when I saw his boat taking shape I had to have one. So I up and built one and I've been building them ever since."

The school Smith attended had a single room and was painted red. It was the same school attended by his eventual wife, Mariam (the name also appears as Miriam, Marian, and Marion) Terry. The two married in 1863 when Smith was twenty and Mariam seventeen. "My parents," said daughter Jennie, "both remembered Abraham Lincoln."

While Gil was away, Mariam Smith became a teacher on the local Shinnecock Indian reservation. At some point after he married, Smith stopped going to sea. He built a house not far from Good Ground at Canoe Place, and became a bayman, supplying restaurants with shellfish and, as a market gunner, with ducks. He carved decoys and built his own duck boats. Smith never lost his love for duck shooting or his appreciation for fine shotguns. Once, sailing Jennie across Great South Bay to his Pelican Island gunning shack, Smith suddenly let go the tiller of his thirty-three-foot P-class sloop *Senta*, raised the Parker gun that lay on the thwart, and casually knocked down a duck, which he then plucked from the water as he sailed past. Smith named *Senta* for the operatic sweetheart of *The Flying Dutchman*, although how he ever came to be an opera buff, or to what depth his interest extended, has gone unrecorded.

At some point before or shortly after the birth of the first of his six children in 1872, Gil Smith began supplementing his gunning activities with boatbuilding. Almost a century later, it would become an article of faith among Smith's admirers that he never apprenticed or worked for another builder. In fact, there is no evidence to the contrary. Smith himself apparently took care to emphasize that he learned the business from the keel up by working out problems for himself—"by his own genius," reporters sometimes wrote. The closest Smith came to admitting working for anyone as a young man was when, in 1936, he told a reporter for the *Patchogue Advance* that he once worked a week for a relative. However, when that relative decided gunning was more pressing than business, Smith decided he would only succeed as his own boss. According to the sparse information he shared with the reporter, he began boatbuilding by "centering his attention on small boats and East Bay skiffs."

The move from Canoe Place to Patchogue in 1876 was the seminal event in Smith family history. The reasons given were that a cousin in Patchogue suggested the town would offer better education for the Smith children and that its location would present Gil with new commercial opportunities. Patchogue boasted a thriving lace mill and a number of boatyards. Rich, seeded oyster beds lay beneath the clear waters on the bay's sandy bottom. The Smiths packed their young children, Amy and Asa, and a kitchen table into their 24' catboat and began threading their way westward through the narrow passages and bays that lay between Shinnecock Bay and the broader expanse of Great South Bay.

In Smith family lore, the early days in Patchogue were remembered more for their disappointment than their promise. Daughter Jennie said that money became so scarce that Smith and Mariam prepared to leave. They had put the kitchen table back aboard the catboat together with everything else and, having raised the sail, were ready to head back to Canoe Place. She remembered her father's words of that moment with perfect clarity all her life: "By the looks of you, you don't really want to leave." They unloaded the boat.

Information regarding Smith's business activities during the early days in Patchogue is sparse. He met Elijah Saxton, a fisherman, landowner, and boatbuilder who had a marine railway on the west side of the Patchogue River. Most probable is that Smith rented space from Saxton. It seems likely that the boats built and repaired during this period included both workboats and yachts. In 1927, Smith told a reporter that a catboat he had built fifty years earlier (1877) was "still in service on Shinnecock Bay." Among the

This photo, taken between 1876 and 1881, shows the busy boatyard of Gil Smith and Elijah Saxton on the west bank of the Patchogue River. Smith is standing by the bow of the unfinished hull. His son Asa stands by the sawhorse. Smith later established his own yard across the river. (Author's collection courtesy of Al Terry Jr.)

earliest boats of which there is a definite record—because it appears in *Manning's Yacht Register*—is the 27'6" x 10'7" x 2'3" centerboard sloop *Reverie* launched in 1878. Notes indicate the boat was altered to a keel in 1882 but converted back to its original configuration six years later.

Smith's timing in the move to Patchogue, where his Amity Street house still stands, was just about perfect. While Smith was getting established, a dramatic change was underway in the sport of sailing. Amateur yachtsmen—middle- and upper-class professionals who styled themselves "Corinthians"—were buying and sailing their own boats. This trend, which started after the Civil War, picked up steam in the 1870s, and really took off during the next two decades. In 1881, Gil Smith received from a Patchogue resident a commission to build a 29' catboat with a 12' beam, 3'3" draft, and a summer cabin. A similar boat was soon ordered by another customer. Smith now moved across the Patchogue River and established his own boatyard on the eastern side next to the thriving Bailey Lumber Yard, which would, among other things, supply the woodwork for decades' worth of New York brownstones.

Although the shop Smith built eventually grew to be about 50' wide and 300' long, he never brought electricity into the building. There was, however, a finished second floor at the eastern end. There, Smith installed the sewing machine on which his wife would, for years, sew the boats' sails. During the lead-up to spring launchings, Mariam hired a housekeeper to help with chores. In this shop, beginning in 1881–1882, Gil Smith began crafting the boats that would make him famous. The locals, recognizing the level of work performed within, dubbed the Smith boatyard, "the piano shop."

Gil Smith employed a variously sized crew of three to ten men, depending on workload. The crew included son Asa, but those familiar with the family recalled that father and son were incompatible. For years, Asa worked as a butcher and grocer, which allowed him to better care for a daughter afflicted with one of the scourges of that era, polio. It is likely, however, that Asa always spent some time during the week or weekend at the boatyard. Although he lacked his father's genius for design, Asa was acknowledged by Gil for his joinery skills and as "the best" varnish man he'd ever seen.

The Smiths' move to Patchogue placed them in the epicenter of a development boom. The Long Island Railroad was a big factor in, and promoter of, development on the island's South Shore. What's more, the people who were coming out to Long Island from the city to live or to build big summer estates were a lucrative mix of professionals with money to spend, and really upper-crust Gilded Age folks with money to spare. Smith's list of patrons would soon include bank presidents, men who were "big" in railroads and insurance, the heads of the Cutex Nail Polish Company and of Singer Sewing Machines, a department store owner, and manufacturers of everything from paper to flour. William K. Vanderbilt had Smith build him a teak-topped float for his waterfront estate.

Smith built a 26' catboat for his own use in 1897 and named it after his wife. *Mariam* immediately caught the eye of Charles G. Hedge, then a railroad vice president and treasurer with offices on Wall Street. He bought the boat as a $650 (about $23,000 today) gift for his own wife and renamed it *Sweetheart*. Once moved to the Hedge's Westhampton summer place, *Sweetheart* promptly defeated two older Smith catboats.

Despite his success, Smith never changed his lifestyle. He went to the shop each day dressed in blue overalls and a bicycle cap, and he worked from 7 a.m. until dark. Those who stopped by regularly all remembered that Smith never ceased work to engage in conversation. The wealthiest of his customers knew him to be a businessman who was as straight as one of his beautifully crafted, hollow masts. Said one of these millionaires to Gil Smith: "When I do business with you, I never pay more than other people, but that is not true with many builders."

After a time, Smith came to be known by townspeople and customers alike as "Boss Smith" or "Cap'n Gil."

The number of boats Smith built is unknown. One lifelong admirer guessed 400. Although he kept ledgers of sorts, Smith himself said he never really counted his output and, when daughter Jennie once asked him, he responded that he had "no idea." What is certain about Cap'n Gil is that, although he occasionally told friends that he was at work on his last boat, he never intended to willingly retire. He was certainly hard at work at age ninety-two when, in the winter of 1935, he suffered a stroke. He recovered enough to return to the shop, but his great gifts had been taken. Asa would carefully check such work as his father did each day, and tidy up as necessary. Gil Smith died shortly after midnight in May 1940, two months before his ninety-seventh birthday. Asa then took over.

The Keepers of the Flame

"Did you ever notice," asked *The Rudder* in an 1898 article about Gil Smith's latest boat, "how localities have certain men who stand out prominently above their fellow beings?" It is fair to say that the sailboat-oriented men of Long Island's South Shore, living in the midst of a number of very capable boatbuilders, took special note of Gil Smith early on, and some do so even today. These are the keepers of the Smith flame. They are men like Roger Dunkerley, former director of the Suffolk Marine Museum (now the Long Island Maritime Museum). The museum was founded in the mid-1960s through the efforts of a group that included, among others, the inimitable marine artist and writer Hervey Gerrett Smith. Dunkerley worked diligently for years with his trustees to preserve remaining Gil Smith boats and supporting materials. On display, among other boats, is Roger's own *Lorelei*, a 25' catboat built in 1915. Roger (and subsequent owners) wisely resisted "slooping" *Lorelei*, thus managing to preserve almost intact what is probably the most original surviving example of Smith's work.

There was the late Tom Madigan, a retired naval commander and expert on Smith's design and construction methods. There is Ralph Carpentier, who found and helped restore for the East Hampton Town Marine Museum the Smith catboat *Senad*, which was missing its transom at the time after having been transformed into a launch. There is Bob Schultz, who acquired a then-leaky Smith R-boat in the 1960s, refurbished it, and remains seriously under the Smith spell even today. There was Paul W. Bigelow who, as a boy of six or seven, went with his father to Smith's shop and would grow up to own

Smith boats and write a credible article honoring the builder. And there were others, like Capt. Corwin, now long passed. Responding to an article on Smith in *Yachting* in 1942, Grayson Lynn named a half-dozen true believers, including Horace Havemeyer, heir to a vast sugar fortune. Lynn opined that Smith "was to boatbuilding what Chippendale was to furniture."

Now, there is Al Terry. A World War II merchant mariner who served on Liberty and Victory ships, Al returned from the Pacific to settle in Bay Port. Al Terry's nominal job was as a Pan Am flight engineer, but his real passion, aside from his family, was the study of everything and anything related to Gil Smith. He became the owner of a succession of Smith boats, which he methodically rebuilt, and then went on to assist others in their projects. He would consult with Barry Thomas, Maynard Bray, and John Gardner on the construction at Mystic of a new 21'6" catboat based on Smith's *Pauline*, built in 1897.

Later, when educator and Apprenticeshop creator Lance Lee fell under *Senad*'s spell—"My fascination began with the aesthetics"—Al Terry became an integral part of building a new version. They named *Madigan* for the man all involved had come to respect, enthusiast Tom Madigan, who passed away when the boat was partly completed. Terry also helped develop the molds for a fiberglass version of the catboat *Moonbeam*, originally built in 1909 (Class B champ in 1910).

Today, on the tree-screened property where Al lives with his wife Louise, the evidence of Gil Smith is everywhere. Al still has the old and much-deteriorated 23' sloop *Melody*, an artfully finished fiberglass replica of *Moonbeam*, and a second, unfinished *Moonbeam* hull. The admittedly dilapidated remains of the R-class sloop *Pauline* reside in the family greenhouse. (This R-class, as with the P-class, was local.) A piece of oak Gil Smith had once salted by leaving in the water at his yard now dangles from a tree in the Terry yard. "It's a reminder," says Al, "to people who don't know about such things."

After a lifetime involved in Gil Smith, Al Terry is still left wondering "how, out of nothing, came these beautiful objects? The beauty," Al Terry has long since concluded, "is in the form." He thinks of Smith as one of three great artists of design. The other two? George Steers and L. Francis Herreshoff.

The Boats

In the most general terms, it might be said of Gil Smith's boats that all were centerboard types; none had more than one mast, and all were gaff-rigged. (The marconi rig for the Smith R-boats was first developed by New Rochelle

Built in 1909 and B-class champion in 1910, *Moonbeam* was meticulously crafted to Smith's high standards and was still providing good sport for her owners in 1939. It was typical for Great South Bay catboats to sail reefed given the locally strong breeze. (Author's collection courtesy of Al Terry Jr.)

naval architect K. B. Sharpe after Cap'n Gil had suffered his stroke.) Smith is, perhaps, most often associated with catboats, which he turned out in great quantity for racing in B (21'6"), BB (25'6"), and AA (28') classes, together with larger (up to 50') daysailing/bay-cruising-oriented models. Many had removable benches, and taking these out was part of each Saturday's race preparation ritual.

The larger boats were typically fitted with a removable summer cabin with fabric side curtains that could be rolled up or lowered as the weather dictated. With their low freeboard, comparatively narrow beam, and underhung rudders, these catboats were quite different in conception from a typical Cape Cod type with its heavier construction, higher freeboard, stone or lead ballast, solid spars, and barn-door rudders. As the Cape Cod cat was conceived for its native waters, the Smith boats were products of their own environment, the shallow, protected waters of the local bays. "They go like the devil and are wetter than the devil," wrote Eugene Connett in his book about a lifetime of Great South Bay cruising.

Despite his reputation as a catboat builder, Smith built many sloops. *Painte II*, for example, was a fifty-footer built in 1904 and offered for sale three years later for the impressive sum of $4,500 (about $150,000 today). In 1905 Smith built a forty-nine-footer with 5'6" of headroom and a 44'6" mast. Al Terry still clearly remembers examining an elegant 50' daysailer named *Iris*—"Not a butt block in the whole boat!" *Iris*'s owner, fearful that his boat's beautiful transom would be defiled should a subsequent owner install an engine, stipulated that *Iris* be destroyed upon his death. She was.

Smith built five P-class sloops, a type originated around 1910. These yachts were, at 33' to 44' on deck, the largest racing boats on Great South Bay. Smith's *Pelican* was an early example, but those who sailed aboard *Constance* and *Edna* engaged in a spirited debate about which of the pair was the finest boat ever built by Cap'n Gil.

Launched circa 1928, the 39' *Edna* was the last boat built by Gil Smith. He was eighty-five at the time. The beautiful *Edna* was a centerboard sloop designed for the local P-class. *Edna*: 38' x 23'6" x 9'6" x 3'3" (board up) (Author's collection courtesy of Al Terry Jr.)

In common with most nineteenth-century builders, Smith never produced any formal drawings, and all lines that survive were taken by others. Smith's boats began as beautifully carved half models, usually two pieces of pine with a thin piece of mahogany to denote the waterline. These models, built to a scale of 1" = 1', typically have five precisely scribed vertical stations on the back. Smith used these stations to reproduce the hull shape on his molds which, no doubt, were faired as he deemed necessary.

According to Al Terry and others who have diligently searched for evidence of some "mechanical device used to take off lines," nothing has ever been discovered. Because no one, not even the keepers of the flame, thought to ask Cap'n Gil or Asa about the lofting process, a certain mystery will forever remain attached to its particulars and to the question of where Smith first learned his method.

The form of Gil Smith's boats slowly evolved over time. Reporting for *The Rudder* in 1897, designer George Farragut Massa noted that "the only apparent change that has taken place within the last ten years is the lengthening of the overhanging sterns. At first they had what is called a 'fan-tail' stern, where the transom is raked under at a sharp angle and came to a point to the rudder post. But now the overhangs run out from four to six feet." Lines taken by Massa from *Lucile* (1891) reveal notably less overhang than that of the later boats like *Mariam* (1897).

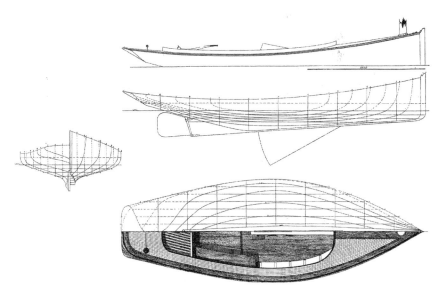

A typical Gil Smith beauty—*Lucile*'s lines show the plumb stem and upswept, graceful stern typical of Smith's nineteenth-century work. *Lucile*: 21'6" x 17'9" x 7' x 1'9" board up. Sail area 343 sq. ft. (*The Rudder*, January 1897)

The shape of the bow also evolved. Compared to 1893's *Lucile* with her vertical stem, *Mariam* has a shorter stem, rounded and with a cutaway forefoot. *Gay B*, designed in 1925, reveals the ultimate expression of the spoon or overhanging bow that Smith began to use and refine about 1901. It was often referred to then as a Herreshoff bow or, in the South Shore vernacular, a "Herrescuffler."

"The sweep of the sheer is now more balanced," says Al Terry of these twentieth-century boats. "We no longer see the big, high bow and very low transom of the plumb-stemmed models. The transom is deepened somewhat and the quarters thickened to further improve initial stability, and the maximum beam moved aft somewhat to increase displacement there."

Like Smith's other catboats, *Mariam*'s modest deadrise (less than on the earlier *Lucile*) and rather hard bilge must have produced a good sail carrier, of special importance since these low-sided open boats carried no fixed ballast. "For ballast," reported *The Rudder*, "they carry clean white beach pebbles under their floors and in bags. These beach pebbles make excellent ballast, as they do not cut the planking or cause the boat to leak or lose sand as she is bound to do in time." Good initial stability was important in a boat like the 26'4" *Mariam* that carried a 536-sq.-ft. sail with three sets of reefpoints. Gil Smith himself was known to carry too much sail in heavier air, diminishing his chance of leading a race.

Using only the finest stock available to him in an era of top-quality timber, Smith planked the boats with Port Orford cedar, which he always called "Washington cedar." Plank stock was obtained from Bailey's in lengths necessary to eliminate butt blocks. Longleaf yellow pine was used for garboards and sheerstrakes, and hazelwood was also used sometimes for the latter. Sawn oak frames were typical before the turn of the century, although alternating steam-bent frames appeared later. Cypress was used often for decks. Honduras mahogany and cherry were used for coamings and trim.

As Smith sought annually to produce faster shapes—typically slightly modifying later boats built from an earlier half model—he also devoted himself to weight reduction for race-oriented clients. Al Terry believes that when curved stems became typical on Smith's racing boats, the builder switched from a traditional keel backbone to one made from a lighter, steam-bent plank to which the deadwood was attached with dowels. On these race-oriented boats, iron nails were used to fasten the planks to the sawn frames, but copper rivets were used on the steam-bent frames, little concern being expressed by owners for the mixing of fastenings. More extreme weight-reduction measures were also taken. Said Al Terry: "The smaller boats had no floor timbers or horn timber. Most had no bilge stringers. The sheer clamp was small in dimension. Decks could be narrow cedar strips nailed to light-weight beams. Spruce spars were, of course, hollow."

How did Smith achieve his signature tumblehome in the topside plank? Al Terry noted, after much study of boats that survived with original construction features intact, that "the sheerstrake was key. The frames back aft were notched for the sheerstrake, which was then given its final shape with a drawknife or spokeshave. The covering board aft continues the tumble."

The end result of Smith's labors was a hull with features that were immediately distinct from the work of other designers. The boats were beautifully finished, most often with white topsides and varnished decks, coamings, and spars. Sometimes, an owner would opt for a black hull. We know that *Lucile*'s cedar planking was painted black and that a gilt covestripe was cut in just below the deck. The cove ended in a scroll on the tumblehome aft. Her cypress decks, hazelwood coaming, seats, and centerboard trunk were all varnished. What a sight she must have been!

As the nature of Smith's skills became known to naval architects in Manhattan, he received contracts to construct several big sloops designed by Cox and Stevens. In 1908, Smith was awarded the contract to build the Sonder (Special) class yacht *Joyette* to a design by Charles Mower to compete in the 1909 edition of a Germany vs. America race series that had begun in 1906. With her designer tending the jib sheets and her builder watching, *Joyette* went on to win that year's event off Marblehead—the Taft Cup.

Measurers came to Patchogue to check the 37' *Joyette*'s dimensions. "Why," said one of them in amazement, "she doesn't vary more than 1/4" in any dimension." Gil Smith, who predictably had not interrupted his work to chitchat with his visitors, simply asked, "Why should she?"

The Legacy

One day in the late 1950s or early 1960s, it occurred to some keepers of the flame to ask why Howard Chapelle had not written up the work of Gil Smith. Chapelle's answer suggested a lack of time, but the fact is that Chapelle was always focused on working craft rather than yachts. Still, he did urge the donation to the Smithsonian of several representative Smith half models.

In 1964, Smith's daughter Jennie sent three half models to Chapelle. These were a 24'6" plumb-stemmed catboat carved in 1890 and the basis for *Senad*, *Bess*, and—in 1897—*Naiad*, the 1906 model for the P-boat *Kid* (named for Jennie), and an undated but possibly 1907 model for the AA catboat *Adelaide II*. Ultimately, the models did not find permanent display and interpretation in the National Watercraft Collection. They were later loaned to the Long Island Maritime Museum where they are now displayed. Another major collection of Smith models may be seen at the Suffolk County Historical Society in Riverhead.

What is far more surprising than the absence of Smith in Chapelle's publications is his alarming omission from the work of yachting historian W. P. Stephens. The latter's sole reference to a Great South Bay catboat in *Traditions & Memories of American Yachting* was an illustration of the twenty-three-footer used by C. P. Kunhardt for a trip from New York to North Carolina and back during 1885–1886. Kunhardt noted that his boat, with a rather clumsily wide transom, was built in Patchogue, but did not attribute a builder.

Thanks to the keepers of the flame, however, quite a bit more of Gil Smith's work survives than that of his contemporaries. For comparison's sake, one need think only of what's left regarding Charles C. Hanley, the New England genius of shoal-draft yachts. We have only half models, Hanley's broadaxe, and photographs. By comparison, the surviving Smith boats, half models, and biographical information represent a bounty of information, although the conservation and interpretation of Smith materials in recent years has not been all one could desire. And then there are the two recreations. The first was Mystic Seaport's *Anitra*, based on lines taken from *Pauline*, a largely original 21'6" B-class catboat built in 1895 and loaned to Mystic by Roger Dunkerley and his trustees. "Thankfully we got a good example of Smith's work!" said Al Terry when that boat was completed.

Neither did Hanley have a devotee like Lance Lee, whose passion and persuasion resulted in the funding to build the stunning 25'6" *Senad*, the second recreation. The plans, drawn by naval architect David Dillion, note support for the project provided by the National Trust for Historic Preservation.

As this is written, the Long Island Maritime Museum is replicating the shape—as interpreted by Edson Schock—if not the construction techniques, of a Mystic Seaport plumb-stemmed catboat attributed to Smith. The plan is to complete the boat on the National Mall at the 2004 Smithsonian Folklife Festival.

What, in the end, are we to make of Gil Smith? He was a very smart, self-taught designer who learned from observation and slowly but steadily evolved hull shapes that made his boats the ones to beat. He was a self-taught builder who created his own construction methods using a variety of woods as he deemed appropriate. He was one of a great many very capable nineteenth-century boatbuilders, most now long forgotten while Smith's reputation has long outlived him. That said, it was a reputation made, nurtured, and remembered primarily in a highly localized area. As the last keepers of the flame pass on, maintaining Smith's legacy could become precarious.

It might be noted, finally, that Smith never bowed to demands to adapt himself and his boats to the internal-combustion engine. He installed not a single engine in one of his sailboats and may have built, perhaps under the pressure of his family, a lone, now long-forgotten motorboat. At some point around his eightieth year, Gil Smith built himself a garage and bought a Chevrolet to go in it. He proceeded to pretty much demolish the garage with his new car, and it wasn't long before the dangerous Chevy was parked more or less permanently.

The story is told, by Al Terry, of a visiting artist who knew nothing of boats but was entranced nonetheless by the shape of the Gil Smith hull in Terry's shop. The curves, the tumblehome, the overhang, the look of the stem—everything seemed to come together for this witness to Smith's work. "What this is," recognized the perceptive if lubberly artist, "is sculpture."

This story appeared in *WoodenBoat* No. 177, March/April 2004.

"LIKE A FISH IN A BASKET OF SAWDUST"

Winfield M. Thompson, Reporter and Sailor

Historians, no matter what their subject, are always on the lookout for reliable, primary source material. For anyone interested in American yachting during the late nineteenth and early twentieth century, the work of newspaperman and sailor Winfield Thompson is an important resource. Thompson was a professional reporter who had a natural instinct for his craft. He knew what questions to ask and always sought factual accuracy. These qualities are all too often lost in today's helter-skelter efforts to rush stories onto the internet or television in what now passes too often for reporting.

When it came to sailing, Thompson was covering matters with which he had personal familiarity and some expertise. He was an enthusiastic small boat owner with a particular love for catboats but a more general interest in anything related to yachting whether small sailboats, the then new-fangled gasoline engine, or the *America*'s Cup.

In the many years I have studied Thompson's work, I have come to value him as a reliable source and, ultimately, as a colleague and pal. The experiences he shared regarding his catboats, his motorboat, his useful little pram, will quickly endear him to any sailor today or in the future.

Writers, of course, are particularly quick to notice a well-turned phrase, a nicely constructed paragraph, the lyricism that emerges in the work of those who know and love the English language. Winfield Thompson's writing, based on his love for small boats and his knowledge of such important matters as when it's time to reef or to slack a catboat's peak halyard, reflects all of those qualities.

"For this book I selected a writer, my collaborator, Mr. Winfield M. Thompson, the product of whose pen in yachting and other fields of literature was a guarantee not only of graceful thoroughness but of a conscientious adherence to facts and all men's rights."

—Thomas W. Lawson, introduction to
The Lawson History of the America's *Cup*, 1902

One June day in 1891, a twenty-two-year-old advertising representative for Joseph Pulitzer's *New York World* arrived in the bustling little upstate city of Watertown, home to, among many other businesses, a popular variety store owned by Frank W. Woolworth. The man from the *World* was named Winfield Thompson. As he began making his rounds through "the Garland City"— so called because of the red, white, and blue bunting that decorated many buildings—Thompson had no idea that his visit would eventually have a far wider impact than the ads he sold.

"In the course of my stay in Watertown," he wrote nearly four decades later, "I called on almost every business house in town." One of those "houses" was a manufacturer of marine hardware where Thompson encountered a "spare young man, with a shock of curly black hair" named Thomas Fleming Day. Seeing Day standing next to a bench piled high with cleats, blocks, and other equipment, Thompson volunteered that he himself had grown up in a seafaring family. He once described his background and how it influenced him like this: "My people were sailors and fishermen for generations, and as a lad I saw enough of sailorizing as a business to convince me that it was not the life for me. The sailor by profession gets small joy out of his business. The amateur sailor, who goes afloat for fun, generally gets what he goes after, and I am happy to be one such."

Such a fellow was bound to gain Day's interest. Then thirty years old, Thomas Fleming Day possessed an overwhelming passion for small boats and yachts of every sort and especially for democratizing the sport of sailing. Not only had he begun publishing a magazine called *The Rudder* in New York City in May 1890, but he admitted to Thompson that he'd been discussing with a Watertown bank, purchasing a "liability in the form of a small publication called THE *RUDDER, Sail and Paddle*." Apparently after very little deliberation, Day acquired the struggling magazine and, that fall, the two publications were merged.

As for Thompson's impressions of Day, he later recalled that "I found in him a peculiarly attractive personality, unlike any I had hitherto encountered [but] after that casual meeting, I saw little of Day for some years." In fact, it would be a decade before Thompson and *The Rudder*'s visionary creator would have anything more than passing contact. Yet, as things developed, that chance meeting in Watertown would prove to be a great day for yachtsmen of that era, and for those of generations to come.

Southport, Maine, is connected to the Boothbay region by a short bridge. These days, except for traffic, it's an easy drive but in December of 1869, when Winfield Martin Thompson was born at Southport, the village was remote and oriented to the sea. In 1871, ice wrecked the little bridge and for the next twenty-five years, only a ferry connected Southport to the mainland. Winfield was one of six children of John Thompson, a fisherman. He attended the local school, worked in a sardine cannery, a hotel, and cut ice in the winter. His first real experience at sea occurred in 1884 when he briefly joined a steam tug whose cook had become ill. Then, probably in March 1885, with ten dollars in his pocket, sixteen-year-old Winfield Thompson signed aboard a schooner carrying lime in order to get to Boston. There he worked ten-hour days in a leather warehouse and attended evening classes for a period of three or four years, earning the equivalent of a high-school education. That achievement behind him, Thompson found the stress of long workdays and evening study had so weakened his health that he was forced to go home to recover.

In the summer after his return to Southport, Thompson met the owners of the *Gardiner Daily News* who were vacationing just off Boothbay on Capitol Island. That chance meeting shaped the course of Thompson's life. He became the local correspondent for the *News* and parlayed that into assignments from papers in Auburn and Waterville. In 1889 and 1890, he published the *Squirrel Island Squid* for the summer residents of that Boothbay area island, before becoming editor of the *Free Press* in Rockland. Thompson then moved to the *New York World* in 1891, and later the *New York Press*.

All this was prelude. In 1895, Winfield Thompson got a job as reporter at the *Boston Daily Globe* whose editors challenged him with a fascinating variety of assignments that he handled with lively curiosity and graceful prose. Sent to Cuba to cover the Spanish-American War, Thompson filed articles untainted by the near-fictional accounts for which that "splendid little war" became known. When he wasn't writing for the newspaper, Thompson produced stories about local history for *New England Magazine* and *Harper's* and wrote *In the Maine Woods*, a book still recognized today for its importance in the state's travel literature. In 1912, Thompson covered the *Titanic* sinking and, in the process, became the first reporter to accurately record the full extent of the casualties.

At some point early in his career, Thompson was named the *Globe's* yachting editor, a post that carried with it a measure of importance beyond what one might today guess. Harking back to the *America*'s Cup races of 1885, photographer Nathaniel L. Stebbins—known to Thompson and his contemporaries simply as "N. L."—noted that "the whole country was interested in *Puritan*, and Boston was as proud of her as if everybody in the city owned a share of her. . . . Everybody was out to see the new yacht."

By the early 1900s, yacht racing was undergoing both social and technical change, but big-time events remained very newsworthy. The yachting editor was expected to deliver timely and insightful stories. International contests like the German-American series that began in 1906, mixing sport with statecraft, and the *America*'s Cup in particular, were big news. As for Thompson, covering yachting in addition to his other assignments kept him a very busy man, but he was earning a solid, middle-class income, and he wasn't doing it by hazardous professional "sailorizing."

In 1899, a wealthy Boston stock investor and manipulator of copper shares named Thomas William Lawson had an epiphany and decided to enter the world of yachting. He bought a sixty-three-foot steam yacht in 1898, commissioned a 148-footer in 1899 and then, in 1900, decided to build a potential defender for the 1901 *America*'s Cup races. Lawson, a carpenter's son from Charlestown, determined that a locally organized campaign independent of the all-powerful New York Yacht Club was the right of every American citizen. The result was the B. B. Crowninshield–designed *Independence* and an abortive Cup effort that raised eyebrows and hackles. Refusing to enroll in the NYYC, Lawson instead joined the local Hull Yacht Club, and *Independence* thereafter flew the HYC's burgee and Lawson's private signal, a white bear on a blue field.

At the time she was launched by Lawley's on May 18, 1901, *Independence* represented a revolutionary conception. The 140' x 24' yacht was of composite metal construction, with nickel-steel frames, bronze plating, a steel upper strake, an aluminum deck, and eighty tons of lead ballast. Ninety feet on the waterline, *Independence* had a "scow-like" bottom with little deadrise and a fin keel with a draft of twenty feet. In practice, Lawson's boat didn't live up to expectations. There was simply not enough engineering knowledge extant to verify that the boat's scantlings were sufficient, and they weren't. Immediate and drastic steering gear failures were followed by structural issues and very serious leaks. What's more, the keel had been located improperly. *Independence* was hopelessly imbalanced.

The fact that he had failed to compel the New York Yacht Club to admit *Independence* to the official trial races for Cup defense only added salt to Lawson's wounds. As a response, he determined to underwrite a book about the Cup in general and his experience in particular. Nobody would do to write the book, Lawson declared, except the yachting editor of the *Boston Daily Globe.*

"He sent for me and offered a considerable sum to write for him a history of the *America*'s Cup," Thompson recalled years later. "He wanted the book put under his name as author, but I would not agree to that, and we compromised at last on the title *The Lawson History of the* America's *Cup*, with my name on the title page as author, and a few chapters, written by Mr. Lawson, separately titled."

In fact, Lawson gave Thompson free reign to write the overall history of the Cup and told Thompson to "forget my personal interest in the book. . . . I do not want to know what you write." Three thousand copies were printed at Lawson's expense in the winter of 1902. Bound in thick white leather with gold stamping, the book was embellished by beautiful typography, line drawings, and evocative sketches and color plates created by yachting artist William G. Wood. In September 1902, the *New York Times* called the *Lawson History* "the most elaborate and detailed history of the struggle for the blue ribbon of the sea now extant." For his part, Thompson claimed the book was "no more than a glorified piece of hack work. . . . But I had put into it a good deal of research."

In fact, the research Thompson undertook was likely unprecedented for such an endeavor. Although Thompson minimized his effort, no doubt because he accepted a considerable sum from Lawson, the book, as all good books should, spoke for itself. Thomas Fleming Day was so impressed that he promptly signed up Thompson to write an article about the yacht *America*. When the story appeared in 1902, it presaged a steady stream that continued for the next twelve years.

These articles in *The Rudder* (and later in *Yachting*) read today almost as if Thompson knew the sorts of questions that a curious sailor of his own time or a researcher of a later era might ask. While he always presented the big picture, Thompson peppered his writing with wonderful detail that now provides us with unusual insights. Thus, when he wrote about the keel schooner *Northern Light*, built in 1839, he included not only the yacht's color scheme—black with cream decks and green trim—but even details of America's first ever "yachting costume" devised by owner William P. Winchester to protect his guests' shore clothes. It consisted of "red flannel shirt, white trousers and straw hat, with a ribbon around the crown made of cream-colored China silk." From historic yachts to portraits of yachting towns and sailing directions on how to reach them, to descriptions of the planned Cape Cod Canal to the history of the Isles of Shoals, Winfield Thompson covered the waterfront.

The following words appeared in Thompson's "Catboats—a New England Product," published in the *Globe* on June 5, 1904.

As one would expect of a writer, Thompson began his search for the motor for his planned powerboat by extensive reading. This charming little drawing, one of several that appeared in part III of the "Flirting with Gasolene" series in *The Rudder*, is a good representation of Win Thompson, a balding, bespectacled man of just under average height. The catboat picture on the wall hints at Thompson's favorite boat type. (*The Rudder*)

> The catboat sailor has but one sheet to handle and no masthead runners, backstays or other rigging. . . . Should he want to reef, or lower his sail, he has the halliards ready at hand in the cockpit. . . . No boat of her inches can hold on longer in a gale, or go through rougher water on the sinister shoals of the cape . . . than the native cat.

The story was based on a trip to the Crosby boat shops in Osterville, Massachusetts. At the time of his visit, Thompson was seriously considering buying a catboat. He had previously—1895–1897—owned a Crosby catboat but had been without a boat of his own since. Unfortunately for Thompson,

Here is Thompson's 25' Crosby catboat *Twister* grounded out for maintenance at his cottage in Southport, Maine, in 1913. It was a dream of Thompson's to have his catboat moored off the village where he'd been born. (Author's collection)

in 1904, a bad stock investment erased his boat money and it was not until he recovered a year later that his plans were back on track. Then, he examined a variety of knockabout sloops and a yawl or two but, finding nothing to his liking, he made another trip to Osterville. There, in the early spring of 1905, he bought a brand new twenty-five-footer from Daniel Crosby. He settled on that size boat because, as he wrote in "A Catboat Sailor's Yarn" in the April 1906 issue of *The Rudder*, anything bigger would have been "too much boat for one man to handle under all conditions."

Thus began Winfield Thompson's very public love affair with the Cape Cod catboat. Now, Thompson began recording what would forever remain the single best contemporary source for everything having to do with a still popular boat type that had, by 1906, enjoyed immense popularity for both work and pleasure for at least fifty years. Every word that Thompson wrote on this fascinating subject is infused with either accurate historical information or practical advice.

Upon first acquaintance, he wrote that his new boat's rig "looked larger than I had expected, although it was in fact moderate, there being but [*sic!*] 575 feet in the sail. I might mention here that as the season advanced both rig and boat shrunk with acquaintance." He learned how to use the barn-door rudder "as an effectual check" on the boat's momentum, how to safely jib, how to take up on the topping lift and settle the throat and peak halyard to make "a bag" of the sail and send "the boat flying downwind."

When he needed a tender to the catboat, Thompson presented his quest in terms that a typical reader of *The Rudder* could identify with. "I found I was traveling the same road as the average yachtsman of my kind," he wrote. "I had seen safe tenders for small boats; but they were nearly as large as the boats themselves. Also they cost much money." Having had experience with several inadequate skiffs, Thompson designed a seven-and-a-half-foot pram based on a Monhegan fisherman's punt. He asked designer Norman Skene to draw the little boat's lines and published them in *The Rudder* in an infor-mation-packed article titled "A Successful Small Tender." To the delighted surprise of skeptics accustomed to tenders half again as long, the Wee Pup proved to be both practical and fun.

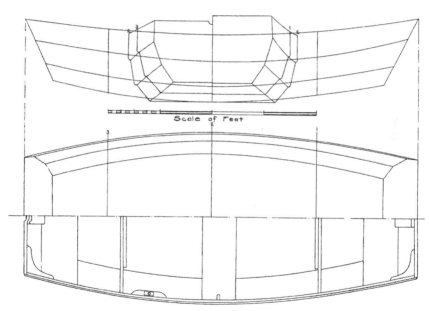

Basing the design on punts he had seen at Monhegan Island, Thompson sized his 7'6" *Wee Pup* pram to fit across the cockpit of his 25' Crosby catboat. The boat proved to be a good load carrier that towed easily. These lines were taken off the boat by naval architect Norman Skene and published in *The Rudder* in January 1906. (*The Rudder*)

Considering his transparent love for *Twister*, it might seem surprising that Thompson sold the boat in January 1907, although the reason would not be unfamiliar. "I was taking on myself the cares and joys of a suburban houseowner," Thompson wrote, "boating was one of the closed chapters in my life. . . . I saw myself chasing a small white sphere over the sward of one of the country clubs of the section in which I had chosen to erect my roof-tree."

The "section" in which Thompson built was Waban, a village in the town of Newton, a relatively easy commute into Boston by public transportation. The cash raised by *Twister*'s sale paid for the lot on which the home was built in 1907 or 1908. The house, at 121 Avalon Rd., featured a skylight salvaged from the derelict schooner *Ramona*, once owned by Civil War general Ben Butler.

There is more to this story than Thompson ever shared in print. In April 1901, Winfield Thompson had married Inez Bearce who'd been born in Lewiston, Maine, in 1871. Inez herself had aspirations as a writer. She had a few short stories published and a few news articles on the arts and drama in the *Globe*. Never once, however, does Thompson mention his wife in connection with sailing, and it is possible that Inez fell into that ever problematic category of spouses who bear an antipathy to boats. Later, Thompson would write "that marriage changes [a man's] boating policy."

Looking back on this period in an article in *The Rudder* in April 1911, he recalled it as a time when "the builder got all my money. I dug in the garden, played a little golf, walked down to the yacht clubhouse [This was the Boston Yacht Club, then actually in Boston before moving to Marblehead.] once in awhile and felt like a fish in a basket of sawdust, cussed a little at my stupidity in parting with *Twister*, went home and tried to forget it. But I just couldn't forget it." Thompson never warmed up to golfing. What's more, it is likely that other conflicts existed in the Thompson marriage besides possible disagreements about boats. The couple took the then comparatively unusual step of divorcing.

Thompson now bought a double-ended Lawley knockabout named *Jester*. Knockabouts, he soon discovered, had little more appeal to him than golf and, in 1910, Thompson bought another catboat. This one was a twenty-two-footer built by Charles C. Hanley during the winter of 1891–1892. Thompson described this splendid boat in "I Buy an Old Cat," published in *The Rudder* in April 1911. In this article, Thompson discussed an odd phenomenon that had emerged and would persist. "Ever notice how keen most chaps are to give an old catboat a bad name?" Thompson asked. He then proceeded to demonstrate that critics of the type invariably lacked personal experience on which to base their comments and were merely voicing hearsay.

Thompson shared important details about C. C. Hanley based on interviews with the builder, recounted *Duster*'s history, discussed the unfortunate tendency among some to add bowsprits and jibs to catboats, and detailed his hunt for a leak. Among the fascinating and typically Thompson tidbits was a comment regarding how *Duster* compared with his Crosby-built *Twister*. Of *Duster*, he wrote: "It was a genuine pleasure to steer her, after handling *Twister*, which was always strong headed [exhibiting excessive weather helm when off the wind]. . . . I may say that every man who handled *Duster* in the course of the season remarked on her steering. Her balance was perfect." Here we have contemporary reporting verifying the genius of C. C. Hanley.

Thompson's only serious concern was that *Duster* had been stored with the mast up and no mast coat, and he worried that moisture may have seeped into the wedges. On August 28, 1910, the thirty-two-foot mast snapped at deck level. Thompson wrote that "I had got my money's worth out of *Duster*, oceans of sport, and plenty of good, honest, fat-reducing work." He concluded his article saying that he was budgeting for a new mast for the coming season. This plan, however, changed.

By 1911, the number of marine engine companies in America had burgeoned from perhaps two dozen a decade earlier to hundreds. Any man with his eyes open could see what was happening and, in the October 1911, issue of *The Rudder*, Thompson began a four-part series he called "Flirting with Gasolene." The very first sentence contained a big surprise about Thompson's personal life.

"Wife said: 'We've got to go somewhere with the baby. . . . Besides, you ought to have a real vacation this year,'" is how Thompson began "Flirting with Gasolene." It was the first time he had ever mentioned a wife in any of his boating articles. The reason he mentioned it now is that, in 1909, he had remarried and Mrs. Thompson (Lena) had given birth to a daughter.

At the same time that Thompson received the doctor's bill, a buyer showed up with ready money, and Thompson impulsively sold *Duster*. As soon as he cashed the check, however, Thompson began to suffer pangs familiar to any sailor. "Being catboatless, at once I grew aweary of the land."

The vacation involved a visit to Southport where Thompson owned a waterfront cottage (still standing) built for him by his brother John. There, among his boyhood chums, Thompson was astonished to learn there were no sailboats to be rented. "Blank looks," he wrote, "told me that I spoke of something that belonged to the dead past." Gasoline launches, by contrast, were available for two dollars a day, and Thompson rented a locally built, Lathrop-powered catboat, the rig of which had been removed. The boat belonged to sixty-four-year-old boat builder Ebenezer Decker, a lifelong friend of

148

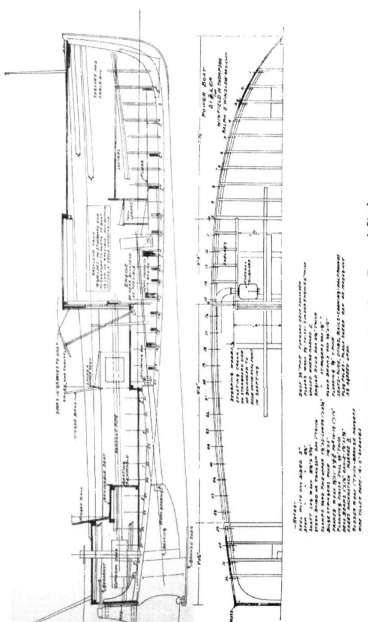

Construction Plans and Scantling Data of Sizzler

The drawings of Thompson's *Sizzler* were made in 1911 by naval architect Ralph Winslow based on Thompson's half-model. A towing bit was provided so Thompson could hitch up any timber that he spotted floating alongshore and bring it home. (Author's collection)

Thompson's who had built the *Wee Pup*. "All you have to do," Decker told Thompson optimistically, "is to turn it over, and it runs until you come home."

Thus began Winfield Thompson's introduction to the internal combustion age. "If anybody was greener than myself when beginning the game I would like to meet him," Thompson wrote. It was typical, at the time, for men to write about their first experience with marine engines in a manner that attempted, and sometimes succeeded, to be humorous. Thompson's approach was to honestly chronicle his travails and let readers decide if they were a source of mirth. "Flirting with Gasolene" is the best single piece ever written on the coming of power and the average man's adaptation to the new technology. With a reporter's eye, Thompson recorded the engines then in use in mid-coast Maine—Lathrop, Knox, Essex, Kennebec, Bridgeport, Palmer, Hartford, and Fairbanks.

"It was not strange that each felt loyal," Thompson noted of Southporters, "to the machine that had seen him through." He described the apparently infinite and sneaky ways in which a make-and-break igniter, vaporizer or carburetor, and batteries and coils could sabotage one's best efforts. He also noted the willingness of every man in Southport to drop everything and rush to the rescue of a fellow with a broken-down motor.

Thompson recognized that a power boat was highly practical "on a coast being much indented by bays and estuaries [where] tides, fickle winds and narrow channels made sailing an uncertain process." As a result, Thompson decided to design a motorboat and have it built by Decker. Thompson carved several half models out of pine blocks that Decker supplied and, when he returned home, he brought the final model to naval architect Ralph Winslow, who lived just south of Boston in Quincy. Winslow took the half model's lines, adjusting them as he judged necessary, and made construction drawings.

Sizzler was a twenty-three-footer powered by a 10-hp, two-cylinder Sterling four-cycle engine selected after much research, a discussion with Tom Day, and endless internal debate about the merits of two-cycle motors vs. four-cycle, different ignition methods, and different brands. Built in Buffalo, New York, the Sterling was a high-grade engine but problems with plumbing and the magneto resulted in a nightmarish six weeks. After that, "with Friend Wife holding down the seat beside me, I had my first uninterrupted ride in the boat."

Thompson seems to have kept *Sizzler* for two seasons before deciding that he really wanted to have a sailboat in Boston. On a cold January day in 1914, Thompson visited yacht broker John Alden and learned, to his delight, that *Twister* was for sale in Plymouth. After his experience with the Hanley-designed *Duster*, Thompson wrote that *Twister* "was not my ideal catboat model, yet it was good enough for what I wanted." Thompson bought

Here is how the Hanley-built *Duster* looked when Thompson bought her. He removed the bowsprit to return the catboat to her original appearance. (Author's collection)

Twister for the second time and began a series called "The Cat That Came Back." In it, he referred to his experience with *Sizzler* as "a misadventure in power-boating" and reported than he'd had letters from men as far away as Durban and Sitka "praying that I stray not from the path of the catboat man."

In 1917, in his twenty-second year at the *Globe*, Winfield Thompson left to become a field agent for the U. S. Shipping Board's recruitment service. Postwar, the Thompsons moved to Whitestone, New York, after Winfield became publicity director for the International Mercantile Company, owner of several steamship companies including the White Star Line of *Titanic* fame.

During the summer of 1920, Thompson covered for the *Globe* the *America*'s Cup races, a contest between Sir Thomas Lipton's *Shamrock IV* and the Herreshoff-designed *Resolute* skippered by Charles Francis Adams. Among his descriptions of *Resolute* was this one: "Every stitch of her canvas was drawing smoothly, every foot of her steel rigging was at the right tension, every man aboard at his station, and her helmsman was as cool at the wheel as if he were steering a little rating boat in a friendly club match off Marblehead Rock."

With that, Thompson's news writing about sailorizing ended. He collaborated on a last book, *The Yacht America*, with the dean of American yachting historians, William P. Stephens, and yachting writer William Swan. Perhaps his final piece dealing with the old days was published in *Yachting* in December 1927. It was Thompson's appreciation of Thomas Fleming Day who had died that August at age sixty-six. In this poetic article, "He Could Read the

Stars," Thompson shared his memories of The Skipper, "a man of simple tastes and manner . . . a philosopher, and a broad one."

In the year following the publication of that article, Thompson and his family departed New York City for the West Coast aboard America's largest steamship, the *California*. This voyage was, essentially, a job transfer. Thompson became field manager for International Mercantile's West Coast subsidiary, the Panama-Pacific company. Thompson remained with the firm until 1932, when he entered an active retirement as a travel writer, did some photography, and assisted Lena in the devoted care of their daughter who, it turned out, suffered from mental retardation. By the time he visited Boston in 1935 to attend a travel writer's conference, Thompson had long since adapted to being a fish in a basket of sawdust. His sailing days were long over and that trip east was his last to New England.

Winfield Thompson died at his home in Los Altos, California, on May 25, 1946, age seventy-six. Although his yachting writing had ended well over a quarter century earlier, it was that work for which Thompson would be remembered. His was a world of schooners and skiffs, *America*'s Cup yachts and catboats. Woven throughout the fabric of his writing was his fascination with old New England, and with the enduring magic of the sea. Who, in his time, but Winfield Thompson could have written about the decline of a once grand schooner as he did in "The Dissolution of *Ramona*" published in *The Rudder* in April 1910? "It was a warm, moist cloudy night in June, with a long old sea heaving in from the bay. . . . Coming aboard at midnight . . . I found the old schooner rolling steadily in the ocean swell, dark as a shadow ship, except for a dim riding light forward. . . . On deck a lone watcher sat on the cabin trunk in the moist dark. The tall spars swept slowly back and forth, describing invisible arcs on the black sky."

Purely Thompson

"Her keel was shaped from an oak stick 56 feet long and 26 inches square. The lead keel was 45 feet long, 2 feet wide and 16 inches deep. The centerboard, of hard pine, with the two upper planks of oak, was 22 feet long, 11 feet deep and 4 inches thick ... The main cabin was 16 by 12 feet, finished in pine and mahogany with two built-in mahogany buffets, large lounges, and ornamental posts sustaining the deck, carved to resemble ships' cables."

—from *"Puritan* at Twenty-Five," *The Rudder*, March 1910

"When, with a friend along, I steered *Twister* in the glowing twilight into the white company of the pleasure fleet at old Marblehead, cast anchor off the town, and after furling the sail leaned on the boom contemplating in the gathering darkness the twinkling riding lights of many yachts; the illuminated clubhouses on either shore; the shadowy old town with the beacons of electric street lamps showing high on its irregular slopes; the illuminated ferry-landing against the rocky shore; the sound of guitar, songs, laughter and mellow hails carrying far across the water; the shadowy passage of tenders plying to and from the floats; and over all the broad, pale shaft of a searchlight from a great steam yacht outside the fleet, I felt that after all the best gifts of yachting are not all confined to the wet sheet and flowing sea."

—from "A Catboat Sailor's Yarn," *The Rudder*, May 1906

"I found that one painting, of three good coats of lead and oil, was enough to keep the topsides in condition for the season. ... *Twister* was planked with hard pine, a wood that presents hardness of surface and lasting qualities second to none, but which does not hold paint as well as soft pine, cedar or cypress. The latter wood is much favored for planking nowadays by the Osterville builders, and I am inclined to think, for good reason."

—from "The Cat that Came Back," *The Rudder*, 1914

This story appeared in *WoodenBoat* No. 199, November/December 2007.

PART THREE

POWER

CHASING THE *DRAGON*

Recreating a Herreshoff Steam Launch

O ne never knows in what guise boat craziness may assert itself. In this story, it is a long-held fascination with steam engines and the designs of Nathanael Greene Herreshoff that led to the creation of a new steam launch true to the spirit of the original. Those lucky enough to have had a ride in *Dragon*, or to have followed her as she steams silently along, have experienced something very special.

Since this story was written, *Dragon* has, as planned, found her permanent home at the Herreshoff Marine Museum (HMM) in Bristol, Rhode Island. Curator Evelyn Ansel updates the story as follows.

> After the first summer of operating *Dragon* with the help of steam engineer Lloyd Beckmann, the launch has served as a static display in the Hall of Boats at HMM, and occasionally as a travelling ambassador for the museum on a trailer. At present we are not operating the boat on the water, mostly due to preservation concerns, light waterfront staffing and above all the availability of a steam engineer with the necessary expertise and time to attend to *Dragon*'s maintenance and operation. However, we are very glad to be able to display this interesting piece of HMCo's steam history. It has become a key interpretive piece in a chapter of HMCo's history that has not historically been thoroughly told at HMM—largely due to the rarity of original HMCo. steam engines. We are delighted to have this little gem, and for it to continue to be a dynamic element in our ongoing efforts to interpret HMCo's steam story.

As for boatbuilder Doug Park, his work on *Dragon* was followed by another fascinating project, the rebuilding of a Herreshoff S Boat using the original construction plans and newly taken offsets. He's busy now maintaining several Herreshoff twelve-and-a-half-footers, a Concordia Yawl, and other wooden boats.

It is a windless, overcast Massachusetts afternoon in mid-July 2017, and a small party has gathered at a harbor-side house on Marblehead Neck for the christening of a most unusual boat. Singly and in pairs, folks wander down the gangway to the float, where the focal point of the day's activities is tied up, cushioned by several big fenders. It's been a great many years now since a steam launch and a catboat provided transportation from "the Neck" across the harbor to the town itself. Yet on this afternoon the steam launch *Dragon* rocks gently alongside, not too far, in fact, from where the steam ferry of yesteryear used to dock.

Now, an occasional wreath of gray, sweet-smelling smoke puffs up from the shiny stack. Slowly but steadily, the needle of the big pressure gauge on the boiler climbs, passing 30 lbs. and inching its way upward. Going for a ride in this steam launch is not a matter of instant gratification. It is a process.

Occupants of passing boats stare with a mixture of disbelief and delight. When they realize they are seeing an actual, for-real steam engine, it doesn't take long for the inevitable question: "Ahoy there, can we hear the whistle?" As the steam pressure rises, Doug Park, the launch's thirty-four-year-old builder, obliges. A pleasant "toot" emerges with a wisp of steam. Then Park opens the firebox door and adds another foot-long chunk of wood. When the pressure reaches 80 lbs. or so, and a christening dollop of Norwegian aquavit has been poured over the bow, it will be time to take people for rides.

"Well," says Ulf Heide, the prime mover behind the project that resulted in the boat, "is this a screwball idea or what!"

The screwball idea had been percolating for a long time. Among the most enduring memories of Heide's childhood in Kristiansund, Norway, were the ferries that plied the town's busy harbor. "The old ferries," he said, "were beautiful steamboats. They took fifteen to twenty passengers, and a captain ran the boat by himself. Where would we be without steam?"

It was a question the businessman and Massachusetts Institute of Technology–trained inventor never stopped asking. For a time, Heide satisfied his steam passion with a friend who owned a small launch used to navigate the twists and turns of the tidal Essex River, about an hour's drive from Marblehead. He began collecting model steam engines, very fine miniatures each with beautifully cast and machined mechanisms. Looking back now, it seems inevitable that the day would come when Heide would chase his dream of owning a steam launch himself.

It was a dream that caught the attention of Bill Park, a friend of Heide's. "He infected me with his enthusiasm and that model collection of his," is how Bill remembers the day he joined the chase. With Bill came his son, Doug, proprietor of Redd's Pond Boatworks in Marblehead, the only

Here is *Dragon*—a scaled-down replica of an 1882 Herreshoff steamer—as she passes below Fort Sewall in Marblehead Harbor. At the tiller is builder Doug Park. (Stan Grayson)

boatshop in the United States connected by name to a victim of Salem's seventeenth-century witch hysteria, the unfortunate Wilmot "Mammy" Redd.

What would become a convoluted chase for a steam launch went something like this: An initial visit to the Hart Nautical Collections at MIT to look through Herreshoff launch plans reinforced Heide's initial desire to find an old boat to restore rather than build a new one. The team visited Mystic Seaport but found nothing tucked away in the museum's fabled Rossie Mill Building (see *WoodenBoat* No. 237) of the right size and style for restoration, even if the museum would have agreed to permit a restoration. Nor did the annual steam meet at Lake Winnipesaukee or an Internet search turn up a promising candidate.

"Well," Heide remembered, "we couldn't find a derelict or make a deal to restore a museum's boat, so we took a suggestion to go to the Herreshoff Marine Museum in Bristol, Rhode Island, and look at the half models there. It was a good move. I never saw a Herreshoff boat I didn't love."

For anyone who knows and loves boats, being in the presence of Nathanael Greene Herreshoff's half-models for the first time is an unforgettable experience. Now, at the Herreshoff Marine Museum, then-CEO Dyer

Jones took Heide and the Parks directly into the model room. "This was fabulous," Heide said, and the models allowed a close study of their shapes.

In the book *Capt. Nat Herreshoff: The Wizard of Bristol*, L. Francis Herreshoff wrote that his father would "do his modeling at night, after his active day overseeing work in the shipyard was over." This habit was established soon after Nathanael made the decision to leave a good job at the Corliss Steam Engine Company in Providence, Rhode Island, and join his blind older brother, John, in establishing the Herreshoff Manufacturing Company (HMCo.) in 1878. Corliss had initially hired Herreshoff in 1869 as a draftsman, but he also became what today we might call a field engineer, setting up and adjusting customers' new engines. Soon enough, he was designing steam engines.

Stationary and marine steam engines were an early stock-in-trade for the Herreshoff brothers. So were torpedo boats and high-speed launches. Although the company also produced many catboats and some larger sailboats after its establishment, Francis Herreshoff noted that his father "concentrated almost all of his attention on the steam launch and steam yacht between 1870 and 1890." Once, Francis asked a machinist with forty years on the job how he had happened to apply for work at the company. The reply: "As a young man I saw one of the Herreshoff steam launches and I just had to come here to work, and have stayed ever since."

The reason why the goal of finding a restorable old launch—one by Herreshoff in particular—proved so challenging is clarified in the book *Herreshoff: American Masterpieces* (Maynard Bray, Claas van der Linde, and Benjamin Mendlowitz, W.W. Norton & Co., 2017), which noted that of 160 launches that the company built, only eight still exist. That's a 5 percent survival rate, compared with 25 percent for Herreshoff sailboats over 20' LWL and close to 37 percent for smaller sailboats. Why so few launches? As tenders for larger yachts, many were hung in davits and saw intermittent use, so they were continually subject to swelling and drying cycles and also to the stresses of repeated launching and hoisting, including bumping against the mother ship.

Among Herreshoff's early launch half-models was a twenty-two-footer with a 5'3" beam. Francis called this "probably the first attempt at the modern powerboat with flat stern . . . that could be driven at high speed-length ratios without squatting." He noted that Capt. Nat abandoned the model after 1878, because "it is probable that the sharp-bowed launches with wide flat sterns were not good sea boats under all conditions." Subsequent designs aimed at improving all-around performance.

As Heide and the Parks inspected potential candidates carved so long ago by Capt. Nat, it turned out that confronting a whole wall of fascinating half-models built to different scales wasn't the easiest way to select which launch to build. The team then revisited the Hart Nautical Collections where they met again with longtime curator Kurt Hasselbalch. There are some 18,000 archived HMCo. documents at the museum, and Hasselbalch soon produced several plans for consideration. Among these was a launch ordered in 1882 by the U.S. government to be carried aboard the U.S. Fish Commission's *Albatross*. This 234', iron-hulled, twin-screw steam vessel, which also carried a brigantine rig, was the first U.S. ship designed exclusively for oceanographic and fisheries research. Alexander Agassiz, among the most influential marine zoologists of his time, led three Pacific expeditions aboard *Albatross*.

Albatross was outfitted with a 26' whaleboat, an 18' "dingey," a Gloucester dory, and a 17' flat-bottomed "spawn boat" used for seining and "general shore collecting." Two additional boats, the largest, were steamers built by the HMCo. One was described as a 25' steam gig and the other as a twenty-six-footer. The drawings for this latter boat, HMCo. No. 94, were among those that Hasselbalch showed to Heide and the Parks. It was this design, the offsets for which Hasselbalch also produced, that became the basis for Heide's new launch.

Thought to be an improvement over an earlier hull form that Herreshoff had found not entirely satisfactory, this boat's overhanging stern has a curved, raked, wineglass transom above rounded, rather than flattened, aft sections. A false keel gives the hull substantial drag aft. "This false keel protects the prop from accidental grounding and provides a structure to bolt the lower support for the rudder," Doug Park said. The hull retained the sharp bow and proportionally narrow beam of earlier models and thus would be a hull easily driven with modest horsepower.

The only problem with "Steamer 94" was that Heide needed a smaller boat that could be more comfortably tied up at his float. Although Herreshoff himself would have fluently made the needed adjustments to reduce the boat's length to 22' from the original's 26'—he sometimes scaled boats from the same half model up or down—it made good sense to the team to have a naval architect produce the 4' length reduction they envisioned. Marblehead yacht designer Doug Zurn was the man they turned to.

"We had Herreshoff's handwritten offsets," Zurn remembered, "so we could feed them into our software program, which generated specific points, all at specific heights off the waterline and at specific frame spacings." Just as Heide and the Parks had felt the thrill of studying models created by the hands of the master, Zurn, too, felt a connection. "What was exciting is, we're full circle. He had chisels and sandpaper to shape his model. We did it on the computer."

Dragon Specifications

L.O.A.: 22.59'

L.W.L.: 20.56'

Beam (maximum): 6.16'

Beam (waterline): 5.25'

Draft at deepest point of keel: 2.13'

Displacement: 3,494 lbs.

Engine: 1882 Herreshoff manufacture single-cylinder, "simple-expansion," double-acting steam engine with 2 ½" bore and 5" stroke.

Propeller: 16 1/2" x 25" pitch at the periphery/21" pitch at the hub.*

*The prop was cast from a 3-D model based on launch #93's propeller, which had been powered by the engine in the *Dragon*.

Despite the impressive refinement of Zurn's software, there was "still a lot of handwork to do under the transom in the wineglass sections, a difficult area in any lofting. We kept working, fairing it all on the screen as they had done on the shop floor. We kept creating and trimming surfaces and brought the frame spacing closer than on the bigger boat." Finally, Zurn printed out full-sized Mylar patterns of each frame and mold. The patterns saved time for Doug Park compared to lofting from scratch, but the hull sections in the area of prop, where the computer software had struggled, needed to be manually lofted and faired.

The HMCo. construction drawing for design No. 94 would have been useful primarily for the experienced builders it was drawn for. The HMCo.'s shop standards of the era were well established, and the skilled artisans knew from experience what the boss expected and how best to do it. Other builders, however, would find it lacking in detail.

A builder today doesn't have N.G. Herreshoff's oversight or one of his boatwrights to look to for advice. Instead, Doug Park had only the profile and plan views, the table of offsets, Zurn's frame patterns, and his own building experience, which had never included recreating a Herreshoff steam launch. "What took the most time," he said, "was determining how it all bolted and screwed together."

Doug Park's knowledge had its foundation in high-school woodshop and backyard boatbuilding. He went on to a stint aboard the schooner *Harvey Gamage*, for which he once carved the nameboards. Leery of boatbuilding as a career, Park went to college and studied physics and after graduation worked for Outward Bound. But his interest in wooden boats persisted, and despite misgivings, he enrolled in the International Yacht Restoration

School (IYRS). There, he began learning the craft from an extraordinary group of versatile and dedicated instructors including Warren Barker, Jennifer McNally, and Walter Ansel. "Every project," he remembered, "was more exciting than the one before it."

At IYRS, Park got practical experience in lofting, first with a Beetle Cat and then a 12' Elco dinghy. Lofting got more challenging when, during his second year, Park was on a team assigned to take the lines off *Ruweida V*, an out-of-shape 38' Starling Burgess–designed, R-class yacht built by George Lawley and Son in 1926. After two years at IYRS, Park followed Ansel to Mystic Seaport as a shipwright on the *Charles W. Morgan* restoration. Each shipwright was given a specific responsibility, and Park was assigned to repair the starboard side of the 1841 whaleship at the turn of the bilge.

It was during his year on the *Morgan* that Park was offered the chance to acquire Redd's Pond Boatworks, where as a teenager he had worked on occasion for its proprietor, Thad Danielson, a skilled champion of traditional construction. "It was tough to leave the *Morgan* because of the depth of knowledge on that crew," Park remembered. "Of course, I can work my own way now, but one misses having others to bounce ideas off of. But they've been supportive and so has my dad."

Some years ago, a construction crew at the Charlestown Navy Yard discovered a treasure trove of old, hand-hewn timbers buried in the clay soil that had protected them from oxygen for, as near as anyone could tell, over 100 years. Some of this white oak and live oak found its way to Redd's Pond Boatworks, where Park fashioned it into reinforcing knees for the stern of Heide's launch. The skeg and keel were made of spare Danish oak left over from the ongoing restoration of the 1885 schooner yacht *Coronet* in Newport, Rhode Island, adjacent to IYRS. "That oak," said Doug Park, "came from the Danish royal forest. The trees had been planted with shipbuilding in mind, and they grow for 100 years before being harvested."

The launch's planking is cedar except for the distinctive sheerstrake, molded in the Herreshoff style, which is of mahogany. The deck planking is also mahogany. The hull's lines are faithful to offsets Capt. Nat took from his half model. The interior layout differs markedly from the original, which had two cockpits. The forward one was the province of the skipper and engineer, with the steering wheel, boiler, and steam engine. The aft cockpit was reserved for the crew from *Albatross* who were involved in research. "We changed the interior, by removing the bulkhead, moving the engine aft of the boiler, enclosing areas under the benches for storage, and continuing the trim and finish of the aft cockpit to the forward half," Doug Park said.

Since the boat would be operated by only one person, the steering arrangement is based not on a wheel mounted forward but on tiller sticks located amidships on both sides, within easy reach of the boiler. In practice, the setup has proven to work well. The materials used in the *Dragon*'s cockpit, and the design of all the moldings, panels, and turnings, followed HMCo. practices as closely as possible.

As work commenced on zero-degree days during the winter of 2014–2015, Park grappled with ways to get his oak frames from the steambox and onto the molds without cooling down so quickly they would break. His solution was to paint each piece of stock beforehand so the heat would be retained a bit longer. Park was confident he could work his way through whatever challenges were involved with construction, including building the tricky stern. But one very important matter had yet to be resolved: The steam launch had no engine.

"We went ahead with the boat and trusted we'd find a suitable engine," Bill Park said. "The goal was to find an antique engine appropriate to the boat."

It was a remarkably optimistic move considering the rarity of original, operational, antique, marine steam engines. The fallback option was to buy an engine kit. But one day, while Doug Park was scouring the Internet for information about vintage steam launches, he stumbled across a note regarding what purported to be an actual HMCo. single-cylinder steam engine. The engine—rescued from a British Columbia sawmill and restored—was owned by a retired steamboat captain in Mississippi who had it displayed like a sculpture in his living room.

"The engine wasn't for sale," Bill Park said, "so we came up with a number, thinking he wouldn't go for it. But he did." Soon, the engine was on its way to Redd's Pond Boatworks. Scarce as such an engine would be, this one would have an uncanny connection to Heide's new boat. Engraved on the polished cylinder head were the words "Herreshoff Mf'g Co. No. 93 Bristol R.I. 1882." This engine had originally been installed in the boat that immediately preceded launch No. 94. "It was the great coincidence of all coincidences," Heide said.

"Steamboat enthusiasts are an eclectic group," according to Lloyd Beckmann. "But typically they are people who like to work with their hands." Beckmann should know. For about the past thirty-five years, his shop in North Kingstown, Rhode Island, has made and supplied steam engines, custom-made boilers, fiberglass launch hulls, and everything related to them. Beckmann's knowledge and appreciation for the steam game puts him in a unique position to comment on *Dragon*'s engine.

Dragon's varnished oak coamings, mahogany decks, and cherry seats create a striking impression. Here, Kurt Hasselbalch (left) of the Hart Nautical Collections and boatbuilder Doug Park discuss some fine points of the engine and boiler installation. (Stan Grayson)

"It is one of two such engines I know of, and the other is in a museum," Beckmann said; a third engine is believed to be in the hands of a replica engine dealer. "What impresses you is how well thought-out it is. It is light yet sturdy. Even the drip pan is structural. Herreshoff used shape to build in strength. The all-brass engine could be 30 or more lbs. lighter than a comparable 2 1/2" × 5" engine with a cast-iron base," he said, noting that the numbers refer to the bore and stroke dimensions.

Beckmann supplied the boiler for Heide's boat and described it as a "vertical-fire-tube boiler," in which more than sixty tubes heat the water around them. The boiler is fundamentally different from the coil boilers HMCo. used in No. 94 and other boats of that era, in which a long, single coil of tubing, made in the company shops, contained water and steam and was heated by the fire surrounding it. That design—invented by Herreshoff's older brother James in 1873 and later refined by Capt. Nat—permitted comparatively rapid heating. Steam could be raised, apparently, in under five minutes. But, as always, there are trade-offs.

"The vertical-fire-tube boiler is a good answer for small steam applications," Beckmann said, "because it's reasonably low in height and has a small footprint, which aids boat stability while leaving enough room around it so as not to cramp the boat's cockpit. Although it takes longer to bring up to temperature than the coil boiler that Herreshoff used, it is better for the boiler's long-term service life to raise the temperature slowly." The HMCo. itself abandoned coil-tube boilers in 1885 because they were so hard to build and the circular tubing so difficult to clean.

The term "steam engineer" isn't bandied about much anymore, but it implies a person possessing quite specialized knowledge who's on considerably more intimate terms with a steam engine than is the operator of a turn-key, internal-combustion machine. In *The Steam Launch*, Richard M. Mitchell noted that the steam launch operator "has a clear idea of the weight of firewood he will have to carry onboard for an hour's run, the intensity of fire he needs for full-speed operation, and the way energy is transferred from the firebox to the boiler water, the engine, and the shaft and propeller."

A license isn't required for steam hobbyists running small craft, but poking around *Dragon* quickly reveals there's a lot going on. Lift a floorboard and you discover yellow- or red-handled levers mounted to valves at key spots along a lengthy network of skillfully formed copper piping. Levers and valves are on the boiler, too. There is also a sight glass that shows the water level, a bow-mounted water tank and downstream from it an open "hot well." Steam that has returned to its liquid state while flowing through the condenser—a copper tube that runs along the outside of the keel—is piped back to the hot well.

"The system isn't 'closed,'" Doug Park said, "but if you don't let the hot well spill over, blow the whistle too much, or build too hot a fire and have the high pressure relief valve blow too much, you shouldn't need to add any water."

Once the boiler has reached adequate pressure of about 80 psi, Park deals primarily with three components. First, there is the throttle controlling how much of the steam goes into the engine. Second, there is a water pump run by the engine that feeds the boiler. Third, a lever beside the engine is a "make-up pump" operated manually when the engine isn't running to keep the boiler at what Park called "a good level."

But those are just the most commonly used controls. "There are a few backup safety valves that you close when you're not running," Park said, "but you make sure they are open before you start running." One is a shutoff valve for the throttle and there are isolation valves for both water pump lines. "They are closed when you are done operating so that when the steam in the boiler condenses, the resulting vacuum doesn't suck all the water out of the pump lines, which would make you have to prime them with water before they will work properly again. Everything else has valves, too, but you generally don't need to use them unless something were to break, such as the whistle, the water level sight glass, the condenser pipe, the pressure gauge, etc."

Eventually, the preparations for *Dragon*'s maiden cruise around Marblehead Harbor are complete. The pressure gauge shows 80 psi, and we cast off with a half-dozen smiling guests aboard. It doesn't take long at all to get a sense that the boat rides smoothly and makes very little noise.

But the best way to appreciate *Dragon* may be to watch her from another boat. With the engine's four Clydesdale horsepower in harness, power is instantaneous upon opening the throttle, and because the engine is "double-acting" with steam driving the piston both up and down, the shapely launch slips right along. Park had estimated her top speed would be six and a half knots, but his GPS showed her making seven. In the choppy sea running outside Marblehead Harbor, *Dragon* went about her business with little fuss.

What impresses everyone who studies the launch under way is that she seems to glide as effortlessly as a fish. The bow stirs barely a ripple. The wineglass stern leaves only a small, flat wake. Such disturbance as there is comes mainly from the stout bronze rudderstock. Observing this beautifully crafted boat in action provides a thought-provoking answer to her owner's rhetorical question posed at the outset of this story: "Where would we be without steam?" Well, we'd all be a bit poorer without this fascinating throwback that celebrates Capt. Nat's genius even as it recalls the evolving technology that powered the industrial revolution.

As this is written, *Dragon* has been donated to the Herreshoff Marine Museum. There, she'll be docked not far from Capt. Nat's recreated model room. It would be worth a trip to Bristol just to see her and to think about where we'd be without steam. Ask nicely, and they're sure to toot the whistle.

This story appeared in *WoodenBoat* No. 261, March/April 2018.

TIME MACHINE

Exploring America's Oldest Marine Engine

first became involved in writing about antique marine engines in the early eighties when Roger Taylor, president of the International Marine Publishing Company, came up with the idea for what he called "a get-greasy book." The result was *Old Marine Engines: The World of the One-Lunger*. Although the topic might at first seem esoteric, it turned out that there was a solid core of interest among old-timers who had personal experience with the early engines, a growing number of enthusiastic collectors, and those who simply were fascinated by the engines' technology and the histories of the long-gone manufacturers.

Old Marine Engines sold well and was followed by two more editions and two new books: *Engines Afloat from Early Days to D-Day* and *American Marine Engines: 1885–1950*. All that research and writing really made me appreciate the miracle of the Sintz engine recounted here. Not only is it a fascinating mechanical object but also its survival intact was extraordinary.

Like all the pioneers, inventor Clark Sintz had to solve the inter-related problems of how to get fuel and air into the engine cylinder, ignite it to produce an explosion, and exhaust the burnt gases. He had more success in the mechanical realm than in business, but that was typical of most of his competitors. Still, Sintz will always rank among the great pioneers of what would later become known as "the internal combustion century."

"The manufacturers of Sintz gas engines have had a broader and more successful experience in building marine gas engines than any other builder in the United States. The result is the most perfect launch engine made."

—Michigan Yacht and Power Company brochure, circa 1902

As any engine collector or student of America's marine-engine industry could tell you, authentic examples of the early machines are exceptionally rare. Chances of finding an intact engine from what is arguably the industry's most dynamic period—roughly 1900–1916—have for years now been, let us say, negligible. Chances of stumbling upon a pre-1900 marine engine in anything like original condition would be essentially nonexistent.

That reality is what makes the 1893 Sintz at the Penobscot Marine Museum in Searsport, Maine, so unusual. In fact, when I first learned of this largely unheralded artifact, it seemed too good to be true. I had extensively researched the engine's ever-elusive creator, but that did little to help explain what this particular Sintz might really be. Finally, one sunny August morning in 2009, I had the chance to meet the old engine face to face.

Tap tap. Clink clunk. Hissssss. I looked high and low for signs that something was amiss. The engine didn't entirely match the patent granted in November 1893, but detail changes between drawings and a working engine weren't then unusual. This Sintz is almost certainly both the oldest and most original marine engine in North America, and it has a remarkable story to tell. It's the tale of a largely forgotten man and a profound turning point in the technological, economic, and cultural history of the United States.

The Great Fair

In 1893, the hottest ticket in the country gained you entry into one of the greatest world's fairs ever held. Chicago's Columbian Exposition sprawled over 623 acres along the Lake Michigan shoreline. Twenty-two years after the city's devastating fire, the whole world came to Chicago. The fair had everything: art, history, technology, recreations of Columbus's ships, even a big wheel built by T. H. Ferris that enabled people to get an overview of the whole show.

Visitors were amazed by a streetcar powered by a Daimler gasoline engine, the tram gliding around a circle of track like a Lionel around a Christmas tree. Inside the Transportation Building was a five-acre display hall designed by Louis Sullivan and Frank Lloyd Wright. Here were all the latest bicycles, an Etruscan chariot, a full-sized mock-up of an ocean liner. Clark Sintz was there, too. Then forty-three years old, the mustachioed inventor didn't have the name recognition or financial clout of Gottlieb Daimler or Daimler's U.S. licensee, piano-maker William Steinway. But the 18' launch and engines Clark Sintz brought to Chicago would make him an intriguing and very influential figure at the dawn of the internal-combustion century.

The well-known Truscott Boat Manufacturing Company had an exhibit close to Sintz's. In a 1945 article in *The Rudder*, James Truscott remembered his family's involvement with Sintz and the great fair. "The earliest American gasoline marine engine was a two-cycle model developed by Clark Sintz. . . . The engine having shown considerable promise, Truscotts made a sales arrangement to show it at the Columbian Exposition; one, the small size, in a yacht tender and a larger one in a demonstration launch in the lagoon."

Among the twenty-five million people who attended the fair was an advertising genius named Ora J. Mulford. Even as he built one of Detroit's most successful ad agencies, Mulford pursued his passion for boats and, especially, the promise of motorboats. Mulford ordered a Sintz in Chicago and was soon showing off his gasoline launch to anyone in Detroit who might be interested. In what would soon become the "motor city," that included quite a crowd. Later, nine years after the fair, Mulford and the Sintz engine would be brought together in circumstances that neither he nor Clark Sintz would ever have guessed.

The Prodigy

The grandson of a German immigrant, Clark Sintz was born on the family farm in Springfield, Ohio, in 1850. Like many internal-combustion pioneers, he learned mechanics from steam engines, and from blacksmith and machine shops. He built a tiny engine using the barrel from an old black-powder pistol when he was twelve, a real steam engine when he was eighteen. Then, in 1876, Sintz attended the Philadelphia Centennial Exposition and witnessed the Otto engine on display. The 2,200-lb, 2-hp Otto was a horizontal-cylinder, stationary engine. It operated (at a leisurely 160 rpm) according to the four-stroke principle—intake, compression, combustion (power), exhaust—on which Nicolaus Otto owned a patent until an 1886 lawsuit overturned it.

Seeing the Otto changed Clark Sintz's life. It not only focused him on gasoline engines but on developing engines that ran according to the two-stroke principle not affected by Otto's patent. What's more, although Springfield had no navigable waterways, Sintz recognized the big potential market for marine engines. Sintz claimed that he built a horizontal-cylinder, two-cycle engine intended "for marine work" in 1884 and installed it in a 25' boat. It's now unclear if this recollection was accurate. An alternative date for the

This portrait of Clark Sintz was taken during the 1893 Columbian Exposition in Chicago where Sintz demonstrated his pioneering two-cycle engines. (Author's collection)

"first American designed Marine Gasoline Engine" that other sources have attributed to Sintz was 1887, the boat a 30' launch designed by well-known naval architect Frank Kirby. (As always, claiming a "first" is risky. San Francisco inventor Daniel Regan almost certainly had built a gasoline launch in 1884.)

Like most inventors, Clark Sintz had more mechanical genius than capital. In 1888, Sintz joined Springfield businessman John Foos and a wealthy windmill maker named P. P. Mast to form the Gas Engine Co. The stock-in-trade here was stationary engines. Sintz remained only until 1890, then sold out and established the Sintz Gas Engine Company.

Although it may now seem surprising, inventors and investors were then uncertain about whether marine engines or automobiles offered the best chance for financial gain. For at least a decade, the relationships between marine-engine makers, boatbuilders, and automobile entrepreneurs were interwoven in often complex ways. Clark Sintz was involved in all three businesses, but it was his marine engines that made the biggest impression.

His brochure pointed out vital advantages of internal combustion over steam. "It requires no boiler, coal, wood or [licensed] fireman."

It was a Sintz marine engine much like the one featured here that caught the eye of a wealthy furniture manufacturer in Grand Rapids, Michigan, named Addison Barber. In Sintz, Barber saw an investment opportunity and with Barber's money came his title as treasurer of Sintz Gas Engine. In December 1892, Clark Sintz moved his shop from Springfield to Canal Street in Grand Rapids, then known as "the furniture city." There, the Grand River gave access to "the big lake." Sintz soon took the opportunity to invite members of the local fishing club on a significant voyage up Lake Michigan to Petoskey.

The Daimler and the Sintz

By the time of the Columbian Exposition, the Daimler engine had become world-renowned, the first gasoline engine practical for self-propelled vehicles. Gottlieb Daimler and his brilliant engineer, Wilhelm Maybach, had been refining the engine ever since its 1886 debut in a lapstrake launch on the Neckar River near Cannstatt, Germany. Obsessed with secrecy, Daimler had the engine concealed beneath an ornate, ventilated box. To confuse spies, he hinted the boat was influenced by Thomas Edison and had an electric motor.

The Daimler was a four-cycle engine with a primitive but successful float-feed carburetor. Atop the engine stood a Bunsen-burner-like device that warmed the hot tube ignition system—glowing metal tubes that ignited the fuel-air mixture. James Truscott remembered the Daimler as "a very bulky encased affair, yet perhaps the best offering of the time."

Sintz's brochure stressed the two-stroke cycle engine's inherent advantage over a four-stroke cycle engine like the Daimler. It "has an impulse at every revolution, while all other gas engines have but one impulse to every two revolutions, hence our engine . . . develops just twice the power of a four-cycle engine."

In the Sintz, as in all classic two-strokes that followed, the piston opened and closed ports in the cylinder wall or crankcase to allow the ingress of fuel and air and the outflow of burnt gases. No valves, valve springs, pushrods, camshafts, and cam drives were needed, an important advantage in those early, carbon-encrusted days of cranky, expensive engines and mediocre lubricants. The two- vs. four-cycle debate continued for some two decades before four-cycle engines matured and prevailed.

Unlike the Daimler, Sintz's engine had electric ignition of a type known as "make-and-break." The system featured a set of mechanically controlled

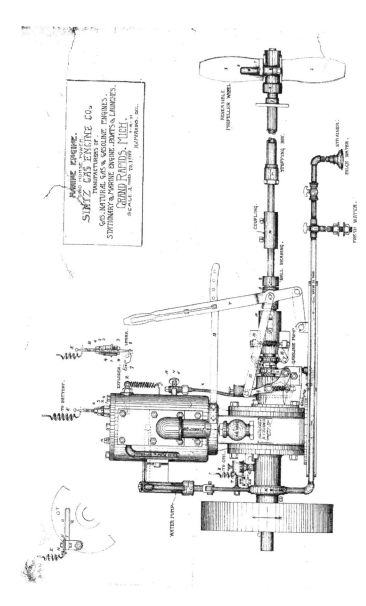

A revolutionary but still comparatively primitive invention—the Sintz two-cycle marine engine. The igniter atop the cylinder head made mechanical contact with the "exploder" inside the cylinder that was opened by the rising piston and closed by a spring. Speed was controlled by the bronze lever that both forced fuel into the cylinder base and adjusted the propeller pitch. In the neutral position, the blades stood at zero pitch and the boat stood still. Once set, speed was maintained by the governor on the rear portion of the crankshaft. (Author's collection)

contact points—the "exploder" in early parlance but soon defused to the less-scary term "igniter"—within the cylinder. The igniter was wired to a battery, switch, and low-tension coil. When the points were snapped open by the Sintz's rising piston—the "break" part of the operation—a spark jumped the gap. Taking aim at hot tubes, Sintz's catalog stressed that his engine did "not require a flame to ignite the charge." While this was true, the make-and-break was then subject to vexing electrical gremlins, something both Maybach and Sintz well understood.

The Time Machine

When attempting to understand the Penobscot Marine Museum's 1893 Sintz, it is helpful to discard any knowledge of contemporary engine technology, or even that of, say, 1912. Instead, it's best to try and approach the engine as it would have been understood, more or less, in its own time.

The elaborate Ellis Lubricator on the engine's starboard side shows the challenges Sintz faced in this regard. The topmost reservoir was filled with medium-grade lubricating oil. The sight-feed oiler below it was adjusted to deliver six to eight drops per minute into the cylinder. Sintz warned customers that too much oil would foul the igniter and stop the engine. The lowest oiler was a shutoff. (In 1909, mixing oil with gasoline was introduced by Pierce-Budd, a maker of two-cycle marine engines in Bay City, Michigan.)

The 1893 Sintz also used drip-feed oilers for the crankshaft bearings. Although normal practice on other engines, such oilers were not sufficient for a two-stroke gasoline engine. A two-stroke's crankcase had to be tightly sealed; otherwise, the fuel/air mixture compressed within the engine's base could be pushed right out the crankshaft bearings as they wore. Soon, adjustable grease cups became standard to both lubricate and better seal the crankshaft.

How did air and fuel vapor enter the cylinder? A prominent feature of the 1893 Sintz is the fuel pump that fed a "supply valve" on the cylinder. Air was drawn in *separately* by the rising piston through the "air valve" on the crankcase. The air was compressed by the descending piston and forced through a transfer port into the cylinder where it mixed with a timed shot of gasoline. The mixture was then compressed by the rising piston and ignited.

How was speed controlled? Not like we'd expect. As the 1893 Sintz had neither mixing valve nor carburetor, there was no throttling capacity in the conventional sense. Instead, the engine had a governor like those on stationary engines. Mounted aft on the crankshaft, the governor engaged or disengaged the fuel pump by means of a cam. The instruction manual explained: "When the governor balls are fully expanded, the cam will be out

Rare indeed is the 1893 Sintz at the Penobscot Marine Museum. The knob-equipped fittings on the side of the cylinder adjust the drip-feed oil lubricators. (Matthew P. Murphy)

far enough to miss the roller that operates the [fuel] pump lever, and when the balls are closed, the cam should be in such position that ... the roller will have a bearing on the cam." Desired rpm (up to 400) could be adjusted by either tightening (faster) or loosening (slower) the nuts that tensioned the governor springs.

In practice, both boat and engine speed were controlled by the engine's big "shift lever" that simultaneously adjusted propeller pitch *and* the position of the governor's cam that engaged the fuel pump. "[M]oving the lever forward one notch gives a small pitch to blades and moves boat slowly, the pitch of wheel and speed of boat increasing as lever is moved forward, the governor controlling speed of engine until lever is hooked in last notch; when in last notch, the cam that operates the gasoline pump is thrown in full and the full power is given to the wheel." Rather clever.

In 1893, one couldn't go to a local auto-supply store and buy a fresh storage battery. The "Sintz Battery" was the then-usual earthenware crock full of homemade electrolyte. Owners were instructed to blend pulverized bi-chromate of potash, warm water, and sulfuric acid. Such batteries lasted four to six weeks, longer if one was lucky. In 1896, the National Carbon Company introduced its Columbia Number Six and groups of these one-and-a-half volt dry-cell batteries replaced the cumbersome crocks.

As for the "exploder," the Sintz manual offered a page of advice and warnings about adjustment and the need to keep things clean and insulated. To maximize battery life, the exploder contacts were brought together—the "make" in the make-and-break system—for only a fraction (one-tenth) of the crankshaft's rotation.

Of course, starting the Sintz wasn't a matter of inserting a key and pushing a button. The owner's manual explained the process. "Open both stop cocks in the gasoline pipe, open thumb-screw [the knurled knob on the "gasoline valve"], work the pump lever up and down until gasoline appears at the thumb-screw. Put the handle on the crank shaft . . . then turn the flywheel towards the starboard, turn briskly, and the engine will start and leave the crank in your hands."

If too much fuel was admitted prior to starting, it had to be expelled by removing a threaded plug in the cylinder head and cranking the 120-lb flywheel several times. After running the engine for an unspecified number of hours, owners had to watch for stretched governor springs and then "shorten up springs." Because dirt was ever a threat to block the fuel pump, gasoline was to be "strained through a cloth or fine wire strainer when put in tank for use." The fuel pump plunger needed regular packing "whenever . . . it commences to leak."

While Clark Sintz was adept at manipulating the engine, ordinary mortals found it challenging. James Truscott remembered: "This was long before the days of the carburetor or the jump spark [spark plug] ignition and it was really a man's job to keep an engine running. . . . Critical adjustments were constantly needed to keep the sensitive affairs in operation."

A wealthy New Orleans boat enthusiast named Arthur Duvic learned firsthand what Truscott was talking about. In 1893, Duvic purchased a Sintz-powered 25' launch. With the boat out of the water, Duvic recalled that he was able to get the engine running reliably (probably because there was no load on it) but it took days to learn how to keep *Clothielde* going on the Mississippi. Eventually, however, Duvic made a run to Biloxi, a ninety-mile trip up-current at an average speed of 5 mph. The event marked what would become the steady decline of steam on the rivers. Commerce would gradually be dominated by legions of owner-operated "gas boats" and later diesel towboats.

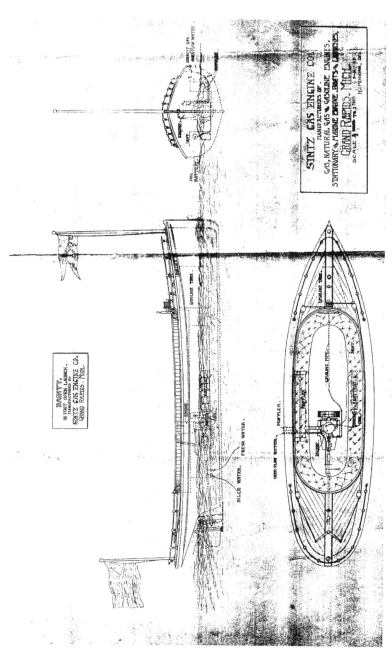

It was not unusual for early marine-engine makers to offer completed launches. These drawings show the 18' Sintz launch *Dainty* and the layout of the engine installation. (Author's collection)

The Provenance

In February 1893, fifty-three-year-old John Allen Jewett of Head Tide, Maine, ordered a 4-hp Sintz engine to install in his Sheepscot River scow, a gaff-rigged vessel known locally as a square-toed frigate. Such boats carried freight, produce, and firewood. The Sintz cost Jewett $369, a sum that probably represented as much or more than a half-year's wages for a working man.

A planned narrow-gauge railroad caused Jewett to cancel his plans, and he stored the engine. After slumbering for almost a century, this Rip Van Winkle of a Sintz was sold by Jewett's grandson. Fortunately, the new owner couldn't start the engine, and he sold it to local antique engine enthusiast Jim Sutter who had immediately recognized the Sintz's importance. Sutter had the engine thoroughly cleaned and lubricated, reunited it with its original Sintz-patent propeller, and then donated the outfit to the Penobscot Marine Museum in 1989. That is how this Sintz miraculously escaped hard use, cobbled-up replacement parts, repainting, a saltwater-ruined cylinder, two World War scrap drives, the local dump, and pilferage. Talk about survivors.

The Sintz Gas Engine Company

By July 1894, about eighteen months after moving to Grand Rapids, Sintz Gas Engine employed sixty-five people, a significant number for such a pioneer business. The company's four-story 45' x 80' building at 242 Canal Street had a woodworking shop on the second floor. Here, Sintz launches were built, ranging from 16' to an impressive 46' model. That December, shareholders voted to more than triple capital to $100,000, very roughly equal to about $2 million in today's money. By then, however, Clark Sintz had already become unhappy with the company.

In January 1914, *Power Boat* magazine published a brief article by Clark Sintz in which the inventor called the monies that made possible his move to Grand Rapids "inducements." He claimed that "finding the [Sintz] organization unsatisfactory, I sold out in December, 1893, built a new engine under the name 'Wolverine.'. . . I did not use my own name as it might cause the mixing of the mails of the Sintz Gas Engine Co."

A great deal went unsaid here. It is probable that Clark Sintz envisioned a new engine while Barber and shareholders preferred to improve the existing one of which, O. J. Mulford would later write, "several fortunes have been spent." Sintz's new engine was also a two-cycle but completely different from the 1893 model. Probably because of legal concerns, the Wolverine patent was issued to Sintz's older son, eighteen-year-old Claude, in December 1894.

Although Clark Sintz's *Power Boat* article suggested his departure from Sintz Gas Engine was total, this was not the case. In March 1896, a Sintz carburetor patent was assigned to his old company. In a Grand Rapids *Evening Press* article published on December 27, 1902, Sintz claimed a connection (perhaps as consulting engineer) to Sintz Gas Engine long after his departure. In this story on "Sintz's New Auto," the inventor claimed that he "only severed his connection when arrangements were made to remove it to Detroit." State records indicate that Sintz Gas Engine remained in Grand Rapids through 1901.

Ever the inventor rather than the business executive, Sintz also sold his share in Wolverine, probably in 1902. He then established a company to build automobiles. In 1904, this company went bankrupt and it took fourteen years for Claude Sintz to repay his father's debts. After the failed automobile venture, Clark Sintz moved on. He worked for a time in Central America for the United Fruit Company, maintaining equipment. He also designed machinery, transmissions, and an after-market carburetor for the Ford Model T.

The Legacy

Well-satisfied with his Sintz engine, O. J. Mulford eventually became the company's Detroit sales agent, working out of his Woodward Avenue ad agency. But this was just the beginning of Mulford's efforts in the marine industry. In late 1899, Mulford and a wealthy partner named William Pungs formed the Michigan Yacht and Power Company. Also involved was Detroit boatbuilder Alfred Seymour.

The first marine engine brought in-house for manufacture was a four-cycle designed by an artistic mechanical genius named Charles Brady King. King had also bought a Sintz engine at the Columbian Exposition. In 1900 King accepted a buyout offer from Ransom Olds who was using his own engine business to fund his pioneering automobile. The four-cycle King/Olds marine engines were successful, and King worked for Olds until a fire gutted the factory in March 1901. Olds then sold the King tooling to Michigan Yacht, and King went along to supervise production.

On February 4, 1902, Mulford and Pungs took another big step and acquired the majority shares of Sintz Gas Engine Co. The Sintz operation was now moved to Detroit and consolidated with Michigan Yacht at its riverfront plant on Jefferson Avenue. "The consolidation of these two firms has brought together the largest and most complete Yacht Gasoline Engine Building Plant on the Great Lakes," reported *Beeson's Marine Directory* in 1902.

Michigan Yacht could now offer its boats—including luxurious launches up to 60' long—with King four-cycle engines, Sintz two-cycles, or other brands if a customer so specified. Mulford turned his formidable copywriting talents to a new Sintz brochure. He wrote: "it is conceded by all experts to be the most efficient marine engine manufactured ... we have sold more power for launches and boats than all other makes combined."

Whatever the impressive scope of Michigan Yacht/Sintz Gas Engine, Mulford and Pungs had differing ideas about the company's direction. Mulford was already easing out by the beginning of 1903. The business transitioned to become the Pungs-Finch automobile company (1904–1910).

In 1906, O. J. Mulford and two partners founded a new marine engine firm in Detroit. They introduced competitively priced, easy-to-run two-cycle engines with Schebler carburetors capable of operation "in the hands of the average pleasure-seeking boat owner." This company was named for Mulford's investor partners, Paul and David Gray. The Gray Motor Company—Gray Marine Motor Co. as of 1925—became one of the best-known and longest-lived of all America's marine engine builders.

After Clark Sintz and his sons Claude and Guy sold Wolverine, that company grew steadily. Claude remained with Wolverine until it moved to Bridgeport, Connecticut, in 1907 to gain better access to export markets. "There was a time," he wrote, "when the sun never set on the Wolverine motor." Wolverine remained in business until 1955.

In 1902, when the Grand Rapids newspaper did its story on Sintz's automobile, the inventor piped up that he didn't think cars should be permitted to travel on public roads at much more than 20 mph. His inventive life was brought to a sudden end when he was struck and killed by an automobile in Bay St. Louis, Mississippi, in 1922.

In his 1892 patent filing, Clark Sintz had written: "[The] object of my invention is to provide a means whereby an explosion may be secured at each piston stroke." Sintz never enforced his patent for a two-cycle engine and neither, apparently, did the Detroit attorney who acquired the patent in 1906. By then, the two-cycle marine engine was fast becoming a way of life for commercial fishermen and yachtsmen from the Midwest to the East and Gulf Coasts.

In 1912, an insightful engineer and *MotorBoat* magazine contributor named A. E. Potter looked back on the marine engine and how it had so quickly changed the nature of waterborne commerce and recreation. Based on his own firsthand knowledge, Potter wrote: "The early developments of two-stroke-cycle motors were made in the vicinity of Grand Rapids, Mich., gradually extending towards the Atlantic seaboard."

What Potter was suggesting, without coming right out and saying it, was that all the pioneer companies—Palmer, Mianus, Lathrop, Bridgeport, Truscott, and the rest—benefited directly or indirectly from Sintz's concept for a "substantially valveless" two-stroke engine. In the end, perhaps Clark Sintz's greatest legacy was the capacity of his engine both to instruct and to inspire.

How Rare Is the Penobscot Marine Museum's Sintz?

There are five Sintz engines of which I am presently aware.

1) In 1892, two Milwaukee men, Gottfried Schloemer and Frank Toepfer, purchased a Sintz that they used in a horseless carriage. They got the machine to work although it wasn't really practical. The vehicle survives in the Milwaukee Public Museum. The engine, however, was much modified for easier operation by subsequent owners.

2) The Sintz purchased by Elwood Haynes survives in restored form in the important 1894 Haynes-Apperson horseless carriage at the Smithsonian.

3) A Sintz marine engine, incomplete and probably built circa 1896, exists in private hands.

4) A Sintz marine engine, said to be of 1896 vintage, remained for decades the property of O. J. Mulford, Gray Motor Company, and finally the Gray Marine Engine Division of Continental Motors Corp. Its whereabouts are unknown.

5) The Penobscot Marine Museum's 1893 Sintz is complete and original including even Sintz's patented reversing propeller and the associated linkage. It is by any measure an exceptionally rare and important artifact.

This story appeared in *WoodenBoat* No. 213, March/April 2010.

THE MAN FROM MOTOR BOAT LANE

Joe Van Blerck and the Van Blerck Motor Company

As the popularity of the internal combustion marine engine grew, motorboat racing soon became an important sport. Races began being held on rivers and lakes throughout the country, among the most important being the Gold Cup, first run on the Hudson River in 1904 and organized by the Columbia Yacht Club. The highest-level competitions quickly attracted wealthy enthusiasts who could afford the expensive boats that reflected the very latest in hull-design theories and the most advanced engine technology.

The challenge for the engine designer was to develop machines that would produce the highest horsepower at the lowest weight. Of course, the engine had to be sturdy enough to reliably finish the race, too. So the search was on to not only increase horsepower and rpm but also build engine components incorporating the best metallurgy and finest casting and machining techniques. Among the best-known engine designers of this early period was Joe Van Blerck.

During the years 1914–1918, Van Blerck engines were a staple of Gold Cup competitors and Joe became a colorful personality sought out by newspaper reporters and magazine writers who covered the sport. Then, too, his engines were used in a variety of both custom cruising yachts and production powerboats. These days, Van Blerck's name is doubtless recognized by only the best-informed powerboat enthusiasts, but he once stood at the center of the sport and his story is well worth knowing. A mechanical genius, Joe was an inimitable pioneer. Men like Van Blerck don't come along often.

"One of the best-known and most-liked men in the marine motor industry is Joe Van Blerck, who began building marine motors in his backyard in Detroit, about five years ago."

—*Motor Boat*, September 25, 1914

In 1913, the fastest motorboat in America was a twenty-six-foot, single-step hydroplane designed by John Ludwig Hacker. This fifty-three-mph boat, *Kitty Hawk V*, was powered by an inline twelve-cylinder engine that was some twelve feet long. The engine's 1710.6-cubic-inch displacement, a whopping twenty-eight liters, was twice the volume of the typical diesel in one of today's commercial fishing or larger pleasure boats. Producing 250–270 horsepower at a weight of some 1,900 pounds, the big twelve's power to weight ratio was about 7.6 pounds per horsepower. This was an exceptional figure at a time when an exotic Roberts two-cycle racing engine had an hp/weight ratio of almost 12:1 and a typical runabout engine 28:1.

Kitty Hawk V's motor was designed and constructed in a Detroit shop run by a stocky, thirty-seven-year-old Dutch immigrant named Joe Van Blerck. His obvious genius had, by the mid-teens, made Van Blerck popular with both wealthy customers and boating journalists. The latter enjoyed writing about a man who had left a land of wooden shoes and windmills to carve out a unique niche in a new world of machine tools. During an unusually vibrant era in motorboating, Joe Van Blerck, sleeves rolled up on his blacksmith-like arms, swearing in his Dutch-accented English, made for good copy. For a time in America, from about 1910–1916, Van Blerck was *the* man when it came to high-performance marine engines.

How all this happened remains something of a mystery. Van Blerck emerged from obscurity into the limelight only to fade as the engine industry and the expensive game of top-level motorboat racing evolved. Piecing together Joe's story is hampered by the callous destruction of whatever papers and documents he thought to preserve during a career that spanned four decades. Today, his pioneering innovations are recognized primarily by a small group of cognoscenti, a sad legacy for a man who once stood—in a dapper three-piece suit and a bowler hat—at the center of American motorboat racing and the market for high-end yacht power.

Josephus Christianus Wilhelmus Van Blerck was born on August 16, 1876, in the Dutch village of Oudenbosch, well south of Amsterdam. Most Van Blerck men had, for generations, been master smiths and that is the only hint we have regarding how Joe came to his vocation. In 1901, Joe married Dympna (anglicized as Dimphina) Goddine. Together with Joe's brother Johann, the couple emigrated to the United States in 1902. Why leave home?

Joe Van Blerck in his Monroe, Michigan, factory in 1914. The in-line twelve is destined for installation in ball-bearing mogul Henry Timken's 23' *Kitty Hawk VI*. (Author's collection)

For an ambitious young man focused on the great internal combustion engine revolution, the big opportunity lay elsewhere than the Netherlands.

The Van Blercks' move to Detroit placed Joe in the single most dynamic place on earth for a man with his interests. Not only were technical developments occurring at an intense pace, but many of the men who would make fortunes in the automobile industry would soon spend great sums on racing boats and lavish motor yachts. Joe's first years in Detroit—1902–1906—represent a tantalizing puzzle. He appears in no city directory until 1907 when he is listed as superintendent of a Woodward Avenue garage and subsequently as a machinist. Then, suddenly, in 1910, Joe emerges as president of the Van Blerck Motor Company. The shop was located in an area of marine-related businesses, slips, and boathouses then known generally as "Motor Boat Lane." Van Blerck's shop was at the foot of Hibbard (now Marina Drive), a street ending just off the Detroit River opposite Belle Isle.

How did a Dutch-born machinist become proprietor of what *immediately* became known as a technologically advanced marine engine company that bore his own name? "The Van Blerck Motor Company had its birth in the woodshed at the back of Joe Van Blerck's somewhat humble residence in

Detroit," reported Rex Wadman in *Motor Boating* in December 1917. "He first built a small single-cylinder motor, then his friends persuaded him to build a two-cylinder engine, then he went on to a four-cylinder, to a six, to an eight and then a twelve-cylinder of the same [5 ½" x 6"] cylinder size."

Wadman, who actually had become Van Blerck's advertising manager and, later, sales manager, was in the perfect position to document Joe's history. Unfortunately, Wadman was more interested in creating a marketing image than he was in recording accurate dates and details for posterity. Wadman suggests Joe was in business in 1907. Joe himself always suggested 1909, which seems to be essentially accurate. As for the friends of Joe Van Blerck, Wadman mentioned no names. Doubtless, he was referring to Joe's wealthy customers, investors, and boat-builder colleagues.

According to an anonymous, flawed, but still useful document in the Algonac Historical Society, the first engine Joe sold was a four-cylinder bought by James W. Gilbert, an Algonac merchant. Gilbert is believed to have installed the Van Blerck in a 30' x 4'6" boat named *Ecce* (Latin for "behold" and pronounced A-che). *Ecce* had been built in 1905/1906 in Toledo to a design by Philadelphia's E. H. Godshalk Co. and was originally equipped with a Roberts four-cylinder, two-cycle engine. When *Ecce* was sold by her original owner to newspaper heir William Scripps, she was re-powered with a Scripps. Then, probably in 1908, Gilbert bought the engineless hull from Scripps, and the Van Blerck was installed. *Ecce's* twenty-one-plus mph performance was impressive at a time when the slender "auto-boats" racing for the Gold Cup were running at from sixteen to twenty-four mph. The second Van Blerck engine went, it is thought, to Chris Smith, an entrepreneur, jack of many trades, and fellow member with Gilbert of the Algonac Business Men's Association. *Dart* was timed at twenty-three mph and promptly found a buyer.

If word of Joe's engines had spread forty miles north to bucolic Algonac by 1908–1909, Van Blerck's tinkering was already known in Detroit. There his magic woodshed was frequented by a succession of curious, sometimes famous men. What little oral history survived within the Van Blerck family consistently linked Joe's beginnings to Henry Ford. "Before entering the marine engine field in 1910, he was associated with Henry Ford in the development of the Ford car," reported the *Brooklyn Daily Eagle* in its obituary of Van Blerck. "Mr. Ford and his young son Edsel often spent many pleasant evenings with Mr. Van Blerck when he was building his first marine engine in the backyard of his Detroit home."

Although no paper trail remains, Van Blerck's connection with Ford was a persistent topic of conversation as long as Joe and his son, Joe Jr., were both alive. As a boat-crazy teenager in Freeport, New York, in the early 1940s,

Mario Scopinich hung around the boatyard and shop the Van Blercks then owned. It was a hotspot for a wealthy clique of hydroplane racers. The group included band leader Guy Lombardo, and Joe Jr. himself, who enjoyed great success with both a 225-cubic-inch and seven-liter hydro. "We all heard quite a few times that the old man had worked with Henry Ford," Mario remembered.

What was the nature of Joe's "association" with Ford? We can only conjecture that Van Blerck combined such gifts as a machinist with natural engineering talent and that he was recognized as a unique artisan. Possibly, Van Blerck worked on a consulting or vendor basis with Ford and C. Harold Wills—the multi-talented engineer who helped make a reality of Ford's vision for the Model T. The car's design principles included a lightweight but high-strength chassis and engine produced on an assembly line using interchangeable components.

From the very start, Van Blerck catalogs stressed the importance of metallurgy, light weight, and the virtues of an assembly process in which the workmen "become so proficient in the production of one type of motor only that they become masters of the particular work in which they are engaged." These subjects all became a kind of mantra within the automobile and engine industries.

Kitty Hawk V's fascinating engine was strictly a special order model—officially a C-12 Special—but it retained the basic architecture of the four-, six-, and eight-cylinder engines that launched the Van Blerck Motor Company. The business became official in 1910 when Joe allied himself with James Haggerty, a wealthy investor who'd made a fortune in the brick business. Haggerty retained principal ownership of the company's 511 shares of stock while Joe and his wife initially each owned five. The staff was ten men and a female secretary. (Detroit's Gray Motor Company, one of the larger marine engine firms, then employed 170 people.)

These "first generation" Van Blercks, while not revolutionary in design, were of such quality that their performance was greater than mere specifications might suggest. The engines were, like many of that period, T-heads—the cylinder head was flanked on one side by the intake valve and on the opposite side by the exhaust valve. The resulting combustion chamber was too large in surface area for ideal efficiency but there was room for dual spark plugs fired by a Bosch battery and magneto system. This tended to mitigate the combustion chamber's poor shape while reducing the chance for a total ignition-system failure. What's more, valve timing could be adjusted to permit the rush of the intake mixture to sweep out exhaust gases, improving efficiency. The valves were easily removed for de-carbonizing (then a

Chris Smith built the 20' *Baby Reliance III* and powered her with a Van Blerck C-12 Special that had high-compression pistons and could achieve the then-high 1,800 rpm. Here she is on the Mississippi River at Davenport, Iowa, during the 1912 racing season. Smith would go on to found Chris-Craft. (Author's collection)

persistent issue), and the camshafts, one on each side, could be fully enclosed and efficiently lubricated.

A good T-head engine was durable, quiet, and easily maintained. It was also handsome, for the architecture possessed a pleasing symmetry. The Van Blerck line included 650-rpm B models intended for launches, cruisers, and commercial applications; 1,000-rpm B-Specials and 1,200 rpm, lighter weight C-models for faster boats; and the 1,600 rpm C-Special models for racing. All had individual, cast-iron cylinders. On the higher-rpm C- and C-Special models, however, each cylinder's water jacket was cast with an open area that was then covered by a thin brass plate secured with numerous machine screws by a worker using a brace and screwdriver bit. These cutaway cylinders reduced overall weight by about 100–200 pounds.

The cylinders were bolted to a robust aluminum crankcase (iron on the B) engineered for stiffness, a trait by then recognized as desirable for longevity. Ever attentive to metallurgy, Van Blerck specified crankshafts of shock resistant chrome nickel steel; connecting rods were drop-forged of "special" steel; pistons were turned of "best quality" iron ("semi-steel" on racing models); bearing shells were manganese bronze "lined with the best [they had a high percent of nickel for wear resistance] Babbitt obtainable." The C- and C-Special models had force-fed lubrication, which Van Blerck realized early was a key to reliability for racing, and the system had a built-in strainer. At the time, this feature was rare on any but a few high-performance brands.

Joe Van Blerck's neighbor at the foot of Hibbard was a struggling boat-build-ing firm named the Detroit Launch and Power Company. The company's president, John F. Hacker, owned a nearby ice dealership and it was Hack-er's son John L. who was general manager of the boatbuilding effort. The younger Hacker proved more interested in naval architecture than business and the company failed, probably in February/March 1911. If a successor firm, Hacker-Pouliot Boat Co., ever opened, it seems to have lasted only a few months.

When his own efforts in Motor Boat Lane folded, Hacker was taken on by Joe and, in a *Yachting* article, was referred to as "Mr. J. L. Hacker of the Van Blerck Co." The senior Hacker recorded in his diary that, in August 1911, he went over to see his son "Johnny" at Van Blerck's shop so they could "wind up" the affairs of their failed boat-building efforts. Evidence suggests that John L. then lived above the Van Blerck shop and, oddly enough given his recent performance, his title at Van Blerck's was business manager!

A Hacker-Van Blerck relationship may have predated Hacker's employ-ment by Joe. Current information suggests that, in the winter or spring of 1911, Hacker received a commission from Lee Counselman, chairman of the car-building firm Chalmers, for a racing boat of the emerging hydro-plane style—a boat that would largely skim atop the water rather than slice through it.

Kitty Hawk II was built under Hacker's watchful eye by Louis Mayea who would go on to found his own Mayea Boat Works and use *Kitty Hawk II* in his own advertising. The boat was powered by a six-cylinder, 80-hp Van Blerck. During her first season in 1911, *Kitty Hawk II*'s dominance made her a genuinely famous boat.

"Dear Mr. Van Blerck," Counselman wrote, "Mr. Hacker called me up Saturday and asked if I would send him a photograph of the cups and pen-nants won by *Kitty Hawk* this year. . . . I think the greatest victory of all was won by the motor . . . finishing every time without engine trouble of any kind."

In 1912, *Kitty Hawk II* was purchased and upgraded by Henry Timken whose roller bearing invention gave rise to factories employing thousands and great personal wealth. Timken enjoyed owning fast boats and became a staunch fan of Hacker designs powered by Van Blerck engines. In 1912, Hacker designed for Timken a big runabout named *Kitty Hawk IV* for use at the inventor's vacation home in San Diego. *Kitty Hawk V* followed in 1913 and *Kitty Hawk VI* in 1914. Timken joined a fast-growing Van Blerck customer list that included wealthy businessmen, actors, and a senator, among others, and Timken also became an investor in the Van Blerck Motor Company.

It soon occurred to Rex Wadman that customers' boats represented a wonderful marketing opportunity and the company began publishing annual "boat books." These artfully produced brochures contained designs by the best-known naval architects of the era. There were racing hydroplanes by Adolph Apel, George Crouch, William Fauber, Jack Beebe, and, of course, Chris Smith. The Smith-Ryan Boat Company, like the Van Blerck Motor Company, opened in 1910 and Van Blerck supplied the power for several of J. J. Ryan's racing boats including a C-12 Special for *Baby Reliance III*. *The Boat Book* also depicted fast runabouts by Lawley and Chris Smith; express cruisers by J. Murray Watts, Matthews, Weckler, A. E. Luders, Carlton Wilby, William Hand Jr. (one of Hand's was for Sarasota circus entrepreneur Charles Ringling), and a variety of fine yacht-building companies.

Not to be ignored were more work-oriented boats that included a forty-foot tender to the presidential yacht *Mayflower*. Built at the Portsmouth Navy Yard and equipped with an eight-cylinder Van Blerck, it took President Wilson on his tour of the Panama Canal. A twin-hulled thirty-two-foot Hickman Sea Sled with twin Van Blerck eights hit forty mph with twenty-four men aboard. During World War I, the Greenport Basin and Construction Company built nineteen sixty-foot "scouting" boats, each powered by a trio of Van Blercks. For Yale University, William Hand designed a coaching launch. It was built by George Lawley and named, inevitably, *Boola*.

As for John L. Hacker, he remained with Van Blerck for a year and, then in his mid-thirties, departed in June 1912. But he continued to design numerous boats for Van Blerck patrons.

On the morning of June 7, 1912, the Van Blerck Motor Company was largely destroyed by fire. This potentially devastating blow was countered immediately by the finding of a new facility a mile or so inland on Leib St. With demand growing—129 people were by then working at Van Blerck's—plans were now made to build a new facility thirty-five miles south of Detroit in Monroe. This factory, built of steel, concrete and brick, was opened on December 10, 1913. It contained five dynamometers—Van Blerck was perhaps the first manufacturer to certify horsepower—and was organized to permit efficient production of 1,000 motors a year.

The move to Monroe was accompanied by management changes. Several articles about Van Blerck contained some references suggesting that Joe was overly involved in too many areas. In September 1914, *MotorBoat* reported, "Joe continues as president of the company, but being relieved of the executive duties has time to follow his natural inclination as engineer and master mechanic." Charles B. Page, an 1899 MIT graduate with a dozen years experience in the engine industry, now became vice president and treasurer.

The sales, production, and advertising departments were also placed under experienced new managers. A revised marketing thrust was aimed primarily at the runabout and express cruiser markets.

Whatever Joe Van Blerck may have felt about the new company organization, he had already recognized that, good as they were, his existing engines, with their separate cylinders and camshafts to which the lobes were attached by "pins," could be improved. An entirely new model line was introduced for 1915 consisting of the E (runabouts and express cruisers), E Special (higher compression and more advanced timing for competition), and EE (workboats and pleasure cruisers up to sixty-five feet). These engines had semi-steel cylinders cast in pairs (en bloc), permitting the previously external oil lines to be internal. The crankcase on the EE was iron—on the E and E Special, manganese bronze for added strength. Only the oil pan was aluminum. The camshafts were now innovative single-piece forgings that would "settle forever the trouble of loose and broken cams and defective timing." Like the engine, the reverse gear was pressure lubricated. It was a positive-acting, multi-disc-type unit so the operator didn't have to worry about the boat creeping one way or another with the gear selector in neutral.

These fine new engines, however, were only part of what America's "master marine engine maker" was up to. Joe had secretly been concocting an engine that burst into public view in 1916. Dubbed the "Twin Six," (the same name used by Packard for its V-12) this was an engine of astonishing conception. It was just eight and a half feet long. Gone was T-head design, replaced by overhead valves driven by an overhead camshaft. Beautifully enameled, the engine looked particularly lean as the two spark plugs per cylinder were located inside the V. Twin high-tension magnetos were mounted at the aft end of the cylinders. Joe must have been working on this 2,545-cubic-inch V-12 as early as 1914 yet its overall design would remain contemporary through World War II. Tooling alone cost $12,500, close to $350,000 today, and a heavy expense for a small company.

At a time in America when the average worker earned about $690 per year, when a new home cost $3,200 and a straight-eight Duesenberg marine engine cost $5,300, the Van Blerck Twin Six engine carried a list price of $7,250. That price included a reduction gear unit, for Van Blerck was a pioneer in the technology. Brilliantly, he recognized that a lightweight engine running at comparatively high rpm while turning a big propeller at a comparatively low rpm was the key to overall performance and packaging. The concept worked on boats as diverse as racing hydroplanes, fast runabouts, and a 109-foot Herreshoff schooner named *Mariette*. Despite its comparatively compact dimensions and light weight (versus, for example, a contemporary Winton) the Van Blerck eight-cylinder in

The beautifully finished Van Blerck Twin Six was introduced at the 1916 New York Boat Show. The overhead cam, twelve-cylinder engine was rated at 300- to 500-hp. depending on rpm.

Mariette could produce a sustained 10-mph cruise speed while taking up relatively little space.

Illinois Senator George Harding bought the first Twin Six for his Ramaley-built forty-five-foot, forty-five-mph "express-runabout," *Mouser II*. C. Harold Wills, Van Blerck's old acquaintance from his time with Ford, bought five of them! Four went into his cruising yacht *Marold*, another into his Gold Cup racer *Baby Marold*, an ill-fated boat that burned, sank, and, after being retrieved, exploded and killed one of the men who had built her. Industrialist, developer, and art collector August Heckscher bought two Twin Sixes for his 110-foot *Cabrilla* and became an investor in the Van Blerck company. Other Twin Sixes went into naval "defense boats."

In January 1916, with orders flowing in at an increasing rate, the entire west side of the new factory was expanded and, for a time, both day and night shifts were necessary to meet demand. Joe Van Blerck continued to look ahead. In 1916, the company unveiled an overhead cam, V-12 aero engine that produced 185 hp and weighed only 580 pounds, an hp/weight ratio of 3.13:1. A nomenclature change occurred, probably for the 1917 model line, relating to the marine engines' bore/stroke dimensions. The 5 ½" x 6" "E" models were labeled the "I" and the 6" x 6" the "J". (The "J" was still on the U.S. Navy roster powering launches in the mid-thirties.) For 1918, the "M" models appeared. The most elegant of all Van Blercks, the "M" continued the T-head layout but added a counter-balanced crankshaft and an enclosed flywheel.

It was during this busy, productive period that the Van Blerck Motor Company took an exceedingly bad turn. On October 1, 1916, vice president and general manager Charles Page quit and left the marine engine business. Van Blerck sales were then about $1 million. Now, things fell apart. The year 1917 was the last year in which Joe Van Blerck's signature appeared on the company's annual report. In 1918, all the Van Blercks' stock, 310 shares, was listed in Dimphina's name. Suddenly, Joe was out of the Van Blerck Motor Company.

What happened? Regarding Joe, the most plausible suggestion might be that his constant, probably insistent, efforts to innovate finally ran afoul of management. Perhaps, too, a mutual unhappiness developed over the general direction of the business. One suspects that, despite all the talk of standardization, what Joe Van Blerck loved more than anything was continual technological advance and competition.

As for sales, the airplane engine apparently went nowhere; the Twin Six seems to have been produced only for a year or two; and Model D and DD engines aimed at fire equipment, trucks, and stationary applications, had a negligible or even negative impact. The postwar drop in government sales must have hit the company hard as it did others. Then, too, while Van Blerck's engines were built and priced for the well-to-do, the postwar recreational marine market trended in the opposite direction. Demand increased steadily for lower-priced engines and production boats. The high-end racing scene, meanwhile, became dominated by relatively low-cost, war-surplus Liberties and other converted aero engines. Diesels made inroads into the sales of big gasoline engines for large yachts.

Many companies adapted. Sterling, perhaps Van Blerck's most serious competitor, survived the postwar challenges, soon gave up on racing, and would live through World War II. Kermath and Universal relentlessly standardized a few engines for the mainstream market, then expanded and prospered. The Van Blerck Motor Company, its liabilities far exceeding its assets, closed in 1922. That July, the factory where Joe had once wielded a big shovel during ground-breaking ceremonies, was sold for $70,000 and became home to the Detroit Stoker Company.

Sometime in 1919 or 1920, Joe Van Blerck embarked on a two-decade odyssey as a famous but itinerant engine designer. He, his wife, and three children went first to Akron, Ohio. Joe carried with him plans for a thoroughly modern, 425-cubic-inch four-cylinder marine engine, the J. V. B. This one was an L-head (intake and exhaust valve on the same side of the block), less grand but also less costly to manufacture than previous models. The $1,000

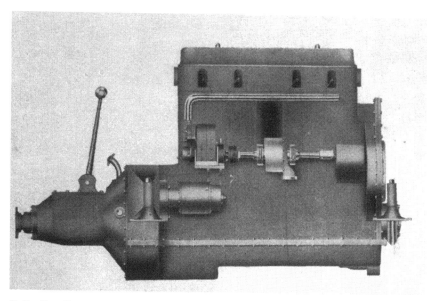

Reflecting the utmost in clean, sleek, 1920s design, the L-head J.V.B. was offered in 38- or 60-hp models and was the standard engine in Elco's Cruisette. (Author's collection)

J.V.B. was built by the Wellman-Seaver-Morgan company and purchased by, among others, Elco for its thirty-six-foot Cruisette.

In 1921 or 1922, Joe moved to New Jersey where the Van Blerck Motor Corporation opened in Plainfield. Here Joe built a line of rugged L-head two- to twelve-cylinder medium-speed engines—the Model N. At some point, probably in 1928, Joe moved to Red Bank, New Jersey. There, Van Blerck Motors converted Continental engines for marine use and Joe built the impressively conceived, overhead cam, all aluminum, 33-hp, 165-lb. Van Blerck Jr. Finally, Joe moved his family to Long Island, eventually settling down for good in Freeport where he owned a boatyard and built the building that housed Joseph Van Blerck and Son. The company produced a line of remarkably fabricated copper exhaust manifolds and also built the exhaust systems installed on the Packard V-12s that powered Elco PT boats.

Joe Van Blerck died at his winter residence in Fort Lauderdale on September 5, 1949, age seventy-four. He'd been in ill health for several years but *MotorBoat* magazine doubtless spoke for many when it noted that the death of "one of America's pioneer marine engine manufacturers came as a shock to his countless friends in boating, and in the marine engine field."

High-engine-technology well ahead of its time, the ninety-cubic-inch Van Blerck Jr. had a lightweight aluminum block, and a chain-driven, overhead camshaft that operated four valves per cylinder. It was intended in part as an alternative to bulky, less fuel-efficient outboard motors. (Author's collection)

Van Blerck's career spanned the great age of marine engine development and Joe spent so much of it on the cutting edge that, one must assume, he shed some blood. Like all gifted innovators, Van Blerck saw things that were beyond the vision of most, a gift not always easy to reconcile in a corporate environment. His great strength was doubtless an innate sense of what would work in an engine, and how to translate an apparently far-fetched idea into an artful reality of cold steel, aluminum, and bronze.

Today, Mario Scopinich is one of the few living men who actually saw Joe Van Blerck. A teenager in the early forties, and focused mostly on helping Joe Jr. with his race boats, Mario retains one overriding impression of Joe Van Blerck as an old man. "He didn't work much when I knew him," said Mario. "He spent most of his time in his shop. The thing about him was— you knew that he was a man who could just make anything."

Where Are They Now?

Time has not been kind to old marine engines. While quite a few authentically correct single-cylinder "one lungers" survive, most of the multi-cylinder "big iron" was sent to the scrap yard long ago. Some classic engines by Scripps, Sterling, and even a magnificent Speedway have made it through and are still in use, the throaty burble of their exhausts and their mighty torque a reminder of bygone days. Make no mistake—an antique powerboat equipped with a modern diesel or gasoline engine is authentic in neither substance nor aura. But let's face it—appropriate engines for restored motorboats really are rare.

While a Van Blerck C-Special, Twin Six, E-Special, or "M" would certainly have been worthy of preservation by America's greatest museums, none were. Amazingly, however, a surviving Van Blerck does occasionally surface. Several years ago, while researching a book on internal combustion engine development, I asked the owner of an unusually fine stationary engine if he owned any marine engines. "No," he answered, "but I know someone who's found one."

"Do you know what brand?" I asked.

"Oh," he answered, "I think it's called a Van Blerck."

An hour later, we were standing in a shed filled with old outboard motors, a motorcycle or two and a disassembled six-cylinder Van Blerck C-Special. It was missing its transmission (too bad!) but retained its original brass builder's plate. The engine had escaped destruction by being put to work in a remote Maine sawmill and it was now in the process of restoration.

A find like that is the stuff of dreams for collectors but, absent incredible luck, the realization of the quest is rare indeed. Fewer than ten Michigan-built Van Blercks are currently known to exist, one of which is still reliably powering a cruiser. It is to be hoped that, one day, a prime example will wind up at the right museum where a knowledgeable curator will have it appropriately displayed and dramatically interpreted for future generations.

This story appeared in *WoodenBoat* Number 197, July/August 2007.

LEGENDS OF THE RIPS

In Search of the New England Bass Boat

A mong the most intriguing aspects related to boat design is how and why different hull shapes and rigs emerged that adapted them to specific local waters and applications. In the United States alone, the historical record includes dozens of such craft including, to name but a few, the Chesapeake Bay Skipjack and Crabbing Skiff, the Friendship Sloop, the New Orleans Lugger, the Cape Cod Catboat, the Hampton (New Hampshire) Boat, and the Columbia River Gillnetter. In San Francisco, the fisherman's colorful lateen-rigged felucca began an evolution that resulted in the famous Monterey Clipper with its reliable, heavy-duty Hicks engine.

The small sailboats used by New England sport fishermen in pursuit of bass underwent their own evolution with the coming of internal combustion. I don't recall what event prompted the idea to explore the origins of what became referred to generally as a "New England bass boat." But a summer's morning in 2012 found me boarding the ferry that runs from New Bedford to Cuttyhunk to meet a man who could help.

It soon became apparent that defining such boats—initially intended for use by fishing guides along the coasts from New England to New York and New Jersey—was not a simple matter. Nor did these wooden boats, designed for coastal waters, have anything in common with the bass boat genre as it's generally understood today. The original New England bass boats were conceived and built by a handful of independent-minded men who had an instinct for what was required. Their staunch, wooden boats and the fishing guides who ran them would become the stuff of legends.

"Coot throttled down for trolling and the *Sea Coot* moved into the rip
... the evil churning of the rip over huge submerged rocks."

—"The Striped Bass, a Detective Story,"
Gerald Holland, *Sports Illustrated*, August 27, 1956

On August 17, 1913, a one-time New Bedford police-officer-turned-businessman named Charles Benjamin Church sailed out of Cuttyhunk Pond in pursuit of bass. Church and his brother-in-law Carl Kraut battled through big swells in Canapitsit Channel and, once in Vineyard Sound, they turned east. When Church reached a spot he reckoned promising, he lifted out the boat's sprit rig and Kraut took the oars, skillfully backing stern-first through surf to within just two feet of the Nashawena shore.

The shallow water beneath them was full of big, seaweed-covered rocks, the tide ebbing hard against the wind. "It was awfully rough . . . I could hardly keep my feet," Church wrote later. Using a century-old German silver reel, Church began casting his live-eel baited hook and soon snagged a fish so heavy that he feared his 11-ounce bamboo rod might break. The 60" bass weighed 73 pounds, a record that stood for some 69 years.

Church referred to his craft only as "a 13-foot smack boat," the term then generically applied to fishing craft of many types. However, the fact that this boat was thirteen feet long, had a quickly removable sprit rig, and was able enough to carry two full-grown men in potentially dangerous conditions suggests it was a Woods Hole spritsail boat. Such "big little boats"—generally a bit over thirteen feet long and approximately six feet in beam—were well-adapted to those who wanted to go beyond surf casting and hunt striped bass among the Elizabeth Islands.

The development of small powerboats allowed fishermen to pursue stripers with significantly less labor than in Church's day. Now, fishermen could rather quickly reach promising spots including the tide rips around Cape Cod, Nantucket, Martha's Vineyard, and off the western end of Cuttyhunk. There, Sow and Pigs reef—"the Pigs"—became as famed for stripers as it was for shipwrecks. While a variety of boats were initially used, quite specialized versions began emerging during the late forties, boats born of their unique environment and the habits of their quarry. This was the purpose-built New England bass boat.

The *Rudy J.*

"There are always waves in Buzzards Bay," said the recorded announcement aboard the Cuttyhunk Ferry as we headed toward the hurricane barrier that protects New Bedford Harbor. But on this August day, almost exactly

Heading home, Capt. Jim Nunes steers toward Canapitsit Channel at Cuttyhunk. The *Rudy J.* measures 24 ½' x 8 ½' x 18". Her high freeboard, hard chines, modest deadrise aft, twin tillers, gasoline engine, and foredeck spray coaming are signature features of the classic New England bass boat. (Stan Grayson)

ninety-nine years after Charles Church caught his famous fish, the bay lay smooth beneath a gray and windless sky. For months, I had been poking into what initially seemed a reasonably straightforward project. But as time passed, the essence of the subject occasionally seemed as elusive as a wary fish. Soon enough, the question popped to the surface—exactly what is a New England bass boat, anyway?

Capt. Jim Nunes was waiting for me at the ferry dock in his green golf cart. The seventy-nine-year-old guide is tall—as a young man, he'd been scouted by the Boston Celtics—and sturdy, toughened by years fishing in an open boat. Often his customers kept him so busy that he fished a 161-day season without time off, yet he never grew tired of the chase. "Bass," Nunes said, "they're one fish that every time you think you know something about them, you learn different."

Soon enough, we arrived at the docks where Cuttyhunkers keep their boats. Once, a long time ago now, these slips were home to all the great ones: the Ballentines and Brownells, the Winslows and MacKenzies. Now though, they're all gone, all save one. Jimmy Nunes' *Rudy J.* is the last wooden bass boat at Cuttyhunk.

Lying in her slip, the 24 ½' *Rudy J.* gives an impression of power, heft—she displaces some 5,500 pounds or more—and purpose. One gets the feeling this boat could handle the very worst Buzzards Bay can dish out. This, it turns out, is a good thing, for Nunes allowed that he fished "regardless of weather. No matter how bad, there's always a place to fish. The customers would go if I would."

The *Rudy J.* has generous flare forward, contributing to a comparatively dry ride and the buoyancy needed to resist plunging too deep in heavy seas. The hull is hard chine with very modest dead rise aft resulting in a stable platform when trolling. "A round bottom rolls like hell and that makes for tough fishing when you're going slow," Nunes learned. The gray painted decks have been fiber-glassed—fish blood is easily washed off—and the stern cleats are mounted out of the way beneath the gunnel. There's no windshield, just a vee-shaped spray coaming. "I didn't want or need a windshield," Nunes said. "At night, especially, it hurts your ability to see all around the boat and it can get in the way. No real bass boat had a windshield."

There was that term—"*real* bass boat."

The only significant projection on the *Rudy J.* is the antenna, something added in the late sixties when there was spare cash for a radio. Out of Nunes's memory bank, an anecdote surfaced regarding a self-sufficient Cuttyhunk fisherman who wouldn't have a radio. "Bob Tilton and I were in our boats fishing at night at Devils Bridge off Gay Head. I headed home and so did Bob but unknown to me, he ran out of gas. He had with him two Boston doctors who were his customers. He raised the engine box and used that like a sail and came across Vineyard Sound. He got through Canapitsit that way, too, and Coot [Irwin Winslow "Coot" Hall] went out and got him."

Like a real bass boat, the *Rudy J.*—named for Jim's father and mentor Rudolph Joseph Nunes—has forward and aft tillers and throttles, giving a fisherman maximum flexibility. Nunes, however, only uses the forward tiller when his back is bothering him, but then he can perch on the engine box and steer. Aft, he is in perfect harmony with the boat's Chevy V-8 and knows the rpm instinctively from engine sound. Some years earlier, he was using the aft tiller and crossing Buzzards Bay with an eager fisherman aboard when the *Rudy J.* was overtaken by a black sky and northerly winds exceeding fifty knots. "It was all white water and foam," Nunes said. "The seas were eight or nine feet high. Well, when you're running the boat in conditions like that, you don't have time to be scared."

The *Rudy J.* was designed and built by a Mattapoisett man named Enoch Winslow. Jim Nunes had seen Winslow's first bass boat, a teak-decked beauty owned by Cuttyhunk guide Lloyd Bosworth. "You could tell right away that Lloyd had something special," said Nunes, who at the time was running a John Luhrs–designed Jersey sea skiff, an able boat planked lapstrake-style with plywood. "It had a windshield. It was a good boat to start fishing with but Buzzards Bay is a tough place and that boat was light and took a beatin'."

Winslow's son-in-law, Roger Thompson, remembers Enoch as "naturally gifted, a self-taught master carpenter, just a genius." Winslow built a catboat in 1903 when he was fifteen years old and, after service in the field artillery in World War I, he began building boats in a shop on Barstow Street. "He'd design using half models built of unfinished pine scaled one inch to the foot," Thompson said, "and would build carvel, lapstrake or other methods." The *Rudy J.* is of batten-seam construction, the mahogany planks bronze-fastened to closely spaced white-oak frames. There is a 4"-wide oak keel with a substantial skeg.

By the mid-1960s, when Nunes met Enoch Winslow, the boatbuilder was in his late seventies and still spent every Monday working as assessor for the town of Mattapoisett, a post he held for sixty years. Nunes and Winslow shook hands on a $5,500 price, but Winslow later reduced that amount by $500, saying he'd finished the boat—"the best one I've built"—more quickly than expected. "There were no plans," said Nunes. "It was all in his head." The original engine was a six-cylinder, 165-hp Crusader.

The number of bass boats built by Enoch Winslow is unknown but it was a relatively small part—perhaps a half-dozen—of his total production that included cruisers of various sizes and dozens of skiffs. Such a figure was a fraction of that built by a man whose career began in earnest about five miles northeast of Mattapoisett in Marion in 1947 and would continue with single-minded purpose for some two decades. The emblem on the back of his boats' transoms left no doubt about their purpose. It said "Cuttyhunk."

"His Whole Life Was Boats"

One early November day in 1968, a bass-obsessed writer for *Sports Illustrated* named Dan Levin drove from Boston to Harwich on Cape Cod to go fishing with famed guide Irving "Bud" Henderson. The temperature was in the high 30s and a 25–35 mph northeast wind was blowing. While others remained in port, Henderson—who apparently graduated from the same guide school as Jim Nunes—headed out with Levin and two other striper zealots. At 6:15, in a rip off Monomoy, a wave broke completely over *L'il Darlin'*, Henderson's 30' MacKenzie. Henderson warned the fishermen not to look aft as it would be too frightening, and continued the thirty-mile journey toward a hotspot for migrating stripers southeast of Nantucket.

Levin's "Rough Day Off Old Man Shoals" gives an unusually dramatic picture of an able skipper handling a big, able bass boat offshore. "The wind was blowing the tops off the waves and filling and refilling the cockpit with foam. Now there were 10-foot swells . . . at the bottom of each one we lurched to a dead stop. . . . Bud Henderson stood at the wheel, operating the manual windshield wipers, speeding up or swerving to avoid a breaking comber and eating apples."

Born September 12, 1902, in Noel, Nova Scotia, Ernest J. MacKenzie went to sea at age twelve, and eventually became a captain under sail. But it was MacKenzie's fascination with the challenge of improving the boats used by Cuttyhunk fishing guides that defined his life. In the early 1940s, Mac was living in Marion, Massachusetts, and working on the 312-acre Stone Estate. The circumstances that prompted the building of his first boat in 1944 (the year he became an American citizen) are now unknown but changes in his employer's affairs were likely involved. By 1948 or 1949, MacKenzie was on his own, building seven stout-looking, lapstrake sixteen-footers in a barn on Hiller Street in Marion. As a young teenager, Bill MacDougall watched MacKenzie at work. "He was a short man," said MacDougall, "perhaps 5'6", and I remember him standing in wood shavings up to his knees."

MacKenzie soon relocated two miles away to Marion Boat Works where he built a series of twenty-two-footers. Some years later, a brief photo caption in the local newspaper read: "The Cuttyhunk style bass boat was

Ernest J. MacKenzie, circa early 1960s. "His hobby was work," said his onetime partner at Kingston, Thomas Stott Jr. (Author's collection/Howard Benassi)

developed at the Marion boat yard." MacKenzie left Marion with his friend, engine mechanic Charlie Picket, to set up shop as the Cuttyhunk Boat Yard in South Dartmouth. There, MacDougall and Picket's son had the job of ferrying boats stored or repaired to and from Cuttyhunk. There, too, according to Steve Purdy's *WoodenBoat* article (*WoodenBoat* No. 197) Mac's friend, boat builder Al Gray, lofted out the MacKenzie 26 while "Mac sat on a bench with a half-model in his hands shouting dimensions."

The South Dartmouth venture was brief. Ernest MacKenzie was a boat builder rather than a businessman, a reality that shaped his career. In July 1951, he found a partner in a well-to-do Plymouth chiropractor. Dr. Herbert Lotz purchased the Kingston boat yard once owned by George Shiverick and set up The MacKenzie Boat Shop, Inc. The flyer headline was "The Original Bass Boat." Eighteen- to twenty-eight-foot models were offered. Unfortunately, this promising arrangement ended prematurely when Lotz died five months later, an event MacKenzie called a "turning point" in his life. Businessman Thomas Stott Jr. purchased the yard in May 1953 but, unhappy with aspects of the new arrangement, Mac moved on.

Sometime in 1955, MacKenzie partnered with fellow Nova Scotian Al Moss—a contractor who'd had much success building A&P markets—as Moss Marine in Fall River. "MacKenzie was a good boat builder," said Joseph Richard Cottreau, a Blue Nose who worked with Mac. "But Al footed the money." Cottreau reported that before he moved to the States in 1956, he had worked on about a dozen MacKenzie twenty-two-foot bass boats in Wedgeport, Nova Scotia. "MacKenzie came and showed us what he wanted," Cottreau said. "The boats were shipped out to Fall River in primer and without engines for completion." During this period, Mac lived weekdays in a trailer at Moss, returning to his Kingston home on weekends. There, the boatbuilder and his son-in-law Howard Benassi machined and polished all the boats' bronze hardware, which was cast from Mac's patterns.

While the Moss Marine years were productive, it was not until 1960 and a move to Al Gray's yard in Taunton that MacKenzie's business affairs and boat production were put on a truly solid footing. Businessman Paul McCusker—who'd bought a large sports fisherman from Gray and who owned Fab-Ri-Kona, a company that manufactured Dexolium, a composite decking material—saw to that. It was McCusker who funded what was now known as MacKenzie-Gray. "That's when the MacKenzie really turned into a production boat," said Paul's son Peter McCusker.

The decision was now made to focus initially on the 23' and 26' models, the sweet spot in the market. "Al Gray and Mac got in touch with customers to find out what they liked and didn't like," said Pete McCusker. "They lofted out the hull and then made changes. They gave the stern more flare, opening space in the cockpit. They raised the chine forward. They added a bit of deadrise aft. The changes were very successful."

Al Gray's son Chris went to work at the yard when he completed high school. "My father thought through boat production to the limit," he said. "There were patterns for frames, floor timbers, stems, and planks, and a jig for the windshield. A boat could be completed in two weeks."

The classic MacKenzie was mahogany-planked over sawn-oak frames, with copper-riveted laps, and bronze screws and keel bolts. (At some point, galvanized steel was used, apparently for cost reasons, in floor timbers and chine logs.) The substantial oak keel was cut away in the deadwood area, contributing to maneuverability. Longtime enthusiast and co-founder of the MacKenzie Boat Club, Jeff Rutledge said a 22' MacKenzie was "the best boat I ever ran. It would zip around like a fish." Directional stability, lift, ride quality and strength were enhanced by the signature reverse lapstrake bottom. (The plank edges face away from the keel rather than toward it.) Guide boats had splash coamings like Nunes's Winslow but graceful windshields were a prominent feature of the other models.

This shot of a MacKenzie twenty-three-footer, probably taken on the Taunton River, was included in the 1967 brochure of the Cuttyhunk Boat Co., located in Hyannis, Massachusetts. "This is a great boat for the family or fisherman," said the brochure. Often painted white, dark green, or dark blue, with a varnished windshield frame and transom, the boats were eye-catchers. (Jeff Rutledge)

Cuttyhunk guide Bob Smith was a friend of MacKenzie's whose *Susan B.* was a fire-engine red twenty-three-footer, a size Jim Nunes called "the best Mac for fishing. You could get very close to the beach. She was wet but she could take a pounding if you could. The feeling here was if you had one, you had arrived."

In 1967, when Paul McCusker moved production to Falmouth Rd. in Hyannis, MacKenzie himself was no longer involved, having suffered a serious eye injury while working in Taunton. At Hyannis, much of the production involved the thirty which, like the twenty-six, was also available in trunk cabin versions. "I thought the trunk cabin was a much better setup for most people than the flush deck because there was a lot more light and room below," said Pete McCusker.

By the late 1960s, a 26' MacKenzie with a 265-hp Palmer V-8 listed at $11,855 (about twice the price of a Cadillac Sedan deVille) before options. Then "materials prices quadrupled in the early '70s," said Pete McCusker, "and the energy crisis hit in '74 and '75. My dad was never going to lessen the spec or build a fiberglass boat but costs were increasing as customers decreased. Dad waited until everyone had jobs and closed the doors."

MacKenzie left no record of how many boats he built—200–250 seems a reasonable guess—or the many changes, especially in pre-Taunton days, that now fascinate or perplex MacKenzie enthusiasts. "Very early boats had fewer side strakes," Rutledge noted. Pre-Moss boats had commercially made rudders and bow chocks. "He changed the rudder design ever so slightly for maximum performance [on the 26]," said Benassi. "Also, there were two different struts used on the 23s." Pre-Taunton boats had caulked decks while Dexolium was introduced at MacKenzie-Gray. Windshield framing evolved. But the bass boats' basics were constant and listed in the Kingston-era flyer: "Lap Strake . . . Vee Bottom . . . Outside Keel . . . Dual Control."

Ernest J. MacKennzie died on February 22, 1995, age ninety-three. Howard Benassi remembers his father-in-law as a man who often worked fourteen-hour days, perhaps taking a Sunday afternoon off. "Once in awhile," Benassi said, "he'd take his Jeep and dog and the family [Mac and his wife Lulu had three daughters] to Saquish beach. We'd go fishing sometimes in Mac's 15' plywood skiff. His whole life was boats."

"He Drew on the Floor"

"Now," said Jim Nunes, "I'll mention another of the real bass boats we used to have here, the Ballentine. Coot had one. In fact, he had two of them. They were seaworthy."

Among Cuttyhunk's best-known guides, "Coot" Hall was a slender man, shorter even than Ernie MacKenzie, who wore glasses and a long-billed fisherman's cap. When reporters visited Cuttyhunk to write stories about bass fishing, it was often Coot who they asked for first. "He was," said Jim Nunes, "a nice guy who could sell ice cubes in Alaska."

The Ballentine bass boats—twenty-two- and twenty-four-footers—were the distinctive creation of George Ballentine of North Falmouth, Massachusetts. According to his son Steve, George designed by eye. "He drew conceptual sketches and would sell potential customers on the look. Then he drew it all out on the shop floor."

By the late 1940s, the features most associated with a Ballentine had been finalized. The hull had a rather fine V-shaped entry. Early versions had a straight stem but this soon gave way to a stem with a projecting "beak" or "knuckle" at its top. The knuckle combined with reverse sheer and generous flare to provide a distinctive look. The hull had hard chines and a big spray rail that swept from the waterline well up the side of the bow.

Although these boats were initially built of plywood over oak frames, by the late 1940s, the planking was mahogany. "Most," said Steve Ballentine,

The 22' *Hooligan* was designed and built by George Ballentine. The builder's granddaughter, Amy Ballentine-Stevens, of Ballentine's Boat Shop in Cataumet, Massachusetts, reported that "the style is making a comeback as people who are downsizing realize that a day boat might be used more than their bigger boats." (Tyler Fields)

"had windshields, but not the Cuttyhunk guide boats." The Ballentines had the requisite tiller aft but the forward steering station featured a small bronze wheel. Power was generally a Chrysler Crown or Ace but the quest for more torque saw the introduction of Chris-Craft conversions of the Chevrolet 283 cubic-inch V-8 for the 24-footers.

When *Sports Illustrated* writer Gerald Holland visited Cuttyhunk in 1956, he sounded out Coot over dinner at the Bosworth House where the guide lived summers with his dog Cutty. In answer to Holland's question about the nature of a bass fisherman, Coot replied: "Once a striper fisherman is hooked, he's hooked for life . . . men and women come here to Cuttyhunk from all over."

For years, Coot took them fishing in his Ballentines. When he moved on, it was to a marvelous boat built by an inventive man known to all as "Fred."

"He Was Always Thinking"

On June 16, 1967, Jim Nunes was trolling the Pigs alongside his friend and fellow guide Frank Sabatowski. Although based in Fairhaven at an old tackle shop named the Outdoorsman, Frank frequently took his parties to Cuttyhunk and on this particular trip, he had aboard an experienced fisherman named Charlie Cinto. From the cockpit of Sabatowski's gray-painted Brownell 26, Cinto cast a blue and white Big Daddy Goo-Goo Eyes plug with yellow glass eyes into the rips. He snagged a bass that equaled the weight of Charles Church's seventy-three-pounder.

Sabatowski's *June Bug* was the first of eighteen 26-footers built between 1966 and 1977 by David Frederick "Fred" Brownell in a barn-turned-boat shop in Mattapoisett. Prior to buying the 26, Sabatowski had owned a Brownell 24 but the 26 was significantly larger, permitting a bigger engine. "A handful of guides used the boats," Brownell's daughter Linda said. "But most were used as pleasure boats by avid people."

The Brownells were designed by Walter McGinnis who based the lines on those of his existing Marblehead 25. "The boats had a narrow entry, deep keel and hard chines to keep them from rolling," Linda said. "My father added a spray rail he developed that ran from under the waterline aft and swept up to the bow." To produce this spray rail, Brownell made his own shaper. The boats had fore and aft steering positions. Initially, the cabin coaming had a single porthole but soon Brownell lengthened the cabin and added the now familiar three-portlight arrangement.

The construction method evolved. "Our first were carvel-planked over sawn frames like the Marblehead 25," said Ronnie Lima who worked at

Hatchet II, a 26' bassboat, was built by Fred Brownell to a design by Eldredge-McInnis. (Author's collection/Linda Brownell)

Brownell's for some forty-five years. "Then we did batten-seam for increased strength. Then Fred built a few that were diagonally planked inside and carvel-planked outside using full-length, scarfed 26-foot planks, which resulted in a very fair hull."

Eventually though, Brownell settled on two layers of diagonally planked 3/8" mahogany epoxied together and bronze-screw-fastened from the inside. The hulls were then sheathed in fiberglass cloth set in WEST System™ resin. "Fred," said Lima, "found a machine that would allow him to tongue-and-groove the planks and we'd epoxy the joints." Cabin tops were made of two or three layers of plywood laminated together with epoxy, a process that eliminated the need for interior framing of the top. At some point, Brownell determined the boat should have a larger rudder and he adapted the keel from one of his thirty-two-foot sport fishing models. The change increased the boat's draft by a few inches, permitted a larger prop, and improved overall performance.

"From the time he got up until he went to bed," said Linda Brownell, "my father always wore a sharpened pencil behind his ear. He never knew when he'd need to do some designing." Besides building sport fishing boats as large as 52', Brownell diversified his business by turning the area around the barn into Brownell's Boat Yard. That prompted his invention of highly successful adjustable boat stands and the renowned Brownell hydraulic boat trailer. Said Ronnie Lima, "Fred was a genius. He was always thinking."

The New England Bass Boat

"Most people," Jim Nunes reflected, "never have a boat that will fulfill all their needs. But I do."

Like a Maine lobster boat, a Florida flats boat, a Jersey sea skiff, or others intended to pursue specific quarry in specific waters, the real New England bass boat was developed to meet the specialized needs of the professional fishing guide. Those needs were best fulfilled with a solidly built, hard-chine 22-26-footer. Whoever the builder, the boats possessed shared attributes that included a substantial oak keel to protect a rugged bottom, the rudder, and the prop. They had largely vertical topsides—about waist high in some cases and comfortable for the fisherman—fore- and aft-controls, an open cockpit with no windshield, and the most powerful gasoline engine practical. These boats could venture into tide rips or the shallow water between surf and shore where bass lurk among unyielding rocks. They provided the necessary stable platform while trolling, responded instantly to throttle input, and could turn on a dime.

Ultimately, most who bought bass boats or their derivatives were not the legendary guides who made them famous, but sport fishermen attracted by the boats' performance and functional beauty. Despite their specialized nature, the true bass boat—the Mac in particular—has provided contentment for weekend fishing, as a family runabout or as a no-frills cruiser. The last time I talked to Jim Nunes, though, he was awaiting the arrival of his next fishing party on the Cuttyhunk ferry. As always, he was thinking about tide and wind.

"You want to go when the full tide is starting to drop," he said. "It's nice if that's around evening when it's just getting dark."

Standing aft in the *Rudy J.*, the guide will know just where to head and where, down in the dark water, the hungry fish will be waiting. Even when the light fades, he'll be able to see all around him.

Bass Boats for a Broader Market

Any story of the Cuttyhunk guides and their specialized boats must note other hard-chine designs directed at the broader market. Ernest MacKenzie and his various partners understood the obvious need to reach beyond the professional fishing guide and stressed the "family" appeal of the boats. The popular Crosby Striper was based on a cypress-built twenty-four-footer originally developed in Ft. Myers by Henry and Frank Daniels for guides in southwest Florida. Wonderfully versatile, the Striper was available as both an open boat and a cabin model. Production transitioned to fiberglass. After MacKenzie parted ways with Moss Marine, the latter built the Sakonnet 26, an Eldridge-McInnis design that reflected features of a number of boats including the Brownell. This boat gave rise to the well-regarded fiberglass Fortier 26. On Cape Cod, Spaulding Dunbar (*WoodenBoat* No. 161) developed his Bristol series of boats—including the 21' Bonito Bass Boat—for the Allen Quimby Veneer Co. of Bingham, Maine. These were attractive, mahogany plywood over oak frame boats with Everdur fasteners. Elsewhere, capable builders produced a number of hard-chine bass boats that, in some cases, achieved local popularity. Today, elements of bass boat "style" may be found in several fiberglass designs.

This story appeared in *WoodenBoat* No. 230, January/February 2013.

A WIDE WHITE ROAD

C. Raymond Hunt and the Development of the Deep-V Hull

One pleasant morning in late summer of 2014, James "Sham" Hunt pulled into my driveway with a trunk full of reference materials relating to the life of his father, Charles Raymond Hunt. Soon enough, we were having lunch overlooking Marblehead Harbor and discussing my writing a long-overdue biography of Raymond, whose genius as both a sailor and innovative designer was known to a core of racing yachtsmen, both sail and power, but had yet to be chronicled in the book he richly deserved.

As the writing process progressed, I developed some insight into Raymond's inimitable abilities and the reasons his work hadn't been more widely celebrated. I also took the opportunity to ride my bike around Marblehead, pausing at places where Hunt and his family had lived for a few years beginning in 1947. Having Sham's reference materials reduced my research time by six to twelve months. The resulting book—*A Genius at His Trade: C. Raymond Hunt and His Remarkable Boats*—was published in 2015. A second, slightly updated, soft-cover edition followed in 2017.

This *WoodenBoat* story focused on Hunt's conception and development of what remains known as the deep-V hull and its revolutionary impact on powerboat design. The story drew a thoughtful response from an English powerboat enthusiast who noted that Hunt's deep-V had gained wide acceptance in the UK slightly before it did in the United States. The writer also mentioned that yachtsmen in the UK were surprised that Hunt "does not even appear in your National Sailing Hall of Fame." This matter was rectified two years after the book's publication. In August 2017, at the New York Yacht Club's beautiful Harbour Court facility in Newport, Rhode Island, Ray Hunt was inducted into the National Sailing Hall of Fame.

"Even to one unfamiliar with the type it was obvious she was a wonderful sea boat: 30 feet over-all, built to designs by C. Raymond Hunt of Marblehead in the yard of Richard H. Bertram in Miami by workmen only recently from Havana, *Moppie*'s underwater form was unusual—V-shaped not only forward but all the way back to the transom."

—Carleton Mitchell, *Sports Illustrated*, April 25, 1960

On the morning of April 12, 1960, Dick Bertram boarded a 30' powerboat called *Moppie*. The boat's driver, Sam Griffith, proceeded to steer her into the smooth waters of Miami's Government Cut. Griffith had *Moppie*'s two big Lincoln engines burbling away at just above idle speed as he and twenty-two other racers waited for 7 a.m., when the flag would drop and send everyone off on what the Bahamas Tourist Bureau billed as "The Most Rugged Ocean Race in the World." Also aboard was yachtsman and writer Carleton Mitchell, who had sailed with Bertram in the legendary yawl *Finisterre* to win three consecutive Bermuda Races.

All anyone knew before the starter's flag dropped was that this edition of the 185-mile Miami–Nassau Ocean Power Boat Race was likely to live up to its billing. A northeast wind had not subsided until the previous day, and it was expected that thirty-knot winds would still be blowing against the flow of the Gulf Stream. When the flag dropped, reported Mitchell in *Sports Illustrated*, "I was slammed back into my chair as Skipper Sam Griffith gunned the engines, the fleet dropped astern and the wake stretched like a wide white road back toward our nearest competitors, a road that grew steadily longer." Outside the breakwater, the men donned diving masks for protection against spray and held onto what they could as Griffith opened the throttles. *Moppie* literally took off.

Nothing could really have prepared Mitchell for the violence of it. He had placed a tube of sunscreen 7' away and, for the next seven hours, never felt it was safe enough to try to reach it. "The ocean," Mitchell wrote, "was as rough as I had ever seen it. . . . At times the effect was something like diving from a second-story window into a neighboring cellar piled with bricks."

Griffith held the Lincolns' rpm down as *Moppie* left the Miami skyline behind. "Mitch and I both marveled," Bertram would later write, "at his judgment of the waves as he would throttle back just in time to keep us from leaping off a big one. . . . About an hour out of Miami, the two aluminum deck chairs on which Mitch and I were sitting disintegrated and were thrown over the side."

Moppie's wooden hull had been very strongly built, but 10' seas, mechanical smarts, and the fact that no competitors were in sight suggested to

Griffith—known as "Wild Man" to friends—that he throttle back to fifteen knots. *Moppie* dashed along in this fashion, all alone for an hour, until they spotted spray to the north. The boat churning that spray was Jim Wynne's twenty-three-footer, *Aqua Hunter*, with its two Volvo Aquamatic drives. *Aqua Hunter* was named in deference to her two major pioneering concepts: she was being pushed along by a pair of stern-drives, a concept that was brand-new at the time, and her hull had been designed by C. Raymond Hunt. Hunt had also designed *Moppie*. Mitchell reported this impression of *Aqua Hunter*: "His little vessel was coming off crests, leaping clear with sky showing beneath the entire length of the keel. *Moppie* promptly ran away from Wynne because of our greater overall length and advantage in horsepower."

Bertram's boat, the big Lincolns turning 4,100 rpm in smoother water under the lee of the west end of Nassau, finished the race at 3 p.m., eight hours and ten minutes after leaving Miami. Not only was it a race record, but it also was set in difficult conditions. "She never once rolled a propeller out, something we had often experienced in other boats under similar

In 1960, this 30' wooden powerboat named *Moppie* won a decisive victory in the 185-mile Miami-Nassau Race. That win spurred the wide acceptance of Hunt's deep-V hull form and in turn revolutionized recreational powerboat design. (C. Raymond Hunt Associates)

conditions," Bertram wrote. If anything, Jim Wynne's arrival in second place two-and-a-half hours later was even more impressive, for his boat had less than half the horsepower of other racers. "It was," Carleton Mitchell wrote, "a remarkable demonstration of the efficiency of the Hunt design in rough water."

The "Hunt design" was the newly conceived deep-V hull form, and its performance surprised even Bertram and Wynne. They had anticipated they might have an advantage in rough seas offshore and in the chop on the Bahama Bank. But their boats had outperformed very powerful and well-proven competitors right from the start. In fact, it was not until the following day that the third-place boat arrived. Al Martin, a pre-race skeptic, told the *Miami Herald*'s Jim Martenhoff: "I wouldn't be a bit surprised next year to see a whole fleet of Hunt designs in the race."

C. Raymond Hunt was a yacht designer of boundless creative energy and extraordinary breadth, straddling the upper echelons of both the power and sail communities. Bill Wallace, reporting on the results of the Miami–Nassau Race for the *New York Herald Tribune* (April 17, 1960), observed that "the winner blended Gasoline Alley and sailing's Hall of Fame."

During the 1930s, Hunt had foreseen the market for an affordable racing sailboat and developed a most unusual design, the 110-class sloop. Their cigar-shaped hulls were built of plywood—an unheard-of proposition at the time—and were launched to much skepticism. Within a few years, however, the hard-chined, slab-sided one-design had become the dominant fleet on Massachusetts Bay and beyond. Illustrating his incredible range, Hunt designed the Concordia Yawl, the quintessential New England cruising sailboat, in 1938—the same year he unveiled the 110. Following on the 110's success, Hunt returned to a companion prewar design, the larger but similar 210, in 1946. During the mid-1950s he developed with his lifelong friend Dick Fisher the small outboard-powered boat that became the 13' Boston Whaler.

Hunt had begun work on powerboats during the war years, but the 110 had its influence. Kingsley Durant, a young 110 sailor in Cohasset where Hunt then lived, still recalls an encounter with him. Hunt told Durant that the hard-chined one-designs had an optimal angle of heel that would most effectively present a V-bottom when the boat was sailing. In this encounter, Hunt went on to muse about the possibilities of this shape in a powerboat. Hunt believed that a production powerboat that could run fast and smooth even in rough conditions would have a wide audience. He spent much of the 1950s pondering this idea, and by the spring of 1958 he knew he was onto *something*—probably something big. He'd been studying up on this. He'd been thinking. He'd been sketching out ideas for a hull form that would impress everyone as something distinctly new.

As a youth, Hunt was an unmotivated student, but when a subject fascinated him, he read whatever he could about it. Over time, he gathered together a small number of reference books that he used time and again. One was his daughter Yan's high-school physics book. Another was a collection of boat designs, including three of his own, called *Your New Boat* (Simon and Schuster, 1946). But the most important of the books he kept close by was Lindsay Lord's *Naval Architecture of Planing Hulls*, first published in 1946.

A Massachusetts Institute of Technology (MIT) graduate who earned an MBA at Boston University and a PhD in naval architecture from the University of the Pacific, Lord had developed an early interest in high-speed powerboats that resulted in a number of fast designs, some used in rum-running. During World War II, he achieved the rank of lieutenant commander and spent his time in the Pacific overseeing PT boats, a perfect assignment for a man of his background and interests. Later, working out of his office in Falmouth Foreside, Maine, he designed high-speed naval craft for both the Dutch and the Spanish navies.

Hunt was particularly drawn to Lord's negative opinion of the so-called warped bottom—that is, a bottom whose angle of deadrise flattens as it goes aft, ending with a nearly flat-bottomed transom. Lord favored a "monohedron hull"—one with a constant deadrise aft.

Hunt's purchase of Lord's book led him to visit the author in Maine. "Ray Hunt came here shortly after the first edition came out," Lord told Mystic Seaport oral historian Fred Calabretta, "and a lot of questions he had. I spent a lot of time with him.... Whenever he was doubtful, he would send the plans [of boats he was designing] to me for comment."

John Deknatel, who led Hunt's design firm for forty-five years, called Lord "one of the innovative designers of the time. He used primitive model tests. Eventually, he concluded that you didn't want to have twist in a hull as the PTs did. He did towing tests to show that a hull without twist in the bottom was an improvement. His theory was that the hull should have a constant section from 'midships all the way aft. And he advocated a significant degree of deadrise. But he would change the deadrise depending on a specific boat, its application, the volume, and equipment within the hull.

"Raymond's idea was different. He used the same amount of deadrise [on all of his boats] from 'midships aft. Intuitively, nobody knows how, he determined the deadrise should be 24 degrees. Today, with all our technology, we know this to be near-ideal. Also, rather than change that angle to meet the demands of different boats, he moved things around within the hull—engines, equipment, and so forth—to make the weight distribution work."

To prove his theory, Hunt designed the prototype for what perhaps would become the most influential powerboat ever built, a boat with a whole new level of performance. For decades, ever since the appearance of the first "autoboats"—the early runabouts—during the early 1900s, there had been the search for increased speed on the water. Long, narrow displacement hulls gave way to stepped hulls that would plane, to V-bottoms of various configurations developed by forward-looking and competent naval architects. These hulls combined speed with seaworthiness, but Hunt was onto a whole new level of performance.

The first two boats built to Hunt's new concept were each called *Hunter*, and were built of wood at the Rhode Island yard of Sam Wharton. The design included a centerboard to improve maneuverability at low speed, but the board would lift up automatically when the hull reached planing speed. Hunt also conceived of using water ballast to improve stability at low speed and while at rest. The patent document presenting Hunt's deep-V boats stated that he had conceived of the idea in 1956 and in the spring of 1957 launched a 23' wooden prototype with a centerboard and a 'midship-mounted engine.

Few images show *Moppie*'s innovative lifting strakes better than this one. The strakes increased lift and stability. (C. Raymond Hunt Associates)

A 16' outboard with a "water ballast tunnel" appeared the following spring. The first boat had, initially at least, surface-piercing propellers. Neither of the wooden prototypes originally had what would soon become the deep-V's most distinctive feature besides the deep-V itself: a series of longitudinal bottom strakes. Hunt devised these strakes as the way to both increase lift and add stability.

Designer Waltman Mayo Walters, who would go on to associations with Dick Bertram and speedboat builder Don Aronow, among others, remembered one of Hunt's prototypes. In a 2010 oral-history interview, Walters told Fred Calabretta: "Deep-V boats are not stable at anchor, they rock around a lot, and so he invented this hole in the bottom of the boat and then a floor inside so that the whole underside of the floor could flood. But when you took off, the water would come out. . . . The boat was beautiful. He got into propeller design. I got to watch that because he had a surface-piercing propeller [with a shaft] that fed through the transom, not down underneath. And that worked pretty good."

Despite this experimentation, Hunt's vision for the deep-V concept was not in custom or semi-custom construction. Rather, he envisioned the design's broad appeal, and saw the potential in mass production. Hunt looked to Wharton for advice on who would be qualified to build fiberglass versions. Wharton was a dealer for Dyer dinghies, and he recommended as a builder the genial Bill Dyer, whose facility, the Anchorage, was located in Warren, Rhode Island. There Dyer had become one of the small group of New Englanders who, after the war, were pioneering fiberglass construction as "the future of boating." At the Anchorage, Dyer had begun molding his famous dinghies starting in 1952. Best evidence suggests the first fiberglass Hunter was built in 1956.

Sam Wharton told journalist and yacht designer V. B. Crockett that the Hunter was "the strongest Fiberglas boat ever built. . . . I've tried to break this boat up for two years and I'm tired of trying to do it." Urethane foam was injected into various areas to increase strength and reduce noise. The twin forty-two-gallon fuel tanks were built of fiberglass, and the boat's shaft-log and centerboard box were molded integrally with the hull to eliminate potential leaks. The board, controlled by a lever, was included to add lateral plane and improve maneuverability at low speed. It was also intended to dampen roll when the boat was stopped, so the owner could fish.

But the real revolution, in addition to the hull's V-bottom throughout, was in the hull's integrally molded stringers or strakes. These were the real attention-getter. Based on an interview with Hunt and Wharton, V. B. Crockett described three benefits of the strakes: "(1) To help lift the boat so that she gains speed and rides on the surface; (2) To give added stability and reduce roll (the air between the stringers cushions the motion in rough going); (3) To roll spray down so that the boat is drier in heavy seas."

According to Hunt, two fiberglass 23' prototypes were built. Each had the centerboard and an engine mounted amidships. During the 1958 *America*'s Cup trials off Newport, Rhode Island, one of these *Hunters* served as tender to the wooden Hunt-designed 12-Meter *Easterner*. The boat, flying the Eastern Yacht Club's burgee from a staff on the bow, was often driven by Hunt's son Josh, with Hunt's wife Barbara sometimes aboard. That's where people first noticed the design. Those who noticed the boat—and they were many—observed how smoothly it ran in rough seas without reducing speed. At rest, it looked like a displacement hull, but then as it gained speed the boat lifted out of the water in a manner nobody had ever seen.

Among those impressed by *Hunter* was Miami yacht broker Dick Bertram, who was then in charge of the foredeck of *Vim*, the oldest 12-Meter in the trials. Bertram never forgot the moment he saw *Hunter*: "It was about 11 a.m., July 16, 1958. . . . The wind was blowing a good twenty-plus knots out of the southwest. Seas were running six feet or more. Great weather for 12-Meter sailing, but a little rough for the wallowing powerboats. . . . Well, something very special came hurtling across those six-foot crests. It was Ray Hunt's deep-V prototype. . . . Knifing through those six-foot seas at thirty knots, this little twenty-three-footer stopped every sailor in the fleet in his tracks. No one had ever seen powerboat performance to approach it." Seeing the boat changed Dick Bertram's life.

Another who noticed *Hunter* was V. B. Crockett, who knew a good story when he saw it skipping across the wavetops. Wondering how a boat with such a pronounced V-shaped bottom could possess the necessary stability and not squat awkwardly at high speed, Crockett promptly visited Hunt in his Beacon Street apartment in Boston. He then wrote an article published in the July 1958 issue of *The Skipper* titled "Revolution . . . Hunt Style, New Power Boat Design Counters Old Theories." He quoted Hunt: "She's quite a bit different than the usual power boat, isn't she?"

Crockett described the hull as "a modified V-bottom boat that doesn't have the usual long, flat run common in the conventional boat. Her entrance is easy and her deadrise is carried at nearly the same angle from amidships to the transom. This gives the underbody a deep vee extending the length of the hull." Soon, wherever men gathered to talk about speed on the water, they would use this new term, *deep-V*. Within the marine industry, and among knowledgeable powerboat enthusiasts and racers, the term would always be identified with C. Raymond Hunt.

Besides being the genius behind the deep-V hull, Ray Hunt is remembered as the designer of the classically beautiful Concordia Yawl, the popular 110/210-class sloops, and the original Boston Whaler. His innovative thinking is carried on still by C. Raymond Hunt Associates of New Bedford, Massachusetts. (C. Raymond Hunt Associates)

At the time *The Skipper* published this article, Hunt was willing to talk about the boat, but the profile and plan-view drawings he supplied to the magazine were accompanied by the comment: "Designer Hunt has released only partial plans." Although he remained, throughout his life, overly casual about financial and administrative matters, Hunt did plan to patent his deep-V idea. He was aware of his design's potential and believed he was giving Crockett only an intriguing glimpse of his new boat.

Because of Hunt's planned patent applications, he did not answer Crockett's logical questions about stability, or an unasked question about low-speed maneuverability. But Hunt, as noted earlier, had addressed these matters with a centerboard and with water ballast.

A decade later, when Hunt provided evidence in defense of his patent on the deep-V hull, he didn't mention that a third fiberglass hull had been built, apparently by New Bedford's Palmer Scott, whose Marscot Plastics was a pioneer fiberglass boatbuilder. After that company's assets were acquired by a boat-obsessed Boston insurance broker named George O'Day in March 1958, O'Day concluded an agreement with Hunt, gaining the rights to sell the deep-V boats. This agreement, however, never developed. Crockett's article in *The Skipper* noted: "The Anchorage, Inc. of Warren, Rhode Island, will continue to build the Fiberglas hull. Fairey Marine, a subsidiary of Fairey Aviation, Ltd., in England will build the same design in England using plywood for the hull." Ultimately, though, it would be Dick Bertram, and then others, who would realize the sales potential of the deep-V.

The Marscot-built hull, it is believed, was sold to Florida boat racer and stern-drive pioneer Jim Wynne, probably in 1959. After a trip to Sweden, Wynne had received enthusiastic backing from Volvo for his inboard/outboard concept that uniquely combined the advantages of an inboard engine with the maneuverability of an outboard motor. Volvo marketed its inboard/outboard under the brand name Aquamatic. Those stern-drives, incidentally, neatly eliminated the very real maneuverability problems that journalist Crockett had wondered about. After refitting his new boat with stern-drives, Wynne drove it to the second-place finish described at the beginning of this chapter.

Hunt's friends and admirers in England were just as impressed by the results of the 1960 Miami–Nassau Race as were observers in the United States. At his house in Cowes, Sir Max Aitken decided it would be a grand idea to have a similar long-distance event in the U.K. The race—over a punishing course from Cowes to Torquay on the Devon coast—would be sponsored by Aitken's newspaper, the *Daily Express*. A prize of £1,000 and the Lord Beaverbrook Challenge Trophy would be awarded to the winner.

"This race," reported *Yachts & Yachting* on September 8, 1961, "was something of a triumph for American designer Ray Hunt, possibly better known over here for his beautiful and successful sailing boats, for the first four finishers were to his designs." The top boats were built by Bertram or by Bruce Campbell's Fairey Marine, which had acquired the U.K. rights to Hunt's deep-V.

Although the initial Fairey-built models—constructed of hot-molded plywood—had included the retractable centerboard, this soon proved leaky and troublesome. Revisions were made to produce what Fairey marketed as its Christina, a twenty-five-footer powered by twin Crusader V-8 engines, each producing 325 hp and driving 14" x 17" propellers.

The winner of the 1961 Cowes–Torquay Race was Tommy Sopwith, driving his *Thunderbolt*. Uffa Fox described Sopwith's performance in his book *Seamanlike Sense in Powercraft*. Fox called Sopwith—son of the *America*'s Cup challenger T.O.M. Sopwith—"a most capable seaman, steersman and navigator with a very great deal of courage. He drove this boat around a 190-mile course, through high grey seas with white breaking crests, without knowing whether he was ahead, astern, or where the rest of the fleet was; all had been swallowed up by seas and flying spray and it was not until he had finished that he learned that he was the leader and winner of the race."

In second place was Jim Wynne, driving the far less powerful, Bertram-built *Aqua Hunter*, with twin Volvo Aquamatics totaling 200 hp. "That they came in second was a great feat for men, boat, and engines," said *Yachts & Yachting*.

Soon after his 1958 encounter with *Hunter* in Newport, Dick Bertram purchased a twenty-three-foot Hunter, intending it for family use around Miami. Bertram was a high roller who could afford to do as he pleased. When the *Saturday Evening Post* profiled him in 1961, he claimed to have brokered $5 million worth of used racing motorboats in the previous year. He was known to some of the world's wealthiest men, including Aristotle Onassis and the Aga Khan. "His outfit," said one of his rivals, "has all the gimmicks, big parties, big ads, big talk."

When Bertram showed his *Hunter* to his friend Sam Griffith, a renowned powerboat jockey, Griffith's reaction was, "I didn't think it would run at all. I told Dick Bertram he was wasting his time." But no one really knew what they were looking at. "We looked it over," boatshop owner Al Martin remembered. "None of us thought it would work. We laughed at it."

As he got acquainted with his new boat, however, Bertram became ever more convinced of its potential. He was so enthusiastic that he commissioned Hunt to draw up lines for a thirty-footer, to be built in wood. This boat, *Moppie*, was built in 1959. After its astounding victory in the following year's Miami–Nassau Race, it served as the plug for the mold that would shape the hulls of the Bertram 31 sportfisherman—the first true production powerboat with a deep-V hull. These molded fiberglass hulls, born from a legendary wooden boat, had a profound influence upon the future of powerboats—an influence that echoes far and wide to this day. They were revolutionary, both in hull material, and in hull design.

This story appeared in *WoodenBoat* No. 245, July/August 2015.

PART FOUR

BOAT CRAZY

THE *MUSKETAQUID* MYSTERY

In Search of Thoreau's Boat

I suppose that being both boat crazy and an English major inevitably meant that I would take a special interest in the boat made famous by Henry David Thoreau in his first book, *A Week on the Concord and Merrimack Rivers.* Thoreau wrote the book during the time he spent in his famous cabin at Walden Pond from July 4, 1845, to September 6, 1847. Although *A Week* is far from the sparkling, often controversial but evergreen achievement of *Walden*, the fact that it had as its basis a little voyage never ceased to intrigue me.

Eventually, I reread *A Week* several times searching for clues regarding the boat Thoreau used and pithy thoughts he had about boats in general, sailing, and simply being on the water. Finally, I gave in and began reading through his *Journal* in search of more information that might lead to understanding.

This story was published early on in my association with *WoodenBoat*. It was, perhaps, a bit outside the normal scope of what the magazine publishes or what its readers might expect to encounter. For those reasons, I remain especially grateful to editor Matt Murphy for his enthusiasm and the care with which the manuscript was edited and eventually published.

As it happened, though, readers were receptive to the story and found it thought-provoking. In fact, not long after the story was published, Connecticut boatbuilder David Snediker created a version of what the *Musketaquid* might have looked like. The Concord Museum exhibited the boat in a special exhibition that ran from August 2007 to January 2008. Since then, the story has occasionally been referenced by Thoreau scholars in the never-ending quest to better understand their subject who advised his readers to "simplify, simplify."

"Mr. Thoreau and I walked up the bank of the river, and at a certain point, he shouted for his boat. Forthwith a young man paddled it across, and Mr. Thoreau and I voyaged farther up the stream, which soon became more beautiful than any picture, with its dark and quiet sheet of water, half-shaded, half sunny, between high and wooded banks."
—Nathaniel Hawthorne, *American Notes*, September 1, 1842

"A sailor, I see, easily becomes attached to his vessel."
—Henry David Thoreau, *Journal*, August 31, 1852

One spring day in 1839, two brothers in Concord, Massachusetts, gathered together the necessary wood and tools and began to build themselves a boat. The effort, wrote Henry David Thoreau, "cost us a week's labor." A few months later, on August 31, twenty-two-year-old Henry and his twenty-four-year-old brother John pushed the boat into the Concord River and set off on a trip that would take them up that slow-moving stream to Billerica and the Middlesex Canal. The six-mile-long canal provided them transit through locks to the Merrimack River, which carried them on to Hooksett, New Hampshire. There, they left the boat and journeyed overland to Concord, or New Concord, as Thoreau called it, giving the trip a symmetry of destinations that must have been appealing. They then voyaged home, arriving back in Concord two weeks after they'd left.

Such a journey would now be thought of as a mildly adventurous camp-cruising expedition, but at the time, the venture was quite a novelty—a small boat expedition that was recreational in concept with no visible commercial purpose. In fact, near the end of the trip, Thoreau noted a rowboat clearly being used as "a pleasure boat by a youth and maiden . . . which we were pleased to see, since it proved that there were some hereabouts to whom our excursion would not be wholly strange." It would not be until the post–Civil War era that rowboats and canoes became a more generally popular leisure activity in the area.

Six years after it occurred, this river "excursion" provided the inspiration for Henry David Thoreau's first book, the initial draft of which was written in a 10' x 15' shingled cabin that he had constructed by himself. Thoreau's handiness was well recognized by those who knew him. According to his friend and biographer, William Ellery Channing, Thoreau's skill with his hands was "early developed, so much so that it was even thought to have had him bound as an apprentice to a cabinet maker."

The cabin, about which more detail has survived than the boat, was constructed in the woods at Concord's sixty-two-acre Walden Pond. There, in the summer of 1845, Thoreau began reworking his notes of the river journey, and he recorded a few details of the boat itself. This was the vehicle that, one might say, literally floated the whole idea for *A Week on the Concord and Merrimack Rivers*, a commercially unsuccessful but important step in Thoreau's development as a writer.

Just what manner of boat was this craft of Thoreau's? What were the details of its design? How was it constructed? These questions lay at the heart of a mystery. Although this boat must be counted as among the most important in American letters, reliable details of the little vessel itself are sparse and even conflicting. Thoreau's *Journal*, his daily record of his readings, thoughts, and adventures, includes a quick sketch done in 1851 of a rowboat that caught his attention because it was built in three sections, each one capable of supporting an occupant. However, the author left no drawing of the boat that he and John built in 1839, and those that have appeared in illustrated editions of *A Week* can only be regarded as fanciful. The effort here is to suggest—based on studied conjecture—what manner of boat the *Musketaquid* might logically have been.

Thoreau provided just enough information about the boat to be tantalizing without being explicit. To cite but one example, nowhere in *A Week* does Thoreau

Thoreau and his brother launched their skiff into the slow-moving Concord River, not far from Walden Pond, and headed upstream to the Middlesex Canal (no longer navigable), which connected with the Merrimack River. (*WoodenBoat*/S. E. Bowen)

give even the boat's name nor, apparently, did he bother to paint the name on the bow or stern. However, those who knew Thoreau knew the boat had a name because he told them so. The name was *Musketaquid*, the Indian name for the Concord, a river that frequently overflowed its banks onto the adjoining fields and woods. The name translates evocatively—Grass-ground or Meadow river.

All we know about the *Musketaquid* are a few precious details that appear in *A Week* and in Thoreau's *Journal*. These sources include both information specific to the *Musketaquid* and some more general observations that offer most unusual and tantalizing glimpses into the sorts of boats used in Thoreau's neighborhood during the mid-nineteenth century. In his *Journal*, in May 1840, Thoreau recorded that his boat "was built like a fisherman's dory, with tholepins for four oars. . . . It was well calculated for service, but of consequence difficult to be dragged over shoal places or carried around falls." This "well calculated for service" is another way of saying the boat, probably built of pine and oak, was heavy. When Thoreau wrote *A Week*, he was more forthright and simply said that the boat "was strongly built, but heavy."

As he began organizing and expanding upon his notes for *A Week*, Thoreau added some detail about the boat. Now, he wrote that the craft "was in form like a fisherman's dory, fifteen feet long by three and a half in breadth at the widest part." What are we to make of this information regarding the boat's type and size?

In his *Journal*, Thoreau refers to the boat being *built* like a fisherman's dory while in the book he says that it "was in *form* like a fisherman's dory." But, technically speaking, one term refers to a method of construction, the other to design. Was it one or the other or both? What's more, the word dory, which had entered the language by the 1720s, if not before, would almost certainly have not evoked, in Thoreau's time, the specific image of a Banks fisherman's dory as it would today.

In fact, Thoreau's reference to a dory plays right into the whole clouded history of boat types that would become known as dories. The dory reference begs long-standing questions about when such boats first appeared, and what they looked like. To further put the word "dory" into its properly murky context, it is thought that a Swampscott, Massachusetts, fisherman might have applied that name to what was then commonly called a wherry.

The fisherman, James Phillips, bought a boat from Amesbury, Massachusetts, boat builder Simeon Lowell, perhaps as early as 1795. Phillips's boat predated the signature straight-sided Banks dory by decades. His was almost certainly a round-sided boat with a flat bottom board in the center. Such a hull could be conveniently dragged from beach to water, a key advantage at Swampscott where the boats were used to offload anchored schooners. At some point, the word dory pretty much replaced the word wherry, but the Banks-style dory did not come into widespread use until at least the mid- to late 1850s. With their removable thwarts, these dories could be stacked on the schooners and launched when the vessel reached the fishing grounds, a method that replaced fishermen hand-lining from a schooner's deck.

Thoreau's statement that his boat was built *like* a fisherman's dory does not mean that the *Musketaquid* really *was* a Banks-type dory or even its round-sided predecessor. In his classic *The Dory Book*, John Gardner posited that straight-sided dories appeared in the mid-1830s. But, even if such boats existed in 1839, would a Banks dory's commodious beam and generous free-board at bow and stern have made sense on the placid Concord, a river whose slow current gave rise to the occasional reference to this stream as the "dead river"? Probably not. Might the *Musketaquid* have had more in common with a wherry like the ones built by Simeon Lowell—boats that we might now call a dory skiff? Or was the *Musketaquid* a flat-iron skiff with some local Concord flavor? The latter makes the most sense.

As keen an observer as he was of animals, plants, the weather, and everything else regarding his natural surroundings, Thoreau also took care to record details of the boats he saw on his native river. He did this at various times in his *Journal*. In September 1851, Thoreau had noted: "There are all kinds of boats chained to trees and stumps by the riverside — some from Boston and the salt [water], — but I think that none after all is so suitable and convenient as the simple, flat-bottomed and light boat that has long been made here by the farmers themselves."

He followed this observation in October, writing: "We comment on the boats of different patterns—dories (?), punts, bread-troughs, flatirons, etc. etc.,—which we pass, the prevailing our genuine dead-river boats, not to be matched by Boston carpenters."

So—although he again used the term "dory" (punctuated in this instance by a questionmark!), it is clear that even twelve years after building the *Musketaquid* Thoreau may have used the word quite loosely and might himself have been uncertain about its technical definition. It is also clear that he had long admired what he recognized as the genius reflected in a local type of boat ideally adapted to the specific needs of those who dwelt along the Concord. Further regarding his boat's overall design, Thoreau writes in *A Week*, that his boat was "hardly of better model than usual." Since the usual model in Concord were skiffs, one is again left with the suggestion that the *Musketaquid* was more skiff than dory.

Six years later, Thoreau touched once more upon the subject of boat types in his *Journal*. In February 1857, he noted that the prevalent boat on the Concord "probably has its prototype on English rivers—call it dory,

In 1854, fifteen years after his voyage on the Concord and Merrimack rivers, this crayon portrait of thirty-seven-year-old Thoreau was made by Samuel Worcester Rowse. (Concord Free Public Library)

skiff, or what-not—made as soon as boards were sawed here." This use of the phrase "or what-not" continues the confusion. A true dory was (and is) a basically double-ended boat with fore-and-aft bottom planks and a tombstone-shaped transom. The bottom was assembled first. As explained by Howard Chapelle, the bottom was then "sprung between special horses to the mold of the fore-and-aft rocker . . . The frames are then set up and the stem liner and transom secured." Substantial vertical bracing was necessary to hold the boat's shape as it was generally built right-side up.

All this is substantially different than a flatiron skiff with its transom stern and cross-planked bottom. The skiff could be built upside down, formed around a few frames, and its construction, while not necessarily easy, would not be as involved as the dory's. In this business of labeling boat types, Thoreau is too casual for our purpose.

The size of Thoreau's boat also plays into this consideration of what sort of craft it actually was. What do the dimensions imply about a boat that was "fifteen feet long by three and a half in breadth at the widest part"? They tell us that this 15-footer had only a 42-inch beam, quite narrow by comparison to, say, a traditional 15 ½-foot (overall) dory as built today in Lunenburg, which has a 52-inch beam, 24 percent more beam than the *Musketaquid*. Today's Lowell 15' Salisbury Point rowing skiff, descended from a model introduced after the Civil War, has a 56" beam. Even a graceful sailing dory or dory skiff as built for yachting purposes on Boston's North Shore in the latter nineteenth century was proportionally beamy by comparison to the *Musketaquid*. A fifteen-foot overall length dory with a forty-two-inch beam at the gunwale would have been a seriously tippy boat.

Thoreau's boat was, in fact, more slender than one might expect and, for all we know, may even have possessed less beam than was typical of the local skiffs. Why was the *Musketaquid* so slender? Perhaps because Thoreau, inevitably, looked to nature for guidance in the boat's proportions. "The fish shows where there should be the greatest breadth of beam and depth in the hold; its fins direct where to set the oars." The *Musketaquid's* beam-to-length ratio could well have derived from Thoreau's observation of Concord river pickerel!

The obviously conjectured picture that emerges from all this presently suggests that the *Musketaquid* was a plainly built, flat-bottom skiff. Perhaps the boat had a comparatively narrow transom that reminded Thoreau of a double-ender, but there is no way of telling. We speculate that the *Musketaquid* had three or four flush planks per side that required caulking.

Could Thoreau, even with his apparent carpentry skills, have produced a lapstrake hull in a week's time? While we really don't know, comments about the boat's lack of water-tightness just a few years later, prompts the tentative conclusion—"no." Let's assume a cross-planked bottom for building ease, and two rowing thwarts with tholepins at each.

There is nothing to indicate how much flare was built into the hull or how much rocker there was to the bottom. One can say that flare and rocker must have been adequate for the boat carried two young men and camping gear in the fast-flowing Merrimack without mishap. We don't know if the boat possessed a skeg. One assumes a skeg was included since fish have ventral fins and further, as we'll see, Thoreau was an astute observer of how a boat moved through the water.

Another perplexing aspect regarding the *Musketaquid* is found in *A Week* but not in the *Journal*. Regarding the boat as she appeared on the eve of the voyage, Thoreau wrote: "It had been loaded the evening before at our door, half a mile from the river, with potatoes and melons from a patch which we had cultivated, and a few utensils; and was provided with wheels in order to be rolled around falls."

This matter of "wheels" has suggested to some that the *Musketaquid* must have had a built-in wheel or wheels and therefore was a sort of "wheelbarrow boat." This is an idea that can be safely rejected. Thoreau never again mentions wheels in *A Week*, and such an unusual feature, space consuming and of inevitable complexity of construction, would certainly have been noted by the boat's two subsequent owners.

The first of these owners was Nathaniel Hawthorne. During a sojourn in Concord in early September 1842, Hawthorne purchased the *Musketaquid* from Thoreau for $7, about what Thoreau had spent for the 1,000 used bricks and pair of secondhand windows that he used in building his famous cabin. Hawthorne renamed the boat *Pond Lily*. Later, Hawthorne passed on the now leaky boat to Thoreau's friend William Ellery Channing.

Regarding the wheels, Thoreau was referring to a dolly of some sort. In fact, Thoreau described making a crude dolly in 1852. From a pine log, he "sawed two wheels, about a foot in diameter and seven or eight inches thick, and I fitted them to an axle tree made of a joist . . . and thus had a convenient pair of wheels on which to get my boat up and roll it about."

What of the *Musketaquid*'s color scheme? Here Thoreau does provide some information. "Below it was green with a border of blue, as if out of courtesy [to] the green sea and the blue heavens." But exactly what did "below" mean? Today, such a description might suggest a green bottom (anti-fouling) with a blue boot top stripe. Thoreau, however, was probably referring to a green hull with a blue stripe along the sheerstrake. This color scheme satisfied the writer's opinion that "a boat should have a sort of life and independence of its own. It is a sort of amphibious animal, a creature of two elements, a fish to swim and a bird to fly."

Sailing was magic for Thoreau. In 1851, he wrote: "The sailboat is an admirable invention by which you compel the wind to transport you even against itself. It is easier to guide than a horse; the slightest pressure on the tiller suffices."

The *Musketaquid* was fitted with some sort of sailing rig. Again, Thoreau referred to nature. "The bird shows how to rig and trim the sails, and what form to give to the prow, that it may balance the boat and ride the air and water best." Specific detail of the rig, however, is nearly nonexistent in *A Week*. Thoreau wrote that the boat had "two sets of oars, and several slender poles for shoving in shallow places, and also two masts, one of which served for a tent-pole at night."

It would be hard to imagine that the *Musketaquid* carried anything more ambitious than a small square sail set on a light yard and controlled by braces (sheets) belayed to some convenient part of the boat or maybe just held in each hand. The other rig choices, gaff or even sprit, would seem highly unlikely given their relative complexity by comparison. Nor does Thoreau ever mention trying to sail to windward. What's more, even a modest square sail, together with the boat's narrow beam, would have propelled the *Musketaquid* downwind at a good clip. Thoreau did note of a portion of the trip home that "the wind blew steadily down the stream, so that we kept our sails [*sic*] set." Later he wrote: "We bounded merrily over before a smacking breeze, with a devil-may-care look in our faces, and our boat a white bone in its mouth, and speed which greatly astonished some scow boatmen whom we met."

Although the *Musketaquid* could be sailed, it would be a mistake to assume that the rig and its manner of being set up was anything more than the most basic. Consider what Thoreau had to say about this fifteen years later in reference to another boat. "I rigged my mast by putting a post across the boat, and putting the mast through it and into a piece of post at the bottom, and lashing it and bracing it." One must assume that an oar was used for steering.

As for what manner of sail the *Musketaquid* may have carried, it was not until nineteen years after the Concord and Merrimack trip that Thoreau entered into his *Journal* something specific about the rig of the little boat that he then owned. "I have spliced my old sail to a new one, and now go out to try in a sail to Baker Farm, [located south of Concord on the Sudbury River's Fairhaven Bay]" he wrote on August 22, 1858. "It is a square sail, some five feet by six. I like it much. It pulls like an ox, and makes me think there is more wind than there is. The yard goes about with a pleasant force, almost enough, I would fain imagine, to knock me overboard. . . . I wish I had this a dozen years ago, my voyages would have been performed more quickly and easily. . . . Before, my sail was so small that I was wont to raise the mast with the sail on it ready set, but now I have to rig some tackling with which to haul the sail up."

Thoreau's wish that he had his thirty-square-foot square sail years earlier suggests there had been other boats in his life. In fact, the *Musketaquid* was one of at least three boats Thoreau owned. Ellery Channing recorded that Thoreau built his first boat at age sixteen (1833). Channing wrote that Thoreau "built a boat for excursions on the river, and called it *The Rover*."

Six years later came the *Musketaquid*, which must have been discarded eventually by Channing when her leaks and general deterioration finally became too much to bear. During his stay at Walden Pond, beginning in the summer of 1845, Thoreau had access to a boat there and mentions it in the book, although he didn't say whether he owned it or not. On Sunday,

March 20, 1851, Thoreau makes reference in his *Journal* to a boat that he did own. He offers no detail about the craft but does provide insight into how a self-sufficient amateur of that time caulked and painted his boat.

"Spanish brown and raw oil were the ingredients. I found the painter had sold me the brown in hard lumps as big as peas, which could not reduce with a stick; so I passed them whole when mixed through an old coffee mill, which made a very good paint mill, catching it in an old coffee-pot, whose holes I puttied up, there being a lack of vessels, and then I broke up the coffee mill and nailed a part over the bows to protect them. . . . I had first filled the seams with some grafting-wax [wax used to protect the grafted parts of plants] I had melted."

Thoreau, whose boating season on the river extended from late March through early December, launched this boat on March 22. He found it overly stable and was disappointed that it did "not toss enough and communicate the motion of the waves." He also found the seats were not well positioned and that a heavy stone was needed to trim the boat when two were aboard. The writer was clearly a smart observer of his boat's performance.

"My boat is very good to float and go before the wind, but it has not *run* enough to it—if that is the phrase—but lugs too much dead water astern. Methinks it will not be a bad sailer." What Thoreau was saying was that the boat's bottom needed more rocker (upsweep) in its after section.

Thoreau apparently stored this boat in the cellar of the family home during the off season. How did he get it from the river to the house? Once again, the mention of wheels pops up. On December 2, 1856, he entered in his *Journal*: "Got my boat, which I had before turned up on the bank. It made me sweat to wheel it home through the snow." This entry again suggests a dolly to get the boat from river to house.

Whatever the deficiencies of this particular boat, Thoreau was still using it three years later. In March 1859, he recorded "a strong northwest wind. Draw my boat over the road on a roller. Raising a stone for ballast from the south side of the railroad causeway."

Thoreau was recognized as an accomplished boatman. After his demonstration ride in the *Musketaquid*, Nathaniel Hawthorne wrote in his book *American Notes* that Thoreau "managed the boat so perfectly, either with two paddles or with one, that it seemed instinct with his own will, and to require no physical effort to guide it. He said that, when some Indians visited Concord a few years ago, he found that he had acquired, without a teacher, their precise method of propelling and steering a canoe."

Hawthorne admitted that he himself never developed such a facility with the boat. It is clear that the *Musketaquid*, at least, could be expertly rowed, paddled, or sailed by its builder who took endless delight in his little forays

Boatbuilder David Snediker created his own version of what the *Musketaquid* might have looked like. The Concord Museum exhibited the boat in a special exhibition that ran from August 2007, to January 2008. (Concord Museum)

on the Concord, Sudbury, and Assabet rivers, observing fish, turtles, trees, and flowers. He loved the Concord so much that he sometimes didn't bother with a boat at all and simply hiked in the water "a foot or two deep, now suddenly descending through valleys up to my neck, but all alike agreeable."

Henry David Thoreau died on the morning of May 6, 1862. His sister Sophia was reading to him from *A Week on the Concord and Merrimack Rivers.* The last full sentence spoken by the writer that morning was a line from the book he had written years earlier at Walden Pond after his voyage aboard the *Musketaquid*: "Now comes good sailing."

This story originally appeared in *WoodenBoat* No. 186, September/October 2005.

SLOCUM'S LUCK

A Life of Near Misses
and Good Fortune

first read Joshua Slocum's *Sailing Alone Around the World* when I
was a soldier in Vietnam in 1970. Encountering Slocum's tale of sol-
itary cruising while I was experiencing the war provided a welcome
escape. But the personal details that Slocum deliberately left out of his
book sparked an intense curiosity that only grew as the years passed
and, especially, after I was finally able to take up sailing in the mid-
1970s. On and off for some forty years, I kept reading Slocum's book
and kept digging, usually in vain, for reliable information about him.

During that time, a number of Slocum books and videos appeared
that were so deficient in terms of research, accuracy, or even in a
basic understanding of sailing, that I was dismayed. But it was not until
the early 2000s that the growing availability of digitized materials on
the internet made me think I could properly address a few long-held
questions about Slocum. Such a research tool had been unavailable in
1956 to Walter Magnes Teller whose pioneering *The Search for Captain
Slocum* represented the rare Slocum book that was both objective and
based on original scholarship.

My first effort, "The Man Behind the Legend: Reflections on Capt.
Joshua Slocum and *Spray*" was published in *WoodenBoat* in the Sep-
tember/October 2006, issue. During the next decade, I continued to
seek out the long-hidden and often conflicting details of Slocum's life.
It was a quest that ultimately resulted in the publication of *A Man for
All Oceans: Capt Joshua Slocum and the First Solo Voyage around the
World*, in 2017. Shortly before the book appeared, *WoodenBoat* pub-
lished the following story.

Somewhere in the Atlantic Ocean, probably sometime in 1866, a ship named *Agra* faces a rising wind. Launched in 1862 at the redoubtable Medford, Massachusetts, yard of J. T. Foster and Co., the 174' *Agra* is still a relatively new vessel. She is of a type known as a "moderate clipper," designed to carry more cargo at some sacrifice in speed compared to the "full" clippers, whose heyday is all but finished. Still, *Agra* can move. She has turned in runs of 350 miles per day, only about fifty miles less than the fastest clipper ships. Now, as the wind gusts become stronger, Capt. Shaw tells his mate it is time to reduce sail. The crew is ordered aloft and one of them, a young seaman named Joshua Slocum, begins climbing nimbly to *Agra*'s main upper topsail yard.

In April 1895, some thirty years after he scampered aloft that day, Slocum told a *Boston Herald* reporter the shocking thing that happened to him. He "was gathering in the sail, when a gust struck him, and pitched him off. His fall was broken and his life saved by collision with the main yard, which he struck on his head, cutting a gash over his left eye, which is the only mark of disfigurement on his face."

Thanks to his 1895–1898 solo circumnavigation in his 36'9" sloop *Spray* and his 1900 book about the experience, *Sailing Alone around the World*, Slocum would become a famous man, and he was called upon at times to sit for a portrait. When he did so, Slocum usually, though not always, presented his scar-free right side to the camera. One can only guess what Slocum thought about as he awaited the shutter's click. That he'd made his remarkable voyage in what then seemed to most people to be a foolishly small boat was confirmation of his superior seamanship. But, deep down, Joshua Slocum knew that something else lay behind a portion of his success. Starting with that frightening fall aboard *Agra* that should have ended his life, Slocum had always sailed with an angel upon his shoulder. As the years passed and the near misses multiplied, he gave his good fortune, his angel, a name. He called it "Slocum's luck."

One wouldn't think that Slocum, with his innate and highly developed skills as a seaman, boat handler, and shipmaster, ever had to count on fickle luck. He was the prototypical self-reliant, self-made man. Ever since he'd embarked on his first voyage before the mast aboard a lumber carrier sailing from Saint John, New Brunswick, to Dublin, Ireland, Slocum had relied upon his intelligence, physical toughness, strict sobriety, and a growing mastery of the sextant and mathematics to claw his way from the fo'c's'le to the captain's quarters. He was the perfect example of the sort of man who made his own luck. Nobody knew this better than Slocum himself. "I had studied the sea as perhaps few men have studied it, neglecting all else," Slocum wrote in the fourth paragraph of *Sailing Alone around the World*. He wasn't kidding.

Slocum's intimate feel for the world's oceans, seas, gulfs, and bays was so highly developed that he was able to recognize when he had entered a specific current within his watery world. To cite but one example, as he approached Brazil in *Spray* when he was homeward bound in May 1898, Slocum wrote in *Sailing Alone* that "Strange and long-forgotten current ripples pattered against the sloop's sides. . . . By these current ripples I was assured that she was now off St. Roque and had struck the current which sweeps around that cape." His inner clock and knotmeter told him his patent log was giving wrong information, so he hauled in the log's spinner and checked it, and indeed one of the blades had been crushed—by a "monster" shark no doubt. (Slocum was both fearful of and ruthless about sharks, luring them to his boat and killing them when he could.)

Slocum could read wave patterns and tell what they meant, those ceaseless, rolling messages that reached him from afar. He understood the barometer and pelagic birds and what each foretold. He was an interpreter of clouds. "To know the laws that govern the winds, and to know that you know them, will give you an easy mind on your voyage round the world; otherwise you may tremble at the appearance of every cloud."

And yet, despite all his knowledge and skill, there were times when only Slocum's luck, such as his fortuitous collision with the *Agra's* main yard, coupled with catlike reflexes and powerful hands, saved the day. In 1865, having sailed before the mast from Boston to Hong Kong aboard *Tanjore*, Slocum was struck down by malaria. Although blessed with a disease-resistant constitution, Slocum became seriously debilitated in Hong Kong and entered a hospital there. Although he recovered enough strength to rejoin his ship when it departed for Batavia (now Jakarta, Indonesia), the fever returned. Slocum, who was then twenty-one years old, had to leave *Tanjore* and enter another hospital.

Now, Slocum found himself weakened and alone in what his firstborn son, Victor, later called "that pest hole of the Dutch East Indies." He might have died there had luck not intervened in the person of a man Victor identified only as "Capt. Airy of the steamship *Soushay*." Slocum himself mentioned Airy in *Sailing Alone*, calling him a "good man." But neither father nor son shared what quirk of fate brought Airy to the hospital where he met the debilitated young Joshua, and took him—"hove down with fever"—aboard his steamship.

Aboard *Soushay*, as she plied the Java Sea, Banda Sea, Arafura Sea, and Torres Strait—waters he would come to know well as a merchant captain— Slocum began a slow recovery. He had so little strength, though, that when the *Soushay* called at Booby Island off the north Australian coast, Slocum had to literally crawl on deck to see the fabled place for himself.

After his initial recovery from malaria—he later told his publisher that he suffered "years of broken health"—Slocum eventually achieved his goal of becoming a merchant ship captain. For the next nineteen years or so—roughly 1869 to 1888—Slocum had ample chances to display his hard-won knowledge of ocean winds, currents, and ship handling while making passages all around the globe. As a ship owner, he brought his vessels—*Pato*, *Amethyst*, *Northern Light*, *Aquidneck* —through terrible storms. Sometimes, the situation involved such danger that he placed his family in provisioned boats in case it became necessary to abandon ship.

Throughout that period, it was Slocum's seamanship and navigational genius that consistently brought him safely into port. Yet, there was a factor of pure luck, too, and it could emerge in odd ways that might sometimes have as much to do with profit as survival. In 1877, aboard his 72' schooner *Pato*, Slocum made a cod-fishing expedition to Russian waters in the Sea of Okhotsk. There, his crew landed so many fish that they ran out of salt, the key preservative. But just as they were about to be forced to abandon further efforts on that rich fishing ground, Slocum encountered a vessel he knew well: *Constitution*, Slocum's first square-rig command when he'd lived in San Francisco seven years earlier. It was preparing to jettison its excess salt and head home. Instead, the salt was transferred to *Pato*, which enabled Slocum to complete filling his ship's hold and sail to Portland, Oregon, where he reaped a good profit from his catch.

What but Slocum's luck could ever account for his safe passage in 1883 through the Sunda Strait—the body of water separating the islands of Java and Sumatra and connecting the Java Sea with the Indian Ocean? Victor Slocum, who was twelve at the time, remembered *Northern Light* sailing through the strait with two other vessels in line behind. Victor never forgot his astonishment at seeing the square-rigged *Wm. H. Besse*, under full sail, shudder to a complete stop in what should have been deep water. It was a mysterious prelude to one of the greatest natural disasters in recorded history.

"She had grounded on a reef which had been cast up by submarine volcanic action in the very spot over which we had passed but a quarter of an hour before. The sea was trembling and in bubbles. A lead that was cast came up from the bottom so hot that it melted out the tallow," which filled the hollowed-out bottom of the sounding lead in order to bring up a sample of the bottom to show whether it was mud or sand. "The *Northern Light* braced her yards and came up into the wind, but as the *Bourne* came up astern of the *Besse* and hove to, to offer assistance, we kept off again for Anjer, which was by this time but a few miles distant."

Slocum stopped at Anjer, known more generally now as Anyer, and then an important Indonesian port, where he learned that the *Wm. H. Besse* would need to be towed to Batavia for repairs that would take several weeks. Upon sailing from Anjer, the *Northern Light* passed the volcanic island Krakatoa, which Victor Slocum wrote "was in the awful majesty of full eruption. . . . Here a bright fire burned, throwing up a column of black steam and ashes which reached a culminating altitude of seventeen miles by sextant measurement. The fall of ashes made the sea all about white with pumice stone. For days after passing it was washed upon our deck by the lively sea."

But neither Victor nor his father had any idea that what they saw was in no way a "full eruption." Krakatoa exploded a few days later on August 26, 1883, with what was said to have been the loudest sound ever heard on the planet. About two-thirds of Anjer disappeared. Tsunamis followed. Ships were carried a mile into jungles, and an estimated 36,000 people were killed. Many years later, Victor's younger brother, Ben, wrote to Slocum biographer Walter Teller, observing that "had we been three days later in that region we would have been suffocated by the fumes."

As the years passed, it was inevitable that Slocum's luck would sometimes desert him. The vagaries of mechanical failures were always a threat. When the rudderhead of *Northern Light* twisted off during a storm off the South African coast, much of the valuable cargo had to be jettisoned to keep the vessel upright as she flooded and the pumps couldn't keep up.

Finally, there came a day in late December 1887 when a fatal combination of current, wind, and a sandbar overcame all of Slocum's experience and skill. While attempting to make his way out of Brazil's Paranaguá Bay in his 138' bark *Aquidneck*, Slocum ran aground after a failed effort to bring the square-rigger about. The uninsured vessel, of which Slocum was sole owner, was soon rendered unfit for anything but conversion to a shabby coal barge.

Although Slocum couldn't have known it at the time, the loss of the *Aquidneck* marked the end of his merchant seafaring career. The grounding also left forty-three-year-old Slocum stranded in Brazil, nearly broke yet responsible for getting himself, his twenty-six-year-old second wife, Hettie (Slocum had remarried following the death of his beloved first wife, Virginia), and his sons Victor and Garfield back to the United States. Slocum's response was not to purchase steamship tickets but instead to build a 35' boat and sail back, a voyage of some 5,500 miles completed between June 1888 and December 1889. Slocum would recount this adventure in 1890 in his self-published *Voyage of the* Liberdade. In designing and building *Liberdade* he was inspired by Chinese sampans and Cape Ann dories, but he always called her a canoe. She provided several examples of Slocum's luck.

Twice during the journey, *Liberdade* narrowly avoided grounding in circumstances that could have been fatal. Caught in a southeast gale somewhere between Cape St. Roque and the Amazon delta, Slocum sought safety closer inshore. In doing so, he sailed right over a shoal. Slocum said the waves "bellowed over the shoal! I could smell the slimy bottom of the sea, when they broke! I could taste the salty sand. . . . This was the greatest danger we had yet encountered. The elasticity of our canoe, not its bulk, saved it from destruction."

A not-dissimilar event unfolded later off the North Carolina coast. Caught in a gale to seaward of the bar at New River, he decided to seek refuge. Twenty-one years after the event, Hettie wrote about it in a letter to a friend: "We went through drawing 2 feet 4 inches of water where at ordinary time it was a rare thing to have more than twelve inches. We were very glad for we had already had enough of it outside."

In 1888, the long, narrow segment of what would eventually become the Intracoastal Waterway connecting New River to Bogue Sound to the northeast was merely a ditch usable only by shoal-draft small craft when the tide served. But after his recent experience offshore, and perhaps at Hettie's urging, Slocum now planned to somehow get *Liberdade* through this sheltered inland route. However, the channel markers that delineate the waterway today weren't there to guide him. He wrote: "I was getting lost in the maze of sloughs and creeks, which as soon as I entered seemed to lead in every direction but the right one."

Then Slocum's luck came to the rescue when they encountered a hunter whose grandfather had dug the ditch and who knew it well. "A bargain was quickly made, and my pilot came aboard. . . . The entrance to the ditch, then close by, was made with a flowing sheet [the sheets being eased with wind abeam or over the stern quarter], and I soon found that my pilot knew his business."

Had it not been for Slocum's luck, *Spray*, among the most famous of sailboats, might have been lost before setting off on the great voyage. In a letter to Walter Teller written in 1954, Slocum's youngest son, Garfield, described an event that might have ended the *Spray*'s career almost as soon as it began. Garfield wrote of a cruise he made with his father to Maine in *Spray*, probably in 1894 when he was about thirteen years old.

While leaving what was most likely Pemaquid Beach, Slocum attempted to make his way past a ledge in light air. It was a situation that any sailor of an engineless boat today would understand and find worrisome. Garfield remembered: "As the *Spray* almost passed a ledge on the leeward, the powerful undertow lifted her and dropped her on the ledge. The waves tried to finish the *Spray*. Some help came quickly to our aid by land and sea. Father threw a coil of rope to some men on shore. He tied me under my armpits, held one end of the rope, and told me to jump. The men pulled me to high ground. Other men, in dories, got the *Spray* off, and towed her to a place where father repaired her bottom."

Slocum presumably entered this event in *Spray*'s log, although he saw no reason to discuss it anywhere else. But he must have recognized the grounding as potentially fatal, since he took the desperate measure of having Garfield hauled ashore through the frigid Maine water. Perhaps there was a reasonably heavy swell that posed a real threat to the boat, and to him as well, for he could not swim. Slocum owed a lot to those Maine fishermen who luckily happened to be present. One suspects that they took the whole event as nonchalantly as he did.

But nobody was present on the night of December 11, 1895, when Slocum mistook vast, moonlit sand dunes on the Uruguayan coast for ocean swells. It was a very rare miscalculation that put *Spray* hard aground on a sandbar about seven miles south of the Brazilian border. With his boat exposed to ocean swells, Slocum managed to launch his half-dory tender. His plan was to row out and drop a kedge anchor in preparation for the next high tide.

But carrying a heavy anchor and 240' of cable through the surf was a precarious task. *Spray*'s tender—a dory that Slocum had acquired and cut in half in Gloucester—shipped water and was in danger of sinking by the time Slocum lifted the big anchor and tossed it into the sea. He did so "just as [the half-dory] was turning over. . . . I suddenly remembered I could not swim." Three times he tried and failed to right his little boat and clamber in without capsizing it again. On his fourth attempt he finally managed it. Now, though, he realized that the current was carrying him offshore and he was in a battle for his life.

What saved Slocum, after getting back into the boat and bailing it, was that he'd managed to recover one of his oars. After attaching a second anchor cable to the buoyed end of the first one, he had exactly enough length to take a single turn around the *Spray*'s windlass. Slocum *might* have planned it that way, but he well knew that Slocum's luck had seen him through yet again.

A briefer yet potentially even more dangerous grounding occurred after Slocum sailed from Cooktown, Australia, on June 6, 1897, to begin his long passage across the Indian Ocean to South Africa. On the night of June 8, after leaving the M Reef lightship astern, *Spray*, "going at full speed, with sheets off she hit the M Reef itself on the north end, where I expected to see a beacon." Had the beacon been operating, Slocum certainly would have seen it. In its absence, Slocum's luck saved him once more: "She swung off quickly on her heel, however, and with one more bound a swell cut across the shoal point so quickly that I hardly knew how it was done. . . . I saw the ugly boulders under the sloop's keel as she flashed over them."

In *Sailing Alone*, Slocum attempted to ascribe this escape not merely to his usual good fortune but in this particular instance to what he claimed was his lucky number: "I made a mental note of it that the letter M, for which the reef was named, was the thirteenth one in our alphabet, and that thirteen, as noted years before was still my lucky number."

However, Slocum didn't share with readers what he meant by his reference to "years before." Nor did his editors at the Century Company, publisher of *Sailing Alone*, query him about it. He was referring to his self-published *Voyage of the* Destroyer. This little book recounted his experience during the period of December 1892 to April 1893, as "navigator in command" of an ironclad warship that was being towed from New York to Brazil. Slocum wrote that *Destroyer*'s crew was composed of "twelve brave fellows." Adding himself to that number brought the total aboard to thirteen. "Curiously enough," he wrote, "that fatalistic number (thirteen) was not thought of before sailing."

The *Destroyer* voyage was grueling for all aboard except for the ship's rats, which, apparently divining what was about to transpire, had abandoned ship. The vessel had been intended for harbor defense only and, when subjected to open-ocean stresses for which she had not been designed, her riveted seams opened up. Slocum and the crew survived only by dint of continuous and exhausting pumping—and Slocum's luck.

In the end, of course, Slocum's luck finally ran out. Because the famous captain simply disappeared, speculation about the time, place, and manner of his going was as inevitable as it was inconclusive. Knowledgeable men who visited *Spray* toward the end—yachting writer H. S. "Skipper" Smith and naval architect Charles Mower among them—suggested structural failure may have been to blame.

Slocum's sons Victor and Ben each had theories about what might have happened. Ben believed that his father, heartbroken and lonely ever since the death of his first wife and soul mate, Virginia, in 1884, finally let the sea take him. Victor posited that *Spray* was run down by a steamship.

In fact, only Slocum's luck had saved him from being run down by a swift, silent sailing ship at night while crossing the Atlantic from Gibraltar to South America on *Spray*'s outbound journey. Collision at night, among a single-hander's worst fears, is the scenario claimed for *Spray*'s disappearance by the Boston chronicler of New England lighthouses and maritime history, Edward Rowe Snow. In an article published in the *Quincy Patriot Ledger* on

April 8, 1959, Snow wrote: "One of the world's greatest sea mysteries, the loss of the *Spray* . . . may have been solved . . . by the disclosure that Capt. Joshua Slocum, who vanished at sea in 1909, may have been run down by a steamer off of the Lesser Antilles within a relatively few hours after he had left the home of a farmer in the vicinity."

Snow's source was Capt. Charles H. Bond, "a master mariner whose background and references are such to make his statements unimpeachable." Nobody involved in the story who might have been affected by what Bond's source revealed was still alive, so there was no longer any reason to hush up the matter. Bond's source, the "farmer" mentioned in the article, had visited Slocum when *Spray* called at Turtle Island (Tortuga) off the northwest coast of Haiti. This farmer, Felix Meinickheim, boarded a local steamship not long after Slocum had sailed and noticed deep gouges in the vessel's bow.

Although the ship's captain admitted to Meinickheim that they had run down a native craft at night, but hadn't stopped, the second mate told a somewhat different story. He said the vessel they had struck was not native to the area and, even more telling, that there was nobody at the wheel. Since Slocum generally took advantage of *Spray*'s self-steering ability to rest, read, and sleep, this last detail is a chilling clue that Snow's report could be true. If so, Slocum's luck deserted him for the last time in the darkness of a Caribbean night. The irony that it was a steamship would not have been lost on Slocum, who had steadfastly refused to abandon sail. "Steam," he once told one of his sons, "was fine for others" but not for him.

This story appeared in *WoodenBoat* No. 256, May/June 2017.

ELECTRIC EXPERIENCES

Small Voyages toward a New World

I n 2018, while savoring a sausage aboard the Scandlines 465' hybrid train-ferry that connects Denmark to Germany, I studied a large onboard display promoting the ferry line's quest to dramatically reduce carbon emissions and create a "green future." Scandlines was then researching zero-emissions electric ferries capable of being recharged during a fifteen-minute layover. Recently, they've added a tube-like "rotor sail" to two ferries that reduces carbon emissions by as much as 5 percent.

Electric or hybrid power in Europe, whether for commercial vessels or yachts, seems to have become, to an extent, a done deal. A pervasive energy consciousness and demand for clean energy is everywhere. *Die Zukunft ist jetzt* read one sign at a recent German boat show—"the future is now." Companies in Germany, the Netherlands, Belgium, Denmark, and Finland are among the leaders in the development and production of marine electric power components.

By contrast, the future doesn't seem to be quite now in North America. However, since the following story was published in 2021, articles about electric power have appeared regularly in *WoodenBoat*. The Classic Boat Shop's Pisces daysailers are a good example of how a service-oriented, boutique shop building a boat whose primary purpose is well adapted to electric power can find an enthusiastic customer base. These days, more new boats are being offered with electric power.

Since this story was published, I have acquired a Honda EU1000i generator and no longer need to rely on shore power to charge *Periwinkle*'s battery. If it weren't for the gasoline needed to run the generator, we'd be entirely off the grid.

241

Seven years ago now, with no particular "green agenda" in mind, I found myself entering a sailing season like none before. Somewhat to my own surprise, I had parted ways with a 5-hp Johnson outboard. Its replacement was a Torqeedo Travel 1003 rated at 3 hp. At about the same time, I ordered from Classic Boat Shop in Bernard, Maine, a new Pisces day sailer. When the time came to choose between diesel or electric inboard power or an outboard, I opted for the electric inboard.

Just like that, I had become an "all-electric" sailor. As I looked ahead to the upcoming sailing season, however, the thought occurred to me, sometimes late at night—"what *have* you done?" While a variety of articles continues to be published about electric propulsion, and while manufacturers' websites extol electric power's virtues, none of that conveys the real-time experience of actually buying into and living with an evolving technology that, at present, remains well out of the mainstream.

A Torqeedo Travel 1003

The 5-hp Johnson was a two-stroke wokhorse that powered a 9 ½-foot, aluminum floor inflatable tender on a one-mile round trip from the yacht club across Marblehead Harbor to my mooring and back. At about 45 pounds, the short-shaft motor was a good 12 pounds lighter than the new breed of four-strokes but there were times when its weight was becoming a burden. There was also weariness with ethanol-related fuel issues and rare but surprisingly expensive repair costs.

The modular Torqeedo weighs about thirty pounds and promised to be maintenance-free. It's easy to carry the battery and tiller in a boat bag in one hand, the power unit in the other. I felt the power difference—3 hp vs. the Tohatsu's 5—would not be a negative since, at full throttle, five horsepower was more power than the inflatable could safely handle with only one person aboard. I was more interested in torque than speed anyway. According to Torqeedo, the type of motor it has developed is known as a "torque motor" and the company name derives from this technology that dates back to 2005.

The Torqeedo website presents a quite detailed description of the frankly near mind-boggling technology and mechanics housed within the outboard's power pod. There, a brushless motor and custom-developed electronics deliver power through a planetary gearset claimed to have a service life of 50,000 hours. All that is hidden away, of course, and it's the big orange, plastic propeller that catches the eye. Designed to take advantage of the motor's torque, it's a variable pitch, variable camber propeller (VPVC) patented by Torqeedo. VPVC means that pitch and camber vary from the hub to the blade tips. The optimized shapes seem to have eliminated cavitation. Its thrust would prove more than ample.

Torqeedo's dealer/service network was, and still is, rather limited. The motor remains predominantly a mail-order item. Seven years ago though, there was a chandlery about twenty miles away that sold Torqeedo. I bought from the dealer, hoping he might add value to the process. In reality, he sold the motor for somewhat less than the $1,995 list price and filled out the paperwork. Soon afterward, the shop closed.

Before using the motor, I tied a length of twine between the lithium battery and the "fixing pin" that secures the battery in place. That eliminates the chance of inadvertently losing the pin overboard. During use, the tiller's digital readout provides percent of battery remaining, range at the current speed, speed in knots over the ground, and consumption in watts. Although I occasionally check speed and generally run at 2 ½–3 ½ knots, I pay particular attention to how much charge remains following each round trip.

A full-throttle trip would likely take the battery down by two-thirds, which would probably trigger a warning beep to let you know. However, at normal speed, the twenty-five-to-thirty-minute round trip leaves about 68 percent capacity remaining. Learning what speed is practical in terms of range and battery capacity is a key aspect of electric propulsion. My conclusion: be moderate, be happy. At home after each use, the battery is plugged into its charger. Recharging takes an hour or so.

In July of the second season, as I was returning to shore, the Torqeedo lost power. We crawled along for a few seconds and then were dead in the water. The culprit was a broken sheer pin. As readers of this magazine well know, gasoline outboards don't have sheer pins that break while one is simply motoring along. Nor is replacing a broken sheer pin a big deal.

Replacing the Torqeedo 1003 pin requires removal of the 17 mm nut holding the prop and the prop itself. But with the pin broken, the prop spun freely and the nut couldn't be broken loose. After a phone chat with a Torqeedo technician, I took the motor to a pal at the local car repair shop. An impact wrench quickly removed the nut.

Back home, I discovered the broken sections of the pin were heavily rusted and the center part was corroded fast in the drive shaft. It could not be simply tapped out without risking damage to the shaft. The solution was a make-shift stand for the power unit, supporting the end of the shaft on wooden blocks, and then tapping out the pin with a punch.

Torqeedo headquarters in Bavaria is not far from Lake Starnberg, one of Germany's many beautiful lakes. The instruction manual advises that after use in salt water, the motor should be rinsed with fresh water. After the pin failure, I immediately began taking the power unit home and rinsing it with a hose after each use. But this has not solved the problem. By season's end, the new pin was showing signs of corrosion. (The 1003 pin is not made of stainless steel.) I subsequently made it a practice to remove the prop and replace the pin every fall, an easy enough job. December 2020, correspondence with Torqeedo revealed that the sheer pin of the newest model, the 1103, has a pin that, by comparison to the 1003, is thicker and made of stainless steel.

On occasion, the motor has refused to operate, displaying an E30 code—"Motor Communication Error"—on the tiller display. The manual advises a protective spray on the battery cable and tiller cable contacts. I do this every couple of weeks and also carry a little can of WD40 in my boat bag. It has also proven helpful to spray the threads of the two cable attachment fittings because they occasionally "seize up" if not lubricated. I carry a cloth in my boat bag to gain a good grip on the fittings.

One assumes minimal maintenance with electric power and in six seasons, the motor has required nothing. Therefore, it was disappointing to discover in the owner's manual that "after 5 years of operation, the shaft sealing ring must be exchanged." The charge for this service is $150. It is preventive maintenance intended to ensure water doesn't get into the power unit. Owners face the choice of a drive to a Torqeedo service center or packaging the shaft unit and shipping it or ignoring the service and keeping fingers crossed.

Verdict: For local use, the Torqeedo has several virtues. It's comparatively light, easy to carry, offers both adequate range and performance, and is quiet and clean. But broken Torqeedo 1003 sheer pins have become a topic on the *WoodenBoat Forum*, other sites, and YouTube. The new 1103, however, would

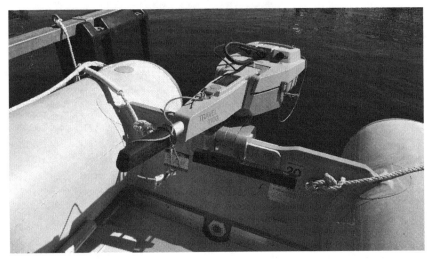

A Torqeedo 1103 mounted on an aluminum floor, 9'6" inflatable. (Stan Grayson)

seem to address this peculiar Achilles's heel, a mechanical miscalculation in an otherwise impressive, high-tech achievement.

A Pisces Daysailer

In the fall of 2013, after a fine demonstration sail in beautiful Somes Sound in a Pisces with builder Jean Beaulieu, the wind died completely. By then, we were nearly back to Jean's mooring in Southwest Harbor. Jean opened the boat's stern locker and, one by one, handed me the three components of a Torqeedo 1003.

It was a simple matter to install the motor on the boat's side-mounted outboard bracket. The Pisces, a thoughtfully updated Herreshoff Fish Class developed by Beaulieu and naval architect Chuck Paine (see *WoodenBoat* No. 249), motored quickly and silently to the mooring. That experience left me dreaming of a new Pisces with neither a propeller aperture nor a single opening in the hull.

Soon enough, reality set it. Marblehead Harbor is tightly packed and a moment's slip-up when making one's mooring alone could easily involve contact with a neighboring boat. The reality was that, both for safety's sake

This Pisces with builder Jean Beaulieu at the helm is speeding along comfortably on a day sail in Somes Sound, Maine. (Stan Grayson)

and for resale value, an inboard made sense. The choice was between a two-cylinder Beta diesel ($16,130) or an electric drive system ($12,510).

The Beta Marine diesel, enclosed in a nicely crafted and sound-proofed box with a varnished table atop it took up more room in the Pisces cockpit than I wished to sacrifice. Nor did the diesel, its transmission, exhaust system, fuel tank and associated plumbing fit my vision for a simple, elegant day sailer. I opted for the electric inboard because it was unobtrusive, quiet, clean, and promised to need little or no maintenance.

The Classic Boat Shop has been installing electric drive systems in cold-molded and fiberglass Pisces for two decades. Early on, Beaulieu conducted a methodical assessment of what battery capacity would be required to deliver the needed amps to a motor appropriate for the Pisces's easily driven hull. "Eventually," he recalled, "the discussion went to lithium which gives you a lot more usable amps with one-third the weight of an AGM battery."

The system comprised a 2-hp motor, its controller, and key switch/voltmeter, all made by the Dutch company Mastervolt. The lithium battery, charger, and power switch are Torqeedo. While some might question whether two horsepower is adequate for a 3,250-lb displacement yacht, this is a non-issue. An electric motor develops peak torque at one rpm. There's plenty of grunt and more than enough speed.

The two biggest issues in going electric were accepting much reduced range vs. diesel and how to recharge the battery. Both matters underscore the

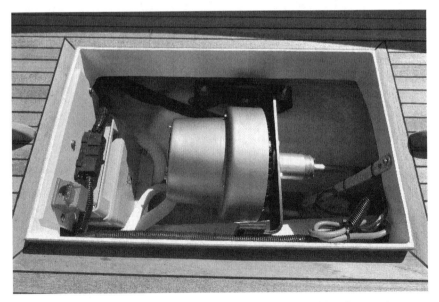

The electric motor takes little space in the Pisces cockpit. (Stan Grayson)

highly personal nature of electric propulsion. With internal combustion, one size pretty much fits all. Not so with electric.

For me, and probably most day sailers, range wasn't important. I explore local waters, generally single-handed, and try never to hurry. If the wind falls light, the Pisces, with its feathering two-blade prop, ghosts right along. A calm spell is less a time to switch on power than to appreciate the beauty of the sea and the islands around Marblehead and Cape Ann, nibble an apple, and await the return of the breeze.

The matter of charging the battery, however, was a real issue since the boat is on a mooring, not in a berth with shore power. Absent that convenience, the single biggest adjustment one must make with electric power is how not to become an obsessive "volt watcher." While "range anxiety" is familiar to electric car owners, an electric-boat owner with a mooring may be disinclined to use the motor thanks to "charging process anxiety."

The working range of the Torqeedo 26-104 lithium battery is from approximately 28.5 volts when full to 21 volts empty. Voltage is indicated on the read-out panel built into the key-switch. During my first four seasons, I tied up twice per season to recharge at a local boatyard float after hours. Charging involves an extension cord that plugs into the charger's socket on the boat's port cuddy cabin bulkhead.

Recharging is a lamentably slow process—about half a volt per hour. Going from 24.5 volts to 28.5 requires eight hours. There are no Tesla-like "superchargers" or FordPass Charging Networks dotted around America's harbors. Generally, I plug in at 25.5 volts so the recharge time is six hours. Torqeedo offers a fast charger that, it claims, cuts the charging time in half at a cost of some $1,995 vs. $599 for the standard charger. If I had it to do again, I'd get the fast charger. The added cost, as a percent of the whole purchase, wouldn't be decisive.

At the time I ordered the boat, the builder noted the possibility of using a Honda 1000 watt generator to recharge. At 29 lb (less fuel) the EU1000i should be easy to handle. Possibly acquiring that generator has been on my mind ever since; however, I'd prefer not owning an ethanol gasoline–powered device requiring some seasonal maintenance.

That said, mid-way through the 2019 season, I rented from Home Depot the smallest Honda they carry, the 2000 watt EU2000i. With its gallon tank full, the generator weighs about 54 lbs. While lifting it into the yacht club launch was not an issue, lifting it onto the Pisces and back out again without marring the varnish or worse was a challenge. It performed well, however, charging as fast as a shoreside outlet. Importantly, a small generator grants blissful independence from shore power.

Although the 2020 season was shortened because of COVID-related slowdowns, I did plenty of sailing. A combination of fair winds and

Charging from shore power. (Stan Grayson)

stubbornness about using the motor meant I didn't recharge all season. When the boat was hauled in mid-September, the panel read 27.4 volts. I'd used barely more than a volt in two months, mostly in motoring very slowly the final distance to the mooring. At present, should I need to recharge during the season, I am leaning toward renting the Honda generator again but leaving it in the dinghy tied alongside during the recharge process.

Even after six years, having the electrical system come to life by pressing the Torqeedo power button for about eight seconds until its LED glows red is still an intriguing novelty. With power on, a conventional red battery knob is rotated to send power to the motor (and LED cabin light and running lights if needed). The main sound one hears underway is the shaft turning in its dripless seal. The boat is so quiet that one learns to caution others unaware of your approach.

During six seasons, the electric drive system has performed flawlessly and required no maintenance. The one problem that arose was caused by human error. Most literature regarding lithium batteries warns against ever fully discharging them as this is said to damage the cells beyond repair. (The Torqeedo 26-104 battery is listed at $2,400 and the latest, improved version, the 24-3500 at $2,999.) To prevent such discharge during storage, the system must be shut down. (As part of my "volt watching," to reduce marginal drain, I shut the system down fully after each use unless bad weather is predicted. In that case, the system is left on as the bilge pump could be needed.)

The shut-down procedure for the Pisces system is as simple as turning it on. The battery switch is turned off and the power button pushed until the red light glows. Now, switching on the key will reveal a blank panel signifying the system is off. Following the third season, however, the system was mistakenly not fully shut down and the battery slowly discharged. If fully discharged, the lithium battery cannot be recharged through the onboard charger.

The result was that the battery had to be removed and taken to the nearest Torqeedo service center, Columbia Marine, about two-and-a-half hours away in Connecticut. There, the knowledgeable technician had a special tool that might, or might not, bring the battery back to life, a process he had performed with success, in similar cases, about a dozen times.

We were lucky. The battery took the charge. The battery was returned by UPS and has been fine ever since. Whether its service life has been reduced, the service center couldn't say, and the ultimate life of lithium batteries remains the source of speculation. On its new Mustang Mach-E, for example, Ford's battery warranty is for eight years or 100,000 miles. Should the battery pack fall below 70 percent capacity during that time, such loss might be deemed excessive and the battery pack replaceable under warranty. As for Pisces builder Jean Beaulieu, he has yet to replace a Pisces lithium battery although many have been in service for eight years.

The lessons I took from this discharged-battery experience are: (1) Lithium batteries represent new technology to both owners and boatyards (among others) and there is plenty of conflicting information or misinformation floating around; (2) Double-check that the electrical system is properly shut down if the boat won't be used for a long period; and (3) The Torqeedo service center saved the day but the availability of more widespread, trained service technicians could only be a positive in terms of customer support.

A fact of life regarding electric propulsion is that, like other electronic devices, components are steadily improved. In a recent discussion about the latest Torqeedo Power 24-3500 battery, builder Jean Beaulieu noted, "an interesting thing about this battery's software is that if there is no current draw for a certain amount of time (47 hours) it turns itself OFF which obviously would have been very useful to you several years ago."

Verdict: An electric drive system engineered and installed by an experienced boat builder, or by a qualified, specialized yard doing conversions, should provide clean, quiet, maintenance-free performance. Know how you will be recharging the battery before buying an electric boat. Be confident in the attention and expertise of those involved in storing and commissioning the boat. Be open to learning new things.

Conclusion

Beginning with the 2014 sailing season, except for a one-time generator rental, I've not burned a drop of gasoline or diesel fuel afloat. Neither have I changed and disposed of oil, an oil, air, or fuel filter, water pump impeller, or spark plug. I've not had to inspect a fuel line, bleed a fuel system, tension a drive belt, or buy an additive to protect gasoline or diesel fuel.

Periwinkle's inboard electric drive system is ready for service at the touch of a button and turn of a key, offering an important measure of convenience and safety. It is unobtrusive, saving both weight and valuable space within the boat, and it is emissions-free. These days, as I sail through the emerald waters around Misery and Baker's Islands or the dark blue sea swells out beyond Half Way Rock, I am inwardly pleased to own a simple, pollution-free boat. Given the advantages of an electric propulsion system, it is, perhaps, ironic that I use it so sparingly and closely monitor the battery's voltage. My time on the water is spent almost entirely under sail and is governed more than ever by the tide and the wind.

This story appeared in *WoodenBoat* No. 285, March/April 2022.

SHARPIE MADNESS

Remembering a Black Skimmer

The attraction some sailors have for "skinny water" is not an entirely rare affliction. Owners of centerboarders who enjoy the solitude and nature to be found where charts show three-foot depths or less at low tide will understand. But there are also those with more extreme ideas about what really denotes a shoal draft sailboat—a boat that will float in a mere foot of water and dry out comfortably as the tide comes and goes. Common traits of those fascinated by such boats is the ability to think well outside the box and accept the meaningful compromises such boats, usually sharpies of one sort or another, require. (The Thames sailing barge and the various traditional styles of Dutch leeboard-equipped vessels are beyond the scope of this discussion.)

Over the years, *WoodenBoat* has published some very fine pieces about sharpies, every one of which remains anchored in my memory. It was the "Presto-style" sharpies developed in Coconut Grove, Florida, in the 1880s by Ralph Middleton Munroe that first captured my imagination and I am far from alone in this. In the January/February 2021 issue, *WoodenBoat* published the intriguing story of a Presto-inspired sharpie designed in Scotland, of all places, by the gifted Ian Oughtred.

But it was Philip C. Bolger's work that pushed me over the edge into sharpie ownership. What's more, even after I sold that boat, I found myself entertaining thoughts of buying *another* one. While I managed to avoid succumbing to the Bolger-designed Dovekie, I took great comfort in knowing that the formidable Peter Duff, whose background was in nuclear physics, had gone so off the deep end that he was actually building and selling them. What's more, he owned another Bolger design, the 33' Black Gauntlet, a predecessor of the boat described in this story.

Although I've always felt myself more or less immune to the influence of advertising, certain books have had a definite impact. Back in the mid-1980s, one such book even prompted me to violate that cardinal rule of boat-selection: buy only a boat suitable for your local waters. Years ago, my local waters morphed from the shallow depths of New Jersey's Barnegat Bay, perfect for centerboard catboats, to the rocky but deep waters around Marblehead, Massachusetts. However, such was the influence of Phil Bolger's *The Folding Schooner and Other Adventures in Boat Design* that I somehow became entranced by a sailboat whose minimum draft was a mere ten inches, more or less.

The boat in question was introduced on page sixty of Bolger's book. The design had been commissioned by marine scientist and boating journalist Mike O'Brien who would later join the *WoodenBoat* staff where he remains on the masthead as the magazine's boat-design editor. Bolger called the design Black Skimmer for a bird that feeds by skimming low with its specially adapted lower mandible in the water to scoop up fish. The Black Skimmer's gracefully rockered flat bottom and wing-like leeboards adapted it perfectly to its intended habitat, the tidal creeks of the lower Chesapeake. One of the book's photos showed Mike's boat, which he built himself, resting in the marsh grass waiting for the tide to float it off the mud. Perfect.

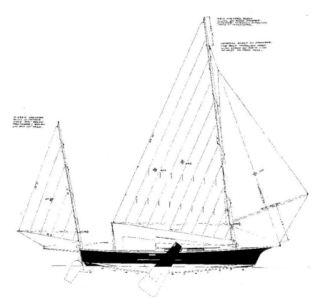

A fascinating boat: Bolger's drawings for his Black Skimmer. (Author's collection)

I perused the Black Skimmer drawings so many times that I knew portions of the materials list by heart: "½"-thick plywood hull with double-thickness bottom; trim molding 1" half-round; leeboards 1 ½"-thick edges well streamlined from about 4" from edge." In my mind's eye, I imagined those streamlined leeboards slicing through the water as we skimmed just above a sandy bottom. The Black Skimmer was still in my thoughts when, in the spring of 1983, I received the latest issue of *Nautical Quarterly* magazine, edited by my friend Joe Gribbins. Among the contents was an insightful article about Phil Bolger written by Joe himself and accompanied by many beautiful photographs. The images included Bolger's inexpensive plywood "instant boats" popularized by Harold "Dynamite" Payson. There also were sophisticated, shallow-draft sailing cruisers, a sleek outboard, and the fiberglass, leeboard-equipped Dovekie then in production by Edey and Duff. A Black Skimmer was included, too. It had been capably built on Cape Cod by Walter Barron who still does business in Wellfleet as the Old Wharf Dory Company. There were three beautiful photos of the boat taken by Ben Mendlowitz.

Needless to say, Joe's article and the photographs further stimulated my interest. By the mid-1980s, I was living in Marblehead but spending a small portion of the summer on Cape Cod. It wasn't long before I arranged to meet the Black Skimmer's owner. He turned out to be a firm believer in Bolger's unorthodox designs and had previously owned a Dovekie. He and his wife had spent a couple of weeks at a time cruising Cape waters in their Black Skimmer, and he gave the boat high marks.

Very shortly after that meeting, a strange thing occurred. On a weekend visit to the Cape, I happened to check the classified boat ads in the local paper and spotted a Black Skimmer for sale just a couple of miles away. Needless to say, that ad convinced me that I was clearly meant to own a Black Skimmer. Soon enough, I found myself watching those "streamlined leeboards" as they sliced through the shallow waters around Osterville. After a brief negotiation, the boat, a five-horsepower British Seagull outboard, and a rust-specked tandem-axle trailer were all mine.

A good friend in Osterville with a peculiar enthusiasm for fixing up boat trailers volunteered to work on mine over the winter while the boat was in the shop of a local builder for a cosmetic restoration. That involved changing the hull color from red to Interlux flat white, painting the cabin top, cockpit sole and seats Interlux Oregon buff, stripping and varnishing the sliding hatch, varnishing the masts and sprit booms, and making sturdy new oak leeboard mounts and mast partners. Both the main and mizzen sails were recent, set beautifully and required no work.

In the shop: *Sand Scraper* nears the end of a cosmetic restoration. (Stan Grayson)

The Skimmer has nice long cockpit seats but, probably for flotation-re-lated reasons, Bolger showed no opening lockers in them. We added hatches port and starboard toward the forward end of the cockpit. As a final touch, the builder crafted two name boards of varnished mahogany with the boat's new name painted in crème lettering outlined with green: *Sand Scraper.*

During that long winter, I began wondering who had built my Black Skimmer. The seller had anecdotal information suggesting the boat had come from, of all places, Chicago. "Why a Black Skimmer on deep Lake Michigan?" I wondered. But, of course, I already knew why: sharpie madness. I began piecing together what little information I had regarding origins. I made a few cold calls and, much to my surprise, discovered an individual who actually knew the boat. He'd taught a boat-building class in the Windy City and remembered the Skimmer.

"That boat was quite a nice job," he recalled.

The boat had been built of good quality marine plywood and epoxy and the bottom had been fiber-glassed up to the waterline. Bolger's materials list called for 500 pounds of "galvanized or enameled" steel plate ballast to be fastened beneath the cabin sole. Indeed, when I lifted the cabin sole, I saw that the ballast had been very neatly installed. In fact, the entire varnished interior was impressive. There was the usual forward vee-berth with storage beneath its red-upholstered cushions, and a portable head at the aft end. There was a little galley on one side and a cupboard on the other. This was a more elaborate interior than the "sprawling space" boat in *Nautical Quarterly* but everything fitted together precisely and each element could be removed.

Early on a Saturday in mid-May 1987, I drove down to the Cape for the launching of *Sand Scraper*. The boat was resting on its refurbished trailer—surge brakes and lights now in working order—in the woods behind my friend's house. Soon enough, we had the trailer hooked up to my Bronco II, hauled the boat out of the muddy woods in four-wheel-drive, and set off for the launching ramp a few miles away at Prince Cove in Cotuit. The plan was to motor back to my friend's dock in Osterville where we'd install the masts and the boatbuilder would drill holes in the new main mast partners so that what Bolger's plans labelled the "semi-collar" could be bolted on to clamp the spar in place.

That first journey was memorable for two reasons. First, it was the only time I've been snowed on while aboard a sailboat. "Welcome to 'spring' on Cape Cod" was the consensus. The second was the outboard motor. By then, I'd had significant experience with two British Seagulls. This one seemed to make more noise than power. I suspected it was down on compression. But as we motored through the still waters leading from Prince Cove to North Bay, every part of that Seagull began to vibrate loose. While my crew steered the boat, I perched on the starboard cockpit seat, special Seagull wrench in hand, adjusting here, tightening there, and feeling like Humphrey Bogart kicking the *African Queen*'s little steam engine to make it behave.

There followed a few trips from Marblehead to Osterville where my friends and I conducted some informal sea trials in shallow East Bay. With her hard chines and leeboards, *Sand Scraper* went to windward in a satisfactory manner and was quite fast off the wind. Sufficient tension of the mainsail luff couldn't be achieved without bending the mast, whose tip was reinforced with carbon fiber. We installed a tack downhaul that solved the problem. A week later, the boat was trailered up to Marblehead and launched.

Right from the start, the British Seagull's days were numbered. I'd long been a believer in the Seagull's simplicity but I had accepted that, charming as it was, the motor was archaic. A carburetor fault with the last one I'd owned, brand new and the latest and greatest with a built-in recoil starter rather than a separate starter cord, had soured me.

By the time *Sand Scaper* arrived in Marblehead, a new Johnson 8-horse-power Sailor was ready to be clamped to her sturdy transom. This two-cylinder, two-stroke was a gem. It started on the first pull and ran quietly and smoothly. On a windless Saturday morning, in fog that allowed less than a quarter-mile visibility, a friend joined me in motoring quietly over to Salem Harbor where I then had a mooring on the Marblehead side.

I quickly became familiar with the routine of preparing a Black Skimmer to get underway. The first step was to remove the mizzen—halyard left attached—from its white sail bag. The mizzen sheet was then fed through the block at the outboard end of a spar that Bolger labelled the "mizzen sheet outrigger." The outrigger was then slid out through a transom slot until its inboard end could be inserted into a sturdy wooden socket mounted on the inner face of the starboard cockpit coaming. The next step was to attach the mizzen's clew and tack to the sprit boom and secure the sprit to the mast. Next, the sail was partly hoisted, the lace line wound around the mast and through the luff grommets. Finally, the mizzen was hoisted fully, the lace line tensioned and the sheet made fast.

Now, the boat sat very comfortably pointing into the wind. Then I'd remove the sail cover from the main and clamber across the cabin top to the open bow well where a Skimmer's anchor and rode reside. Standing securely in the well, one then hoists the main and tensions the downhaul. I never ceased to be delighted at how quickly and smoothly the mainsail, like the mizzen secured to the mast with a lace-line, came down.

I generally departed on a starboard tack. This meant partly lowering the port leeboard before casting off. Free of the mooring, the mizzen would be backed and we'd begin to bear off. Then with a quick easing of the sheets, *Sand Scraper* would be silently ghosting through the shallows where, at low tide, it was 2'–3' deep.

Although a sharpie was certainly not needed in Marblehead, there was a certain method to my madness. Gloucester harbor lies about thirteen miles away and located there is the bridge that gives access to the Blynman Canal and the Annisquam River. The river itself has several tidal tributaries worth exploring but the real attraction is a bit further north. This is Essex Bay with its sandbars, shallows, and channels that wind their way around unspoiled islands. Emptying into the bay is the Essex River itself, somewhat tricky thanks to the tides but also perfect sharpie country.

With a fair wind, the sail to Gloucester took about two-and-a-half hours—off the wind the 25' Skimmer seemed as fast or faster than most cruising boats a few feet longer—but that was the easy part. I always planned to arrive at the Blynman Canal bridge at slack water before the tide turned in my favor. This remains important in a low-powered sailboat for the passage through the Annisquam includes a railroad drawbridge with a tight turn, a winding channel, strong current, and often heavy traffic.

Each time we made the trip through the Annisquam, we passed Phil Bolger's boat, an ark-like ketch that he'd named *Resolution*. Depending upon

Sand Scraper rests at her mooring on the Marblehead side of Salem Harbor, circa 1987. (Stan Grayson)

the tide, *Resolution* would either be afloat or grounded out in the mud. When boating writer Dan Segal visited Bolger for a perceptive *WoodenBoat* article published in 1990 (*WoodenBoat* No. 92), the designer told him that *Resolution* had by then grounded out 6,941 times without suffering damage. Bolger possessed a head for numbers and a mind as precise as it was open to creative, new ways of thinking. "I've reached working hypotheses different from the conventional wisdom," he'd written in the preface to *The Folding Schooner*.

It wasn't long into my Black Skimmer ownership before I contacted Bolger with some questions. He said he preferred to talk in person rather than on the phone so I drove up to Gloucester and, soon enough, was climbing onto *Resolution*, which had a big American flag flying on the mizzen mast. In 1946, Bolger had enlisted in the Army where he served in Japan in an engineering unit of the First Cavalry Division. After discharge, Bolger majored in history at Bowdoin College before beginning his design career but his Army experience had left him with a strong sense of respect for the country and those in uniform.

After Phil's death in 2009, the obituary published in *Bowdoin Magazine* reported: "In 1970 he ripped his diploma in half and mailed it back to

Bowdoin in response to the College's tolerance of a well-publicized Vietnam War protest and student strike." Had I known of his feeling in these matters, I'm sure we'd have talked about Vietnam where I'd spent a year-long tour and, as it happened, had some experience with the First Cavalry Division. Instead, as Phil's Stars and Stripes snapped in the wind topside, we sat on *Resolution*'s green-upholstered berths and discussed sharpies.

I asked Bolger if he thought that the rakish-looking Black Skimmer—which was among his favorite designs out of well over 600—might be successfully marketed as a kit boat. He responded without hesitation.

"No."

He opined that unconventional cat yawls with flat bottoms and leeboards would never have broad appeal or be wise investments. It was a conviction born of experience. The general market wanted headroom and comfort levels a sharpie would never provide, not to mention a keel and more conventional appearance. There was certainly a market among sailors who had a need for extreme shallow draft, but those folks represented a tiny niche. It was, however, market receptive to Bolger's open-minded approach and his delight in divesting a design of any superfluous elements or costs.

"I love to simplify things," Bolger had told Joe Gribbins.

That may explain, among other things, why the Black Skimmer drawings show a V-shaped slot in the bowsprit rather than an anchor roller. I didn't care for how the anchor rode jammed into that slot and added a roller after *Sand Scraper*'s first season.

I don't recall how many times I made the journey to the Annisquam and Essex Bay, but it was less often than I'd hoped. There was the matter of arriving at the canal bridge at the right time and also the trip home, usually a slog to windward. By and by, the sharpie's more troubling aspects began to make themselves felt. She was at her worst in light air in the chop kicked up by powerboats. In those conditions, frequent around the mouth of Marblehead Harbor, the boat was not reliable when tacking. Yes, the mizzen could be backed to help, but it was a nuisance.

The leeboards were an issue, too, not for me but for almost everyone else. The Black Skimmer's leeboards reflect Bolger's goal of simplicity. "The leeboards are hung by an old Flemish method," he wrote, "extremely simple compared with the complex Dutch geometry [usually employed.]" In other words, there is no block-and-tackle. The leeboard's pennant is simply secured to a cleat. You carefully uncleat the pennant to lower the boards and use muscle power to raise them.

I really liked having a boat with leeboards hung by "an old Flemish method." However, the reality is that a Black Skimmer's leeboards weigh about

110 pounds and that's a bit much for many folks to handle. After one person, most unfortunately my wife, got her fingers rather badly pinched by a leeboard pennant and another simply let go of the pennant, allowing the board to wing out away from the hull, I allowed nobody else to deal with them.

Perhaps the Black Skimmer's most annoying aspect, though, was what Bolger himself noted. "[T]hese boats pound and splash noisily at anchor." Bolger, who cruised aboard his own 33' sharpie for eleven years, wrote that "I've found no way to sleep well but to hunt up some smooth little creek."

I was conjuring up ways to mitigate the noise problem when I made the decision to sell the boat. It was a decision driven as much by my becoming weary of inflating and deflating my Avon dinghy each time we went sailing as by the Black Skimmer itself. Later, I even stopped sailing for a few years until a mooring became available in Marblehead Harbor and getting to and from one's boat was no longer a laborious task.

Strangely enough, considering the limited market appeal for a boat like *Sand Scraper*, a buyer soon appeared. He lived in Ipswich and would use the boat in Plum Island Sound and the Parker River, perfect sharpie country. What's more, I recovered most but not all of my roughly $12,000 investment. Based on what Bolger had said about the market for such boats, I counted myself lucky.

I suppose that the relative financial success of my sharpie experiment did much to ease thoughts that buying the boat had been a risky and not particularly sound decision. Yet I have no regrets. *Sand Scraper* was a sturdy boat that never leaked. Maintenance involved little more than varnish and paint touch up. Painting the hull flat- instead of gloss-white had been a mistake for the dinghy left marks on the hull. These were easily cleaned but I began leaving a fender off the starboard side aft to protect the topsides when coming alongside. I never tired of rigging the mizzen, standing in the bow well and raising the main, or putting the boat to bed. That sharpie taught me a lot. I also very much enjoyed the experience of having the occasional knowledgeable enthusiast greet me with a cheerful, "Say, that must be a Bolger boat! I've read about them."

It's now been over thirty years since that time. I would never advise anyone to buy a boat that's not well-adapted to their primary sailing waters. That is something I still think about, especially since I began spending winters on Florida's southwest Gulf coast, where miles of shoal water abound. Often enough these days, I occasionally stop my bicycle under a palm tree and gaze out at Pine Island Sound or San Carlos Bay.

"What a perfect place," I say to myself, "for a Black Skimmer."

This story appeared in *WoodenBoat* No. 292, May/June 2023.

THE GHOSTS IN
THE ROSSIE MILL

The Unseen Boats at
Mystic Seaport Museum

I have never forgotten the moment when curator Dana Hewson flicked the switch in a vast, dark area of the old Rossie Mill in Mystic, Connecticut. "Let here be light!" Suddenly, dozens of old wooden boats emerged. There were rows and rows, stacks and stacks of boats. As we proceeded from one area to another, the dozens became hundreds. Each boat was the "real thing," a genuine, unmolested, documented chapter in the vast story of America's small-craft heritage. For boat-crazy me, the whole place was nothing less than a miracle.

But relatively few people ever got to see those boats. Although the desire to increase accessibility to this hidden collection had existed among Mystic Seaport's devoted staff for decades, there was simply no room to exhibit them. Nor was the mill itself an appropriate venue for visitors. It was cold, ill-lit, and there was too much to trip over. However, Dana Hewson, now retired, also told me about long-held hopes of someday opening the mill. Now, ten years later, it has fallen to Christina Connett Brophy, Mystic's senior vice president of curatorial affairs and senior director of museum galleries, and her team, to make those long-held hopes reality.

"We plan an exhibition space of 35,000 square feet in the southwest corner of the building," Brophy told me in March 2023. "That will be enough to display a large percentage of the collection, perhaps 200 to 275 boats, but not all of it." As this is written, architectural and design plans are underway that will result in an interior facelift of portions of the mill, electrical, water, and roof upgrades, restrooms, an access ramp, and elevator. The mill will become a "Watercraft Hall." Make sure to put this on your bucket list.

Hidden away in a sprawling, brick building in Mystic, Connecticut, is the most important collection of boats that most people will never see. Although it's generally known simply as "the mill," the building's official designation is the Rossie Velvet Mill, after the family long associated with it, and its most popular product. During the first decades of the twentieth century, the Rossie Velvet Mill was Mystic's biggest employer and, in prosperous times, three shifts of textile workers labored there amid the terrible heat and din of 180 steam-driven looms.

Today, though, the mill is quiet and, in winter, its concrete floors radiate a toe-numbing cold. It's long since been a part of the Mystic Seaport Museum and, a couple of years ago, the museum's library was relocated to beautifully prepared rooms here. But much of the old building is given over to boats that, for space reasons, can't be publicly displayed. I first became aware of this situation many years ago thanks to the publication in 1979 of *Mystic Seaport Museum Watercraft*. Here, for the first time, all the museum's boats were revealed.

To say that I was fascinated by the book would be an understatement. Its heft, teal-colored cloth binding, and the smell of its pages remain, to this day, as comforting and familiar as a chat with an old friend. John Gardner, Mystic's then assistant curator and boat-building instructor, wrote *Watercraft*'s foreword. In it, he aptly called the boats "irreplaceable historic documents, and in addition, objects of folk art."

By 2001, when the third edition of *Watercraft* was published, both the book and the museum's collections had grown enormously. "Twenty years ago," Senior Curator for Watercraft Dana Hewson told me in the summer of 2013, "we might take a dozen boats in a year. Now, it's two or three. I don't believe everything out there has been collected, but there probably aren't a lot out there that are consistent with what we look for. We're very selective and, of course, there's not a lot of space."

Today, there are some 450 boats in the mill and, when Hewson first guided me through the building one dark, February afternoon, space constraints were obvious. Boats were stashed in all corners, stacked three-high in places, shoe-horned into every square foot. Even for Hewson, finding a specific boat was a challenge without the printed guide that keys each boat to a specific location within the building's vastness.

An unexpected advantage to seeing the boats here is that they can be viewed without distractions. One need not block out a disruptive background of waterfront condos, jet skis, or even a museum display space. Here, long since removed from water and sunshine and those who'd loved them, the boats exist within no context but time itself. Having studied photos of these watercraft for so many years, I was unprepared for the sense of discovery

I felt when finally seeing them. They seemed at once familiar yet entirely new. Their very survival seemed amazing. What follows are the stories of five boats whose past had somehow become intertwined with my own.

The Catboat *Dolphin*

"Wow," I told Dana, when he flicked on the lights that illuminate the end-most section in an area somewhere seemingly near the center of the mill, "it's Captain Adrian's *Dolphin*!"

Dolphin's accession number as reported in the latest edition of *Watercraft* is No. 1987.138, meaning the boat was acquired in 1987 and was the 138th object accepted that year. Another Crosby cabin catboat at Mystic, *Frances*, has been restored and is on display, but the twenty-one-foot *Dolphin* exists just as she was when Captain Adrian Lane donated her. Both catboats had been built by Wilton Crosby (1856–1935). In 1982, when I interviewed Wilton's grandnephew, Wilton B. Crosby Jr., he told me that Wilton "was born here right on the waterfront [in Osterville] along with the rest of 'em and just fell into it natural. Boatbuilding was the *only* thing to do."

Dolphin was launched in 1917, seventeen years after *Frances*, when Wilton was sixty-one years old, and well after the heyday of Crosby cat-boat production. Still, *Dolphin*'s life story reflects in many ways that of her

Cabin of the catboat *Dolphin*: In 1987, a few years after the author sailed aboard *Dolphin* with Capt. Adrian Lane, the boat was donated to Mystic where she was evaluated as "an excellent example . . . of her famous builder [Wilton Crosby]." (Stan Grayson)

predecessors. Her original owner is unknown but Edgartown fisherman Joseph Mello acquired the boat in 1932. Mello used *Dolphin* for scalloping and, in summer, he took island visitors sailing. He made flannel-lined protective coverings tailored to the varnished cockpit coamings, so *Dolphin's* appearance remained as much yacht as working boat.

When he became too old to properly care for *Dolphin*, Mello, with tears in his eyes, sold to Vineyard Haven schooner operator Bob Douglas. But Douglas soon decided he wanted a bigger catboat and *Dolphin's* next owner was a Spanish American and World War I vet named John Killam Murphy. A lifelong sailor—he was often referred to as "the dean of Connecticut yachtsmen"—and a yacht broker, Murphy was eighty-five when he acquired *Dolphin*.

"I probably never should have bought her," he wrote after the fact, "but I did have fun rebuilding her." Four years later though, in 1965, he placed an ad in *Yachting*. *Dolphin* was purchased by the genial mate of Mystic Seaport's schooner *Brilliant*, Ned Watson, and the boat's skipper, Adrian Lane. Later, when Watson bought himself a twenty-six-foot catboat, Lane became *Dolphin's* sole owner.

Like most catboats, this one was altered over time. Her centerboard was reduced in size, her spars shortened. When she needed a new mast, Lane had it fashioned from a big schooner yacht's spinnaker pole. "Everybody had more working sail in the old days," Lane said when I met with him for a book I was writing in 1981. "They'd take one reef all the time. But I don't reef until it's blowing 20 knots."

On the Vineyard, *Dolphin* once suffered serious hurricane damage that required much of her starboard-side planking be replaced. The boat was somewhat unusual for a Crosby in that her original planking was cedar rather than pine, cypress, or mahogany. But mahogany was used for the new planks, and screw fasteners rather than the Crosbys' typical, galvanized iron boat nails. "They did a lousy job, by the way," Lane told me. "The screws weren't long enough and for years I've been taking out those damn screws and driving boat nails in their place. The old boat nails she was built with—you couldn't get them out to save your soul."

Under Lane's ownership, *Dolphin* presented what he called "something major" every year. "There was a new centerboard and the new mast. I had a new rudder made. We replaced a couple of planks. She's basically pretty sound but I suppose a new keel and some extra floor timbers might be needed."

I went sailing with Adrian one May day when there was perhaps ten knots of wind in Fisher's Island Sound. We beat slowly out of Noank past a spindle with an osprey's nest on it. Lane said the birds were a useful fog signal. *Dolphin* was well-balanced in that breeze, and fresh from a race win the previous Saturday. "There was just one windward leg and the rest were reaches," Lane said. "It was just elegant for catboats, though they are a lot handier and closer-winded than people think."

With a lifetime of experience behind him in sail and steam in most of the world's oceans, Lane knew exactly what he was talking about. "Pretty much all my jobs involved boats," he said. "I probably worked ashore for only five years." Once, in command of a vessel used to monitor submarines' noise levels, some plates let go in the main hold in the middle of the night in January. "We got picked up by Norwegians and taken to Europe."

Lane donated *Dolphin* to Mystic in 1987 and, by then, she'd already been immortalized by the Catboat Association in its Dolphin Award. Despite the many repairs and changes that the then seventy-year-old boat had seen, the survey called her "an excellent example of the art and craft of her famous builder." In fact, rigged up and properly interpreted, she'd make a fabulous exhibit just as she is. For now, though, the old catboat rests in the mill, her big barn-door rudder propped against the port side that shows rust bleeding from the old iron boat nails. If you ever want to know about Crosby catboats, *Dolphin* is a good place to start.

The *Snarleyow*

One day back around 1978 or so, I found myself doing research at the New York Yacht Club's incredible library. Sitting across the table from me with a stack of books and magazines was a gray-haired, studious-looking fellow wearing a pair of large glasses. By and by, we got to chatting and he introduced himself and gave me his card. It read: "John W. Streeter, Yachting Historian." I was in my mid-thirties then, and John seemed elderly but, in fact, he was probably just a couple years older than I am now, and I generally don't feel that old. I recognized, though, that anyone who described himself as a yachting historian was a rare fellow.

John mentioned he was at work on a book, but we didn't have time to discuss the project, and I more or less forgot about it. Then some twenty years later and eleven years after John Streeter's passing, the book was published by the Herreshoff Marine Museum—*Nathanael Greene Herreshoff, William Piccard Stephens, Their Last Letters 1930–1938*. Beneath the title was this: "Annotated by John W. Streeter In the Library of the New York Yacht Club."

This fascinating book, the result of obvious devotion and scholarship, includes thirty-six annotated letters written by Herreshoff and Stephens to each other when they were old men. Letter Nine by Stephens, written August 6, 1935, includes this remark. "I have a yacht . . . a cutter 15 ft. L.O.A. by 3-6 beam designed by John Harvey and built in New York in

1882; she is still sound and seaworthy, the last of the English cutters except *Medusa.*"

This little yacht was *Snarleyow,* a name that, Streeter explained, came from the book titled *Snarleyow or the Dog Fiend,* written by an English naval commander, Frederick Marryat (1792–1848). A line drawing of the boat was included in C. P. Kunhardt's popular *Small Yachts: Their Design and Construction.* In his annotation Streeter noted that "while *Snarleyow* seems to have started cat-rigged, as was the British original, Stephens rigged her as a proper cutter and he sailed steering with his feet, sailing-canoe style [via tiller ropes]."

The grand old man of American yachting history died at his typewriter in May 1946, having more or less completed his epic series of marvelous articles that were later published in book form as *Traditions and Memories of American Yachting.* Stephens was a few months short of his ninety-second birthday when he died and, by then, *Snarleyow's* welfare had been on his mind for many years. Even at the time he wrote that letter to Herreshoff in 1935, Stephens understood how rare his boat was, and that it would one day need a special home. A few months after her father's death, Eleanor Stephens offered the little cutter, some old yachting flags, Stephens's *Field & Stream* articles, and many photographs, to Mystic. The boat, sans rig and the unusual sliding seat that allowed her skipper to adjust his weight fore-aft as necessary, eventually became accession No. 1952.498.

One can never cease to be impressed by nineteenth-century boats. Almost invariably, their structure and details combine incredible delicacy of detail with in-built strength. Of batten-seam construction, *Snarleyow's* still fair hull had been planked with ½" mahogany though years of sanding diminished the thickness by 1/16" inch, or so. The planks are fastened with copper rivets to the battens and to steam-bent ¼" x ¾" oak frames alternating with natural crooks. While her seat/steering setup and rig would be fantastic to have, the sight of this well-crafted, bare hull built 131 years ago is thought-provoking.

Snarleyow's beam of 3'8" makes her beam-to-length ratio quite moderate in comparison to some British cutters of an era when yachts there were taxed according to their beams. For a time in the United States, some sailors became convinced that narrow, deep hulls were far superior to beamier, shallower centerboard types. Kunhardt was among this vocal sect—the "cutter cranks."

The 18'9" x 6'3" x 5' *Fox* ex-*Cockle* ex-*Galena,* another boat in the mill, is also one that the cutter cranks would have loved. She was designed by Marblehead's James C. Purdon and built in town—about a mile and a half from where I write this—at Graves in 1913. Two years later, Purdon sold the

Then Mystic curator Dana Hewson points out some details of the miniature (14'11"), British-style cutter *Snarleyow*, once owned by yachting historian W. P. Stephens. (Stan Grayson)

boat to Marblehead aviation pioneer and yacht designer William Starling Burgess, who gave it to his son Frederic. Frederic sailed this seaworthy little cutter in all weather. (As an adult, Frederic became a physician, and his sister Tasha became a well-known writer and illustrator of children's books. Both adopted the maiden name of their mother Rosamond and were known as Frederic and Tasha Tudor.) While not as extreme as some British-style cutters of their day, this little boat and *Snarleyow* still appear not quite freakishly narrow.

As for Stephens, he seems to have spent too much time with his self-designed and built (1898) *Snickersnee*, a 21'9" canoe yawl, and his writing, to have been a serious cutter crank. But he certainly recognized *Snarleyow* as a historic boat. What we have now in the Rossie Velvet Mill is a little yacht designed in England by a leading architect, built in New York by a leading builder, John C. Smith, and owned and preserved by a beloved man who was recognized in his own lifetime as the dean of America's yachting historians.

The Wianno Senior

"Just look at that," I exclaimed to Dana Hewson. The graceful bow of a Wianno Senior lanced out of darkness into the dimly lit aisle.

"There she is," Dana said.

I walked aft to have a look at the name, *Fantasy*. I was mightily impressed by accession No. 1965.820 for I had recently completed a centennial history of the Wianno Senior and knew that this boat was among the first ones built in the winter of 1914. If you want to know more about the story of the boatbuilding Crosby family, about the development of Cape Cod, about President John Kennedy's favorite sailboat, and about the advent of one-design racing, *Fantasy* is a better prism than most through which to gaze.

One-design classes emerged in the latter years of the nineteenth century and gained ever increasing popularity. Eventually, they replaced the many catboat and "jib-and-mainsail" classes that had previously typified yacht racing. The Wianno Senior was designed in 1913 by Wilton Crosby's younger brother Horace Manley when he was forty-one years old. Manley, the only Crosby to leave Osterville for a time had, with a partner, established a yard in Brooklyn in the mid-1890s. There, he saw the growing popularity of one-design classes. Back on Cape Cod, when the Wianno Yacht Club approached Manley about creating a new one-design, the key parameters included a boat able to deal with the challenging currents, shoals, and winds of Nantucket Sound. It was also to offer some modest cruising potential.

Designed by Manley Crosby and built in 1914, *Fantasy* was donated to Mystic Seaport in 1965. The Wianno Senior Class remains vibrant today. (Stan Grayson)

The WYC got more than it bargained for. There have been a great many knockabout classes but the Wianno Senior is among the oldest and even as other classes faltered, the Seniors sailed on. Why is this so? With her shallow keel, centerboard, and gaff rig, the twenty-five-footer was perfectly adapted to her home waters. Experiments during the mid-1920s with a Marconi rig proved disappointing. "For this little corner of the world," one long-time owner told me, "it's the best-designed four-person boat. It just works for local conditions." Today, third- and fourth-generation Wianno Senior sailors sail in the wakes of their forebears.

Fantasy was bought by Mary Hinkle primarily for her fifteen-year-old son James Gaff Hinkle. While the other boats had buff-painted decks, Mary asked Manley Crosby to paint *Fantasy's* deck canvas green so she'd be able to distinguish it from her porch where she used to watch the races. As for James, he raced the boat for the next half-century, winning a great many trophies. After the war, he served as the Wianno Yacht Club's commodore and, for many years, devoted himself to the demanding task of the fleet's administration.

"He used to say that, when the time came, he'd either scuttle *Fantasy* on Horseshoe Shoal or donate her to Mystic," remembered Hinkle's son, Jim.

In mid-September 1965, Hinkle Sr. chose the latter. "The *Fantasy* has been raced and owned by me for 51 years and is still in good racing trim," Hinkle wrote Mystic, and he went on to list some of the many trophies he'd won. This Wianno Senior is one of only two existing from the original 1914 fleet, and Hinkle had her restored at Crosby's. She slumbers now in the old mill even as newer Seniors, whether wood or fiberglass, still sail out each summer to do battle on Nantucket Sound, skippered and crewed by some of the country's finest sailors and still, by gosh, gaff rigged.

The Hickman Sea Sled

Over time, my writing about the American marine engine industry led to connections with a wide variety of fascinating boats. One that's popped up regularly thanks to its long but checkered history is the Hickman Sea Sled (*WoodenBoat* No. 100). There are three Sea Sleds at Mystic. Accession 1984.56, a double-cockpit sixteen-footer is a brightly varnished and sobering testimony to the fact that it takes more than brilliant innovation to achieve either the recognition of one's peers or business success.

Born in New Brunswick, Canada, in 1878, William Albert Hickman graduated from Harvard in 1899 and returned home to become a Provincial Commissioner and, incidentally, to achieve distinction as a writer of both fiction and nonfiction. Yet by the age of thirty-three, Hickman's interest in boats had led him to establish the Viper Company of Pictou, Nova Scotia. The first *Viper* was a 20'2 x 3" flat-bottom, racing-oriented boat that had nothing in common with Hickman's later work except for his guiding philosophy.

In a 1911 *Rudder* article, Hickman wrote: "In my opinion, unless a speed boat is a sea boat, she is not a boat at all." This search for speed and seaworthiness was Hickman's goal as he developed each successive *Viper*, a process that resulted in his 1914 patent for a hull cross-section shaped like an inverted V. This was the Sea Sled, the product of Hickman's brilliance and ability to think outside the box. "It was the original basic cathedral idea," wrote naval architect Weston Farmer, who well understood Hickman's achievement, noting the design "would suppress the side wash under the hull. The boat would ride on air!"

Riding on air, more or less, meant the Sea Sled could achieve remarkable speed with comparatively modest horsepower, and Hickman also selected the lightest, most powerful engines available—Van Blercks and Hall-Scotts among them—for his inboard models. But the principle held true for the outboard versions, too. What's more, the boats could speed through turns in rough conditions with little or no worry about capsizing or diving into the next wave and possibly not emerging, dangers that drivers of Gold Cup racers learned firsthand.

Hickman's work (which also included development of surface-piercing propellers) met with resistance within the motorboat racing establishment. What's more, even as he created a company in West Mystic to build Sea Sleds, Hickman's post–World War I efforts to secure ongoing Navy contracts resulted in conflict leading to a bitter lawsuit. Ever forward-looking, however, in November 1945, Hickman published drawings of his latest Sea

The unique bottom configuration of the Hickman Sea Sled is evident here. It was among the designs that would prompt C. Raymond Hunt's idea for the first Boston Whaler. (Mystic Seaport)

Sleds. The new boats took advantage of the strength and light weight of "mahogany-faced waterproof plywood."

In 1955, Hickman concluded an initial agreement with businessman Dick Fisher and naval architect Ray Hunt who wanted to build the Sea Sled using Fisher's idea for an unsinkable, foam-cored, fiberglass hull. Soon enough, though, this collaboration failed. Likely as a way to avoid a patent battle with Hickman, Hunt and Fisher kept the squared-off look of the Sea Sled but added a central hull to the middle of the cathedral. The first Boston Whaler, like Hickman's smallest model, was just over 13' long. It emerged in 1958, not long after Albert Hickman's death on September 10, 1957.

The 15'11" x 4'7" Sea Sled considered here was the largest of the outboard models, and this one was powered by a shiny, cast-aluminum, 26-hp Johnson V-45. This boat was a marvelous gift for one Richard Keppler upon his college graduation in 1929. Keppler used his Sea Sled on Schroon Lake where he won a number of racing trophies and enjoyed the boat for over forty years. A deck-off restoration was performed by the second owner.

Accession 1984.56 remains a thought-provoking ghost from the past. The boat is a reminder that being on the cutting edge, as was Hickman, can be as painful as it is satisfying, and that bucking convention without highly developed negotiating ability and plain good luck can lead one into rough seas, indeed.

The Osterville Skiff

My late friend Townsend ("Townie") Hornor was a do-anything, renaissance man sort of fellow, equally comfortable in boardrooms, his big, well-equipped workshop, or afloat. At heart, he was a waterman who grew up on the Osterville shore and developed a keen interest in everything having to do with boats. Among other things, at Harvard, Townie studied with historian Samuel Eliot Morrison, and he was always eager to assist with projects involving past times.

Just about anyone in Osterville needing to dispose of an old boat or have it repaired might contact Townie. One day, in the early 1970s, he was asked if he would be interested in an old skiff. Of course, he was, and he kept the boat for years until, recognizing its importance, he donated it to Mystic as accession No. 1988.24. This was just the sort of apparently mundane, everyday sort of boat that was taken for granted by those who used them. But Townie saw beyond that.

"In the 1930s, and I am sure well before that," he wrote, "everybody [in Osterville] had that sort of skiff as a tender. . . . They were usually painted white or light grey, but a bright one was not unusual. . . . Most had the galvy

At the top of this stack of boats is a humble but functional Osterville Skiff. (Stan Grayson)

[galvanized] patented rowlocks that this one has. . . . A number of local backyard builders built them. . . . The local high school boatbuilding class also built some."

This 11'6" x 3'11" Osterville skiff is a substantial boat. She has hefty knees to reinforce the transom and a foredeck to reinforce the bow. The survey showed some nail sickness where the hull meets the cross-planked bottom, but the sheer clamp is copper riveted to the sheer plank. "This accounts," read the survey, "for the boat not losing its shape. . . . With a little work, it could be serviceable."

Today, one can still see a number of tenders ashore at the Osterville town landing on Bridge Street. But boats like this one are long gone. "When fiberglass arrived in 1947 with its 'no maintenance' expectations, that was about it for the heavy wooden skiff," Townie wrote in his provenance letter to Mystic. "But they were a good stable boat for all seasons."

Of Time and the Mill

"To a large extent," said Dana Hewson, "the boats here are saved for their own, intrinsic value. They are kept for posterity."

The collection—focused on boats from the Chesapeake Bay area, New York state, and New England—is of unending variety. Where else might one stumble upon the boat that gave so many their first experience of sailing—an original Alcort Sailfish? This example was once displayed at a Leominster, Massachusetts, Alcort dealer and its foredeck bears the painted names of company founders Alex Bryan and Cort Heyinger. There's a plywood Dyer Dhow, originally designed for the Navy's PT boats and forerunner of the fiberglass models still made today. There are power dories built by once important companies now all but forgotten. There are motor boats, rowboats, dories, skiffs, and what Hewson noted is "probably the most significant group of shells in the country." There are Barnegat Bay Sneakboxes, racing dinghies, and canoes of all varieties.

"A long-term goal here," said Dana Hewson as he switched off the lights and returned the boats to their slumber, "is to have a section of the mill opened as an exhibit. For now, access can be arranged for groups or for someone building a boat who would benefit from studying those in storage."

For the most part, though, the boats in the Rossie Velvet Mill will continue to await discovery by those historians and devoted visitors who recognize the technology, art, and culture that reside within them. "Here I am," the old boats seem to say. "Pause awhile, now. Think. There are things we can teach you."

This story appeared in *WoodenBoat* No. 237, March/April 2014.

ACKNOWLEDGMENTS

"Herreshoff Catboats"

Thanks to John Palmieri and Evelyn Ansel of the Herreshoff Marine Museum, to the Henry Ford Museum of American Innovation, and to Claas van der Linde.

"Searching for C. C. Hanley"

Thanks to the staff at the Quincy Historical Society, and to the reference staff at Quincy's Thomas Crane Public Library. Thanks, too, to Richard Crockett, editor of South Africa's *Sailing* magazine, to Dave Cox, and to all those in South Africa who responded to inquiries.

"Like a Fish in a Basket of sawdust"

Thanks to John Rousmaniere and Mrs. Jean L. Thompson.

"Time Machine"

Special appreciation to Scott Peters at the Michigan Historical Museum. Thanks to the Collections of the Henry Ford, the Grand Rapids Public Library, the Smithsonian, Jes Hathaway at National Fisherman, John Rex, Richard Day, Richard Durgee, Jim Walkinshaw, and the staff at the Penobscot Marine Museum.

"The Man from Motor Boat Lane"

Thanks to Scott Peters of the Michigan Historical Museum for his generous and knowledgeable assistance. Thanks, too, to Dan Acierno of the Long Island Boat and Motor Works, to researchers Greg Calkins and Chad Mayea, and to the library staffs at the Antique Boat Museum, the Mariners' Museum, the Detroit, Akron, and Brooklyn Public Libraries, the Henry Ford Museum, the Monroe Historical Society, and to Louisa Watrous at the Rosenfeld Collection, Mystic Seaport Museum.

"Legends of the Rips"

Thanks to Jeff Pierce, Charles Robert Smith, Bill Pappas, Ron Fortier, Jonathan Fowler, Bob Steele, and the reference desks at the Fall River, Kingston, and Plymouth Public Libraries.

"A Wide, White Road"

Thanks to Serene Silva and Hunt Associates at Ray Hunt Design. This story was adapted from the book *A Genius at His Trade: C. Raymond Hunt and His Remarkable Boats.* Old Dartmouth Historical Society/The New Bedford Whaling Museum, New Bedford, Massachusetts, 2015.

"The *Musketaquid* Mystery"

Thanks to Thoreau scholar and author Robert D. Richardson Jr. who read the manuscript.

"The Ghosts in the Rossie Mill"

Special thanks to Mystic Seaport Museum's Mary Anne Stets and volunteer Peter Dickinson and, at *WoodenBoat,* James Bartick and Matthew P. Murphy.